Chothe Indigenous Religion and Culture

Chothe Indigenous Religion and Culture:
A Sociological Study

Volume - I

Dr Cheithou Charles Yuhlung

First Published, 2018

Published by

Kalpaz Publications
C-30, Satyawati Nagar,
Delhi – 110052
E-mail: kalpaz@hotmail.com
Ph.: 9212142040

Printed at: G. Print Process, Delhi

Cataloging in Publication Data—DK
Courtesy: D.K. Agencies (P) Ltd. <docinfo@dkagencies.com>

Yuhlung, Cheithou Charles, author.
    Chothe indigenous religion and culture : a sociological study /
Cheithou Charles Yuhlung.
       volumes cm
    Revised version of the author's thesis (Ph. D.).
    Includes bibliographical references.
    ISBN 9789386397768 (set)
    ISBN 9789386397775 (vol. I)

    1. Purum (Indic people)—India—Manipur—Religion. 2.
Purum (Indic people)—Social life and customs. 3. Manipur
(India)—Social life and customs.   I. Title.

LCC DS432.P8Y84 2018 | DDC 305.80095417   23

This Book is Dedicated to

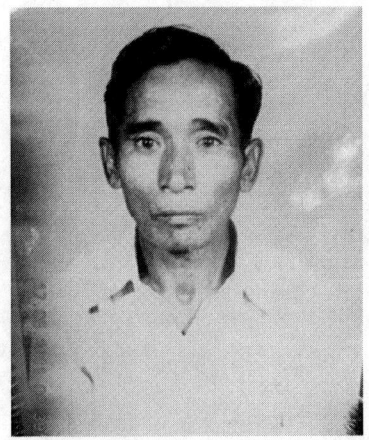

(Late) YUHLUNG ARAMSING CHOTHE
(Died on 17th May 1985)

Contents

$$\boxed{\text{Volume - I}}$$

Foreword 9

Acknowledgements 11

Preface 13

Abbreviation 17

List of Tables 19

Glossary 21

1. **Introduction** 43

 • The Study of Religion: Definition • Brief Profile of the Chothe Tribe • Statement of the Problem of the Study • Objective of the Study • Research Methodology • Chapterisation and Key Issues of the Study • The Confusion of the Chothe and Purum Tribes • Theoretical Formulation • A General View on Religion • Notes.

2. **Introducing the Chothe** 73

 • Introduction: Geographical Location • Historical Background: Genesis of the Chothe • The Three Regional Chothes • Migration • Demography: Factors and Consequences Leading to De-population • Wars and Battles Chothe Involved in the Past • Literacy • Relation with the Neighbouring Tribes and their Influence • Notes.

3. **Chothe Institutions** 114

 • Introduction • Kinship: Marriage and Family • Some Important Persons in the Society • Chothe Economy • Occupation and Employment • Measurements: Length and Volume • Indigenous Rice of Chothe • Chothe Beverage and Wine (Zu) • Types of House • Notes.

4. **Chothe Mythology: The Basic Foundation of their Belief and Practices** 157

 • Introduction: Myth and Legend • Chothe Indigenous Religion • Chothe Genealogical Myth • Brief Analysis of the Chothe Genealogical Myth • The Legend of Chothe Thangwai Pakhangpa • Moirang Ningthourol Lambuba (MNL): Pakhangpa at Moirang • Meitei Mythology of Pakhangpa • Notes.

5. **Chothe Religious Belief System** **215**
  • Introduction • Chothe Pantheon: Cosmic and Nature Worship • Concept of Three Worlds • Soul • Totem: Definition • Superstition: Sign, Omen, Dream and Curse • Some Common Superstitions of Chothe • Dreams • Curse • Taboo • Ghost and Spirit • Notes.

$$\boxed{\textbf{Volume - II}}$$

Abbreviation 267
List of Tables 269
List of Pictures 271

6. **Chothe Religious Practices** **275**
  • Introduction • Rites-de-passage (Birth, Initiation Rite, Marriage and Death Ceremonies) • Re-birth and Re-incarnation • The Sword Bearer (Chaampupa) and the Basket Carrier (Laan-thingpa) • The Death Commemoration Ceremony • Unnatural Death • The Chothe Grave: Design, Symbols and Meanings • Chothe Rites and Rituals • Talisman, Charms and the Fetish • Christian Visionary and Healers • Notes.

7. **Festivals of the Chothe** **339**
  • Introduction • Festivals of Chothe • The Innampei Lin/ Rhin (2006) • The Achui Lin/Rhin Festival • Analysis of the Festivals • Merit Feast (Lohchou-Maichou) • Notes.

8. **Folk Culture of Chothe** **371**
  • Introduction • Chothe Traditional Attire • Chothe Dance • Musical Instruments of Chothe • Indigenous Games and Sports of Chothe • Indigenous Herbal Medicines • Notes.

9. **Factors Responsible for the Decline of the Chothe**
  Indigenous Religion **413**
  • Introduction • The Influence of Christianity on the Chothe Indigenous Religion • Westernisation and Modernisation • Brief History of the Roman Catholic Church among the Chothe • Is the Early Christians Siding away from their Churches? • Notes.

10. **Conclusion** **435**
  • Summary • Findings and Key Issues of the Study • Few Remarks • Suggestions.

References 453
Internet Sources.

Index 523

Foreword

This is a very comprehensive account of the Chothe, one of the indigenous tribes of Manipur. The author, a Chothe himself, has rightly adopted a sociological method in giving a very detail study of the social institutions, religious beliefs and practices and festivals of the Chothe. It is indeed an illuminating book based on the author doctoral thesis. It throws lots of historico-sociological insights hitherto unexplored so far on the dynamic of social changes that have transformed the Chothe from traditionalism to modernism. It is a must reading book.

Professor Lal Dena
Manipur University

Acknowledgements

At the very outset, I thank the Almighty God for His bountiful blessings bestowed upon me throughout my research work and enabling me to complete successfully.

Secondly, I express my deepest and profound gratitude and appreciation to my Supervisor Professor I.L. Aier for his untiring and selfless service rendered to me during my entire research studies. I am indebted to him for his constant guidance, encouragement and support extended to me in the completion of my thesis. For all this and others, he is my mentor, guide and teacher for which I will remain grateful to him.

I extend my heartfelt gratitude to the Head of the Department, Professor I.L. Imchen, and the faculty members Professor Nikhlesh Kumar, Dr D.V. Kumar, Dr B.P. Panda, Dr Shangpliang Rekha and Professor Tiplut Nongbri (former Supervisor) for their help and support.

I also express my sincere thanks to my external experts i.e., Dr Amena Passah, Department of History, and Dr A.K. Nongkynrih, Department of Sociology for their invaluable suggestions and advice for the quality improvement of my work.

I express my gratitude and thanks to Dr Laishram Imoba (Eraibak, assistant-editor) and Gunamani (the Museum curator of Kakching). I am indebted to both of them for helping me in translation and explaining the Chothe Thangwai Pakhangpa the ancient manuscript.

I also extend my sincere love and gratitude to all the Chothe people, especially the informants like; H. Thambaljao, Y. Tomalsing, Y. Maipak, H. Bukunsing, H. Gulapsing, Y. Hongpa, Pr. Roushi, Mk. Neilut, Pr. Wailum, M. Wonchung, Kh. Khedon, Pr. Vincent, Marim Rimlil, Y. Tarik, and Y. Stephen (Damsu), besides many important persons for their cooperation in giving me their valuable time and sharing their knowledge, wisdom, information, opinion and views without which this study would be incomplete. Moreover, I also express my heartfelt thank you to my Chothe friends H. Keidi, Y. Chousana, M. Pandamlung, Pr. Hiramani, Y. Lungle, Th. Jaibunghoi, Mk. Jairus and Y. Chongkan who accompanied and assisted me to different Chothe villages during my extensive and intensive field works and also helping me to capture beautiful pictures. I would also like to say thank you to my NEHU friends; Dr Moyonmi Shimray, Dr Heshu Aji, Nipuni Mao, Kh. Pou, S. Ryan and others for sharing their experiences and ideas.

I express my humble gratitude and thanks to my mother, brothers and sisters, uncles, aunties, and cousins for their constant prayers, moral support and encouragement extended to me throughout my research works. My gratitude and special thank also goes to my elder sister Urumleima (Margaret), and my friend (Late) P. Poujanglung of Ragairong, Imphal for their moral support and encouragement, in fact, it was they who inspired me to pursue this higher research work. Last, but not the least, I also extend my gratitude to all those persons whose name could not be accommodated here but have helped and contributed their knowledge and wisdom in different ways for the completion of this thesis.

This book is based on my Ph.D thesis titled "Chothe Indigenous Religion and Culture: A Sociological Study" published with some modification and addition of data.

Thanking you once again and God bless you all.

Dr Cheithou Charles Yuhlung

Preface

The book 'Chothe Indigenous Religion and Culture' is a monumental work dedicated to the people of Chothe of Manipur, Northeast India. The book describes about the little unknown tribe in a holistic manner about their indigenous religion, customs, traditions, culture, marriage, economy and political systems practiced by them. Besides, it describes their folk cultures like festivals, merit feasts, folktales, folksongs, dance, music, games and sports and factors responsible for the decline of their age-old religion and customs. The book intends for the worldviews and especially, the younger generation of the Chothe tribe to share their knowledge that their forefathers and ancestors practiced such beliefs, practices and customs earlier. According to the Census of India (2011), the Chothe has a total population of about 3585, with a literacy rate of 69.79 per cent. Given their population figure it is also feared that after few years no one would know and remember what kind of social systems they practiced in the past as compared to the present situation as the forces of influences like modern education, Christianity, westernisation, globalisation and neighbouring communities have greatly impacted on their social lives. Therefore, this book would definitely serve as the last complete documented ethnographic work on Chothe that was left incomplete by T.C. Das (1985) the renowned Indian scholar.

In the study, the researcher have presented certain significant historical and sociological findings that would definitely interest academicians, scholars, intellectuals, politicians and laymen worldwide. The study is qualitative and descriptive in nature based on empirical and exploratory approach. The universe of research confines to two districts viz.; Bishnupur and Chandel of Manipur, and is conducted among select village chiefs, elders, senior citizens, leaders and laymen from the eighteen (18) Chothe villages spread into three regional zones. The sources of secondary data comprises of published and unpublished books, manuscripts, journals, newspapers, thesis, dissertations, village and church souvenirs, booklets, etc. which helped in developing the study.

The book contains Ten Chapters divided into Three Sections:

   (i)   Introduction to social institutions comprises of Chapter – One, Two and Three.

  (ii)   Core discussion topics on religion comprises of Chapter – Four, Five and Six.

 (iii)   Sub-ordinate topics on folk cultures, festivals and influences comprises of Chapter – Seven, Eight, Nine and Ten.

Political Map

Location of Chothe villages

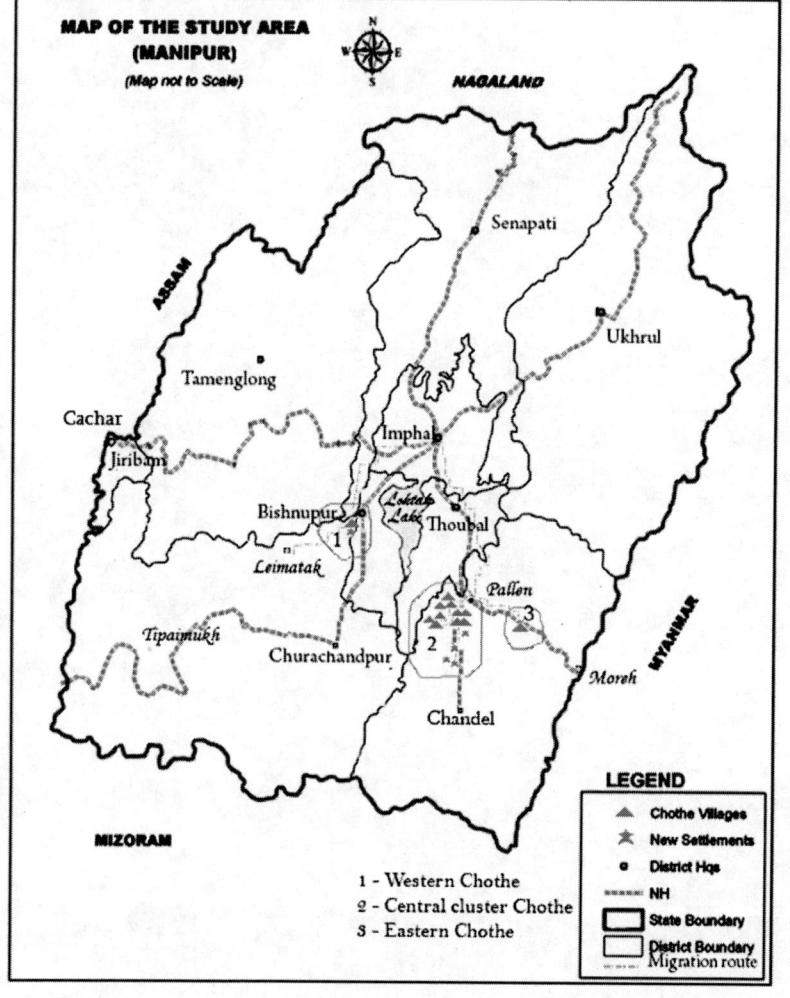

Abbreviation

Chothe Thangwai (Thangmei) Pakhangpa	CTP
Cheitharol Kumpapa	ChK
Moirang Ningthourol Lambuba	MNL
Literally	Lit.

List of Tables

Table 1 (i) : Distribution of Chothe Respondents by Faith 49

Table 1 (ii) : Distribution of Chothe Respondents by Gender (Male/Female, Both Followers of Indigenous Faith and Christians) 50

Table 2(i) : Distribution of Respondents of Indigenous Faith Followers by Age-group 51

Table 2 (ii) : Distribution of Indigenous Faith Followers by Male/Female 52

Table 3 (i) : Distribution of Lamlanghupi Respondents by Age-group (Both Followers of Indigenous Faith and Christians) 52

Table 3(ii) : Distribution of Lamlanghupi Respondents by Male/Female (Both Followers of Indigenous Faith and Christians) 53

Table 4 : Distribution of Chothe Christian Respondents by Denomination.... 53

Table 5(i) : Village-wise Distribution of Chothe Respondents by Age-group (Both Followers of Indigenous Faith and Christians) 54

Table 5(ii) : Distribution of Chothe Christian Respondents by Male/Female 55

Table 6 : Distribution of Education Qualification of Chothe Respondents (Both Followers of the Indigenous Faith and Christians) 56

Table 7 : Village-wise Distribution of Occupation of Chothe Respondents (both followers of the Indigenous faith and Christians) 57

Table 8 : Chothe Population Census of Manipur, India from 1931-2011 (Scheduled Tribe) 62

Table 9 : Chiefs of Ajouhu (Purum Khullen) 81

Table 10 : Khongkhang Chothe Group: Their Villages and its Chiefs 84

Table 11 : Chothe Population by Village: Census of India 2001 and Personal Data 2004 96

Table 12 : Chothe Literacy Rate: Census of India 2001 and Personal Data Sept.-Oct. 2004 105

Table 13 : Chothe Clans and Sub-clans According to Various Ethnographers.. 122

Table 14 : Kinship Terminology 127

Table 15 : The Socio-political Structure of theVillage Council (Hu-bungkung) of the Chothe (See also CLAM, record book p. 5) 132

Table 16   : Fix Amount of Customary Fees for Coronation Feast
(see T.C. Das, 1945:176) 137

Table 17   : Distribution of Occupationas Government employees
(Personal data 2004-05) 147

Table 18   : Distribution of Chothe Occupation: Non-Govt. Employees
(Personal data 2004-05) 149

Table 19(i)   : Chothe Standard Measurement of Volume in Indigenous Units 150

Table 19(ii)   : Chothe Standard Measurement of Length in Indigenous Units/
Methods 150

Table 20   : Variation of Names Referred by Various Ethnic Groups to a
Person 198

Table 21   : Distribution of Chothe Respondents who Believes in Totems 229

Table 22 (i)   : Followers of Indigenous Faith who Believe in Superstitions 232

Table 22 (ii)   : Followers of Christian Persons who Believe in Superstitions 232

Table 22 (iii): Distribution of Chothe Respondents who Believe in Superstitions
(Both Followers of Indigenous Faith and Christians) 232

Table 23   : Chothe Respondents who Believes in the Existence of Ghost
and Spirits 250

Glossary

Abai – A book. Also refers to yam (*abai*) if used in heavy drop tone.

Abai jek – Prohibition of yam plantation. A taboo observed on *Lamleh lethoipa* ritual day.

Abung/ Bungkung – The banyan tree.

Achoi – The yeast cake. Often used in fermenting rice-beers or liquor.

Achui rhin/lin – The post-harvest festival (festival meant for the youths or common festival).

Aek – stool.

Aham/ Kuchu Leiham – A herb (*Goniothalamus sesquipedalis*) believed can dispel evil spirit.

Ahang-yuishom – The black praying mantis. The totem of Chothe *Mareem* or *Marim's* clan.

Ahom rui – The rope of a creeper plant (The Meitei called it *heingang mari*).

Ahu Lungsukbung – The historical ancient settlement near Henglep behind Thangching peak.

Ahu Saishakung – Abandon Chothe settlement near Treasurer Office, opp. Kangla, Imphal.

Ahu Tuisarung – Abandon Chothe settlement near Tipaimuk area (Lit. Hot running water).

Ahu Yangpalkung – Abandon settlement of Chothe, near Lanthabal, Imphal.

Ai-ari jan – The chicken intestine divination.

Aihung – The cock's crow.

Aike /arke jan – The chicken leg's divination.

Aire kung lam – The peacocks' dance, performed during *Innampei rin* festival.

Ai-ring thapa lethoi – The ritual for the exchange of soul with a fowl.

Aishan – Turmeric (*Spe.Curcuma caesia*), lit. Red colour for chicken.

Aithing – Ginger (*Spe.Zingiber officinale*), lit. Pure tree for chicken.

Aithing jan – The ginger divination.

Ajong-pa – Male monkey.

Aju – The rat.

Aju aek – The rat's stool (lit. *Aju*= rat, *aek*= stool).

Akae – The goat.

Akae aek – The goat's stool. (*Akae*= goat; *aek* = stool).

Aku – The number 'Nine'.

A-lung – The heart.

Amot – Banana.

Anam kokna lethoi – The purification ritual for any ominous sign. Casting of the smell to relief from the suppression and depression and chaos in family.

Anha – A bitter shrub plant with small yellow flower (*Spe. Justicia adhatoda*, common name *Adulsa*).

Anleiphon/ Ariphon – A kind of creeper herbal plant (*Spe. Centella asiatica/ Indian* pennywort).

Annajek/ anpak-napak – Any kind of green vegetables.

Antui–The fermented bamboo shoot (*Soibum* in Meitei) used as a delicacy in food items.

Angou – White colour.

Anphui/ Soknoudon – A shrub plant with heart shape leaf (*Clerodendrum colebrookianum*, common name – bleeding heart).

Apa – A man or male or father.

Apate/atun – Younger paternal uncle (father's younger brother).

Apu – Grandfather (any aged old man).

Apute – The younger maternal uncle (mother's younger brothers).

Areng – The king.

Arrang – The paternal aunt's husband (father's sister's husband).

Arrow (Airow) lethoi – The rite of roasting a fowl/chicken.

Arsharah – The spleen.

Arsharahjan – The divination of dog's spleen.

Artui – The egg (any kind of egg).

Artui jan – The egg divination.

Arung – Stone.

Arung junpa – The shot put throw or stone throw (also known as *Tanghung lungthong*).

Asa/Asha – An animal.

Asa arung – The animal's stone.

Asan/ashan – The red colour.

Asei-asi – Taboo, forbidden from doing any kind of evil or wrong things or face death.

Aseipa – The act of prohibition or announcement of taboo on any village purification rituals.

Ashai – The singer/ initiator/ or vocalist.

Ashang – The respondent/s.

Assain or *Ashei* – The Assistant-Priest, who assist the high priest in major ceremonies.

Ashiem (*Tokana*) – Lit. Handmade special gift (some money) given to persons for rendering his/her service in kindness.

Ashina sikan-ongpa – The dismantling (sitting) ceremony of the youth unit or *Nungak-luthei bungkung.*

Ata sari – Seven brothers, related to a folktale of seven brothers.

Atan chom – High jump (lit. *taan* = run; *chom* = *jump*).

Ateirpa – The elder paternal uncle (father's elder brother).

Atha – The wings.

Athem – The appeaser, one who propitiates the deities.

A-thi – The Dead (*Thi* = dead).

Athin – Liver.

Athi-amang tampa – The offerings for the dead or ancestors.

Athi-chup ngei – Lit. The blood sucker or vampire, refers to witches.

Athi laa – The dead/ funeral song.

Athi-lam – Land of dead (signifies hell).

Athi tokana – The death's token or gift.

Athi tongthin – The instruction to the dead.

Atoy – The thigh.

Atun – Lineage/ clan's father's younger brother (agnatic group).

Avan arung/ laihu arung – The heavenly stone/the god's stone (This thunderbolt stone is consider as talisman with a belief that it can dispel evil spirits and used as medicine).

Awa-aampi pun – The main traditional shawl of the Chothe, meaning 'bright motif'.

Bakton – A long tree bean that have high medicinal values, known as *shamba* in Meitei.

Bakuk – Pieces of broken earthen pot.

Baibek – A bird belonging to Koel family.

Balei/barei – The most common flat winnow, having a diameter of 2-2 ½ ft.

Bambu – A Rongmei term for Chothe *Shunglung* the gods of four directions of a village.

Bampuijairik hongpa – The proposal youth coming to whole the night at the girl's house.

Bampuilikhongni – The particular day the youth come to stay at the proposed girl's house.

Bhoot – Ghost or spirit.

Bu – Rice or food.

Buhu – The largest tray basket, generally having a diameter of 3-3½ ft.

Bulum – A handful of warm rolled cook rice.

Bungkung/bung-kung – Around the base of the banyan tree (*A-bung* = the banyan tree).

Bumoupa – Lit. Loss of appetite, or allergic to food.

Bungpi (abung) – The pipal/peepul tree (*Ficus benghalensis*) or refer to a banyan tree.

Butoi rin – The bread festival. Another name for *achui* festival.

Cacharis – Refers to Bodo-Cacharis of Vaishanavist faith, who are locally known as *Mayang* (*Bengali*) derived from *Maihang* meaning 'black or dark face'.

Chaang/chang – The right side or matured or ripe or odd number, or the animal's trap.

Chaam – A knife or sword.

Chaampupa – Lit. The sword bearer, who behest as the God's child/ guardian angel in finding the best burial spot when a relative dies.

Chamtun – Lit. Hilt sword, but refers to the decorated dancing sword.

Chamtun lam – The sword dance. It signifies victory and is performed during *Innampei* festival.

Changchou – A music instrument played by mouth made of bamboo like harmonica.

Changrui/Changloi/Hachari-noupong/Petai – Refers to the junior most supervisor or information secretary, who is a member of village council.

Chapan thapa – An appeasement rite for minor illnesses. It means sending a message in advance to gods.

Chawte/Shote/Zote/Chote/Chothe – It derives from *Kachokte*or *Kachoite* meaning, 'the child I hold/ stirred with'.

Cheiche – The small bamboo forceps (V-shaped) served as spoon to eat chutney (*mashipoi*).

Cheijunpa – The mischievous spirit or ghost that often throws a stick from a bushy hideouts.

Cheitharol Kumpaba (*ChK*) – The Court Chronicles of Manipur (ancient manuscript).

Chiru – An indigenous tribe of Manipur. A cognatic group of Chothe. It is believed to have derived from the term *Chi-ngu* meaning 'salt thief' an event occur in the past.

Ching leihu – Hill gods.

*Chinglang/ngan*or *Checklang* – Thatch plant, tall-stalked very woolly mullein with densely packed yellow flowers grown in hills.

Glossary

Chisai/Chesai/Risai – Uncooked rice in Chothe.

Chithou – Sticky rice.

Chithou-ahang – Black sticky rice.

Chithou-angou – White sticky rice.

Chithou-asan – Red sticky rice.

Chongtak lak – Long jump.

Chote munpi – Name of an abandon settlement near Henglep sub-division, Churchandpur district. Now occupied by New-Kuki the Thadou speaking group.

Chungthieng – Almighty God or the God of the Above in Chothe.

Dai – Cymbal.

Daishin – Pakhangpa's mother. The elder daughter of the great Chothe chief Surou (Tarang or Nungkarakpa or Sanarakpa) and wife Lenghoinu. She is also known as Kamlangtaopi or Thamoilempi or *Leinung Yabirok Yakha Channu* by the Meitei.

Deir – Longy or dhoti (Originally it was black in colour for Chothe).

Doi-ai – Lit. Placing a fowl. It refers to the 'imitative magic'. It means someone buries or placed or positioned or drop something imitative like doll by sacrificing a fowl to deceive or inflict the enemy/ targeted person using magical charm.

Fho – The shield.

Fho lam – Lit. The shield dance. A warrior dance with a shield in celebration of war victory.

Fho-parakpa – Lit. The shield movement. Refers to how a warrior moved skilfully his shield during wars and battles in the past.

Ghalim – A headman appointed by every village themselves among Old-Kukis. An old term used by outsiders/foreigners to refer to the political hierarchy of tribals.

Hachari – *noupong* or *Changrui/Changloi* or *Petai*–The Junior most supervisor or information secretary among the members of village council.

Hachari-ulin or *Changrui* – The senior supervisor, who is a member of the village council.

Haihru/laihu – God (any god).

Hancha – The intermediate leader, among the *Tang-ngarinta bungkung* (matured-adult unit).

Hau – A term commonly used by the Meitei to refer to any tribesman or tribal or hill people.

Heiruk keipa – The purchase of god's fruits and sweets for the benedictory ritual.

Heloi – Lit. The seven sisters' elves. Any spirits that do not touch the ground with their feet.

Hikkai laiwa/mahei – The magical spell that split the lovers or married couple, in Meitei.

Hithang – The junior leader among the *Tang-ngarinta bungkung* (matured-adult unit).

Hloukal or *Phamnei-ngei* – The ruling party or the village council members among the Christian villages.

Hu-bungkung – The entire member of the village council, when judgement is done in public.

Huipithoranga – Chothe mythical cave. Lit. 'The cave where the five men sprang out'.

Huisem – The flute.

Hulak/hurak – The village chief.

Hung – The drum.

Hungchong lam – Lit. The dance of jumping drum, performed during the *Theilhong* the merit or coronation feast.

Hungdoi rin (*Kriton* in Meitei) – Special dead commemoration ceremony, observed in memory of their ancestors.

Hung matheipa – The tuning of drums. Drums are tuned before any major festival begins.

Hushapa – Lit.Village constructors. Refers to the four directions gods (*Shunglung/Bambu*) that guard the village.

Ichang /Aire-chang – The peacock's feather (*Aire* means peacock).

Idou/Aidou – The wild turmeric (*Zingiber cassumunar*).

Imphal – The capital of Manipur. Derived from a tribal dialect 'Inn-phai' meaning the big house in the plain or palace in the valley (*Inn* = house; *phai* = plain). Later some Meitei pronounce it as 'Yumphal' but subsequently became known as 'Imphal'.

Inn – A House.

Innku/eenku – The lineage.

Innku laa – The lineage song.

Innampei rhin/lin – The pre-harvest festival (festival for elders) of Chothe.

Inn chung arrow – Lit. Roasting of chicken on the house roof, connected to a folktale.

Inn-thingpa – The house purification ceremony.

I-phung – The wild-ginger species.

Iring thapa – The ritual performed to exchange the captive soul with a live fowl, especially for a sick child suffering from air borne diseases/ illness.

Ishan jek – The prohibitions of turmeric plantation (*Ishan* mean turmeric, *jek* = trouble).

Ishantui inpa – The drinking the turmeric juice.

Ithing jek – The prohibitions of ginger plantation.

Jai or *Yai* – Sleep or sleeping (*jaipa* the act of sleeping).

Jai or *Yai* (*Jan*) – Also means the talisman stone. Refers to any magical object.

Jai/jan-anpa – Lit.The act of looking at the talisman stone. Refers the act of divination or consulting the talisman stone or crystal ball for any ominous sign. I *Jairik hongpa* – Coming to stay for the night.

Jaitha – The sound sleep. Also refers to the pre-scheduled joint-labour work of rotation, sometime used as *lomjui*.

Kamhao – The Sukte group, belonging to Chin-Kuki-Mizoethnic group, once attacked Chothe and other tribes of Manipur by 17th century.

Kamkeirang/akei – Lit. The striped tiger (In short used as *Akei* means the tiger).

Kamsabut – An indigenous herb commonly use in treatment of malaria, gastroenteritis, diabetes and cancer diseases.

Kangshet – The woman's waist strap, wore above the hip to fasten the sarong/mekhla.

Kansuh Kanrung – Mythical son of Makan man, who led out Chothe people from the cave.

Kehom – Pineapple.

Keirou thou – The rite for the purification of the family (for ancestors).

Keirung-ulin – The senior rice manager or treasurer of the village council.

Khaba-nganba – An ancient term to refer the Khoibu-Maring tribe or Fhalam (*Poi* origin) by valley Meitei of Imphal, believed to have first occupied the Kangla area.

Khamlang-Taopi – The name of Pakhangpa's mother, known before her marriage to Khongding the Moirang king. A nickname indicating a lady originated from the Kham or Khampat land by valley people since she belong to Chothe tribe.

Kharai – The cooked meat package.

Kharam Leishok anganba – The beautiful red flower given to Sunurembi by Pakhangpa as a token of his love, plucked from the abandon Kharam village gate during his expedition. The flower is now commonly known as *Sunurembi Toukhamlei* meaning the forbidden flower of *Sunurembi* after a decree was announced prohibiting any commoner from wearing it.

Khiyang/Khiang/Hiyang – A major clan of Chothe (lit. Lighten after parturition).

Khok – A kind of indigenous tree of soft wood with small leaves.

Khomnoubi lai – Lit. Tender breast milk. Refers to an appeasement rite for the young mother who lack breast milk for the baby.

Khongkap – Lit. Foot pace or steps. The Khongkhang village derived its name after one of the queen of Manipur expressed about the footpath when she visited their village *Mouhulon.*

Khongsai – One of the clan of Thadou speaking group, also commonly known as *Khongjai.*

Khuman – One of the royal clans of Meitei. Earlier predominantly found in Moirang.

Khutchai – The witches the sprinkles/ spread with her hands.

Khutchai mit – Lit. The evil-eye witch.

Khutchei jum – Lit. The witch with pointed index finger.

Khut tang – The standard measurement unit of length, from a man's elbow to the tip of middle finger.

Khut-shei – Lit.Long hands. But here it refers to a witch with long hands by layman.

Koi – The bangles (lit. round) or circle.

Koikung – The centre point of the universe or the epicentre.

Kom – An indigenous tribe of Manipur (a cognatic group of Chothe).

Konjai jaicheipa – The valedictory divination performed at the closing ceremony of the festival.

Konjaijunpa – The forecasting of the coin or lead divination.

Konjin Tuthokpa or *Sentreng* – The Meitei mythical name for *Pakhangpa.*

Korpa – The brass bowl man. Refers to the Hindu priest with the holy brass cup.

Kuchu Leiham – A kind of wild herbs (*Spe. Goniothalamus sesquipedalis*) used as incense to dispel evil spirits.

Kuki – A major ethnic group of Manipur. Believed to have derived from DZO (Lushai) word from 'Tui-Kuk', for Tipperah (Sakchip) Tribe (see Shaw 1929: 11).

Kui-git – Lit. Piercing of the ear. A ceremony performed by member of the council elders to obtain higher status in society.

Kum – The year.

Kum tepa – The counting of years.

Kuptreng or *Ashiba* – The Meitei mythical name for *Sanamahi.*

Kwai –The beetle or areca nuts.

La or laa – A song or the folksong.

Laan – The carrying basket.

Laander – The semi-hole basket.

Laan-kum – A kind of porch or cache of a small basket, where the scrolls/ small bamboo sticks are kept hung in it.

Laan-wang – The haversack basket.

Lai – Gods or deities.

Lajek – The prohibition of weaving or starting a loom for new cloth (when a villager dies).

Lam /Ram – Lit. An area/land (e.g. Lamlanghupi lit. *Lam*- land, *lang* - bright, *hu*-village *pi* – main/ mother) which means the main/ parent village on a bright mound.

Laimaton – The highest peak of *Loiching/Loijing* hill ranges on the southwestern hills, near Bishnupur town, on the northern side of Thangjing peak.

Laisana – Lit. The god's gold. The name given to Pakhangpa's wife, often referred by the Imphal people to mean the queen.

La-lui angou–The white stream of thread.

Laman – The dancing ground or open space in front of the sacred-grove or deities' site.

Lambu tupu (Lampu turpu) – Lit. The old man the owner of land. It refers to the 'geographical or tourist guide' or 'officer-in-charge' of the land in ancient days.

Lamchel – The race.

Lamkang – An indigenous tribe of Manipur, mostly inhabiting in Chandel district.

Lamlanglon – An ancient Chothe village name (lit. the bright frontier land/ mound).

Lamleh lethoipa or *Panthong iratpa* – The special ritual for all the village gates and direction gods where the ritual is performed at the main village road/entrance gate.

Lamta – The month of February-March of Lunar calendar in Meitei.

Lamhel – The forest spirits that guard a particular forest area, commonly known as *Surai-lamhel*.

Lam-meithanpi – The forest fireball spirits.

Lamthi – Refers to the death of a person in wildernesses or outside the village.

Lamthing lethoi – Lit. The rite for the purification of an area/ land.

Langpan – The month of September-October in Meitei.

Leibak –The new recruit of young boys as soldiers, age above 14/15 years who have performed the youth initiation ceremony and inducted to the youth unit ‘of *Nungak-luthei bungkung* as members.

Leibak manpa – Lit. The youth initiation ceremony for both boys and girls (teenage/adolescence) to become member of the youth unit.

Leihu lamjai – The middle-world or the middle path on the way to the God's land.

Leihu mit – Lit. the 'evil-eye' in Chothe, a synonymously term for a witch.

Leihu pottampa (*Heiruk keipa*) – The veneration of the village God (Pu Lungchungpa).

Leining – The woman's headgear.

Leinung Yabirok Yakha Chanu – The named of Pakhangba's mother, commonly referred by the valley people in earlier days (lit. the lady from the interior slanting stream).

Leirema (*Leimaren*) – The god of fertility, wealth and prosperity (the house god).

Leirum – The woman's earring (also refers to a type of cloth/shawl).

Lei-shei – Lit. The witch with long tongue. Refers to a witch that sticks out her red tongue beyond its normal length in her sleep.

Lei-zu/leizu – Lit. The purchase wine. Refers to the country liquor sold commercially.

Lethoi-pa – The act sacrificial offering.

Linglut – The woman's blouse, in Chothe.

Liangmei – An indigenous tribe of Manipur. Considered a cognate of Chin-Kuki group who migrated northwards and assimilated with Rongmei (Kabui) and Teznimi tribes.

Loh – It has several meanings and is use according to the subject in different verb forms. It means visit, gathering or going in group or to burn.

Lohchou-maichou – The feast of merit to obtain higher social status in society.

Loipa – Roaming/visiting.

Lomjui – Lit. The scheduled joint-labour work, especially in paddy fields.

Lomjui jaima – The middle joint-labour group leader.

Lomjui noupong – The junior joint-labour group leader.

Lomjui ulin – The senior joint-labour group leader.

Lomrui – Lit. Working together with comrades/ friends, as part of the joint-labour team.

Lomtun – The festive house, or the family who host the village festival/ celebration.

Loukhatpa – Lit. The act of taking up or accepting. Refers to the traditional 'send of ceremony' of a girl whose marriage was considered invalid because of breach of elopement, where the girl's parent later agreed to accept as their daughter and son-in-law by taking the loyal bride price from the boy.

Lou-houpa – The simple offertory rite for the four directions gods of village deities done after the benedictory ritual of the major festivals (Lit. throwing away of the medicine).

Loumi – The opposition party or the farmer's political group among the Christian villages.

Lu/A-lu – The head.

Lubak – The storage basket in Meitei.

Lui-jand/ Ruijand – The suicide committed by hanging (*Lui/ Rui*= rope, *Jand* = hang).

Luje – Man's headgear, (*Lu* = head, *Je/ jep* = wrapper/d)

Lungchungpa – Literally it means 'one who sits above the rock'. It refers to the Dragon-Python God (also known as *Ruipi Shantai* in Chothe) and when transformed into human being is called as *Pakhangpa*. In Chothe, the Dragon-Python symbolises the 'Rain God', where 'Ru/Lu' means 'rain'; 'Chung or vaan', means 'above'; and "Pa" is masculine gender for 'father/man/male'.

Lung-kang – The rock bed (*Lung*- rock/ stone; *kang*- attic, synonymously refers to bed= *kotkang*).

Lungni – This/ that day.

Lungnik – The tightly knitted winnow, with small holes compared to *Wai-wang*.

Lungleh waishu – The Chothe historic settlement at Lungleh in Mizoram. *Lungleh* means, 'abundant of rocks or stones', and *Waishu* or *Warshu* means, 'let it shine or prosper'.

Lung-pi – The huge rock (the mother rock).

Luplak – The assistant-chief of a village.

Luwang – Royal clan of Meitei, synonymous with Chothe *Thao* clan.

Maan-loh – The demand of bride-price.

Maan shipa – The act of giving the bride-price.

Machampa – To neutralised or null or void.

Maharani – Refers to 'Queen' in Meitei or Bishnupriya (A borrowed word from Hindi).

Mahei jadu – Magical charm (lit. Fruitful or productive act).

Mahei laiwa – Magical spell (lit. Spell the fruitful word of god by tongue).

Mai/ma – North or front side.

Maiba – The Meitei priest (also act as sorcerer).

Maibee – The Meitei priestess.

Maichoupi – A kind of merit feast, identified with an ancient settlement.

Makan – A major clan of Chothe (lit. one that stop the fight).

Maksa – Lit. 'Alliance or compatriot', especially refer only by the wife giver family, lineage or clan members to their brother-in-laws/son-in-laws.

Mameeshi – Lit. 'His Left Shadow', to mean the Human Beings or Mankind.

Manrung – Lit. Payback the earnings.

Mansum – The traditional bride-price. Significant bride-price was a gong in early days.

Mao – An indigenous Naga tribe of Manipur in the north.

Mapi – Lit. His/her grandmother.

Mapu – Lit. His/her grandfather.

Maram – An indigenous Naga tribe of Manipur, who migrated to north in the early days from south. Believed to be a cognate of Chin-Kuki by linguistic and culture.

Maraampa – The lot's charm for the first selected name of a child.

Mareem/Marim – A major clan of Chothe. Lit. merry or happy.

Maring – An indigenous tribe of Manipur largely inhabiting in eastern Chandel district.

Mashi – Chilly.

May-poi – Lit. Blindness remover or Deflector of blurriness of eyes.

May-tum – Lit. A lump of meat. Now refers to meat chutney.

Meruk – The smallest standard measuring basket.

Mee/Mameeshi – Man or ordinary layman or a person (human beings).

Meebo-laa – Commemoration song of their ancestors or lineage head.

Meekhut sem – Lit. Witchcraft act. Refers to the imitative magic involving the handwork.

Mei – It means either 'fire' or 'tail' of an animal.

Mei-aek – Charcoal.

Meingai – The nickname of *Chothe Thangwai/ Thangmei Pakhangpa* use during his childhood, commonly refer by the Chothe.

Meitei – The conglomeration of various tribes living in the Manipur valley, Imphal, who converted to Hinduism in latter 18th cc. (see endnotes of Chapter 3).

Meishei – Lit. Firestick. Refers to the bundle of thatch stalks used as torch in olden days.

Meishei huppa – Binding of thatch stalks into bundles to be used as fire/torch in festivals and other important night occasions.

Ming bohpa – Lit. 'Naming of the child'.

Mithun – Bison.

Mit-trang – Magic or the fallacy of the eye by magic.

Moipung – Big sea shell.

Moirang – One of the ancient principality of Manipur in south. Earlier known as *Kege-Moirang*to mean the 'Chinese stock', later dominated by the Khuman clan.

Moirang Ningthourol Lambuba (*MNL*) – Literary accounts of the kings of Moirang.

Moonah/Kum – Ancient term for year in Chothe.

Mouhulon – An old name for Khongkhang village, derived from a bamboo species *Moupi*.

Mou-rui – Bringing the bride or a girl (to the boy's house).

Mou-shem – The arrangement of a girl/ bride for a marriage.

Muithidang/Yuithidang – Tying and hanging the small bundles of dog meat in a string according to the number of youths.

Muithoi (artui) – Lit. 'Waking up the hairs'. Another serious method of egg divination.

Muipa zuron – Lit. The wine served to tame.

Nachung/ nuku – Chest (*nuku* = breast).

Nashu – East (lit. direction in which the sun rise).

Nashu (Huru) shunglung (Bambu) – The village deity of the east direction.

Nata – West (lit. direction in which the sun sets).

Natashunglung – The village deity of the west direction.

Najui lam – Lit. The dance of women folk. Refers to the dance comprising only girls in *bampui* or *Innampei rin* festival.

Neemjek – Prohibition of *Neem* (a kind of yeast plant) plantation.

Ngaibek – The winter bird.

Ngakha/maha – Small silvery fishes.

Ngaparum-Chingjin – New Cachar road that enter from Kangpokpi side.

Ngavok – The dog fish (*Sp.Channa punctatus*).

Ngoupok – Dried germinating seeds of paddy used in making yeast (*achoi*).

Ni – The sun.

Nik – The traditional girl's longy or sarong or mekla.

Ni-nu – Lit. The mother sun. Mythically the Chothe consider the Sun as female.

Nimok-la – Devotional song of sun worship.

Ningthoujas – Lit. Theroyal (seven) clans of Meitei kingdom. Established after each regional kingdoms leaders accepted the confederacy with the Kangla king as their emperor.

Nom-nompa – Lit. The limping ghost.

Numei – A woman.

Nungak Luthei or *Nungak-lutherbungkung* – The council of girls and boys (youth) unit.

Nunghai laan – Lit. The back swinging carrier basket.

Nungak loh – Refers to the three years marriage labour service served in girl's house.

Noupham – Placenta.

Nouphamphumpa – The act of burying the placenta.

Noukham butha/chathak – The simple rite of offering some food and sweets to the gods/spirits that blocks the placenta during parturition by reckoning the Sun and Moon gods as the earliest.

Ouk/ok – Pig.

Ouk/ok manpa – Lit. Pig catching. It means catch a pig or the pig hunting game.

Pai – Haversack basket.

Pakhang-lakpa – Leader of *Tang-ngarinta* member and Commander-in-chief of the youth.

Pamheide/Pamheiba – Lit. 'The forbidden child to embraced or hold onto one's lap' in Meitei. It refers to King Garibniwaz (Waireng Pamheiba).

Pangal – Refers to Meitei-Muslim (*Meitei-Pangal*) of Manipur (who migrated from Cachar).

Parpa – A major clan of Chothe. Lit. The act of blooming (of a flower).

Pasek – Lit. A deep scar mark. Also means a kind of dimple or a mole.

Pena – Violin or sarinda in Meitei.

Phei – The bow (and arrows).

Phiren-lamta – Months of February-March in Meitei.

Phambakpa – The feast of coronation (for the political leaders).

Phamkeipa – The promotion ceremony designated to the council of *Urinta* and *Tang-ngarinta* members.

Phamtakpa – Designating the political position of the newly appointee.

Phumpa – The act of burying.

Phung – Clan (not lineage).

Phung tlaanglam – Fine imposed for breach of marriage outside the prescriptive clan/village/country.

Pheiroi khapa – Refers to the basket type made on the ground to fence the offerings made to the gods during *Lamleh lethoipa* ritual.

Phuirang – Hornbill. The totem of *Khiyang* or *Hiyang's* clan.

Phiyung – Broom (House broom).

Pipa – The eldest male head of a family (*innsuung*) or lineage's (*innku*) or clan's (*phung*).

Pingprou – The swallow bird. Assumed as the totem of *Rangshai/Riangshai*.

Piepei – A miniature of bamboo basket.

Pot-shem – It means arrangement of materials. Also refers to 'contagious magic', where magical charm is spelled by a priest or the concern person on any kind of object or edible things for personal gain and given to his targeted person or enemy.

Potshempa – The act of arranging materials. Also refers to bride sending off ceremony.

Pumningpa – Lit. The act of body worshipping or baptism or transformation of body. Refers to the ritual of exchange of soul.

Pun – Cloth or shawl.

Pun junpa – Lit. Casting the cloth, a term used at the time of child naming ceremony.

Rai – The navel cord.

Ral-laa – War song.

Ral-thouna laa – The opening song to begin the war.

Ral lu chouna laa – The song of how one chop off an enemy's head (during the war).

Ral-rulna laa – The closing/retreating war song (A symbolic song sung at the end of war).

Rangi – Thatch grasses.

Rangshai/Riangshai – Another major clan of Chothe.

Rashi – Personality or charisma in Meitei/ Hindi.

Rengchangnu – The cicada girl (*Hangi-ngorang* in Meitei).

Rengchang – A person in charge of music and its instruments.

Renglei – Lit.The king's flower. Refers to a kind of herbal plant known as *langtharei* in Meitei [(Bot. *Eupatoriumcammanoi* Linn. (Asteraceae)].

Rhin/rin/Lin – Lit. Festival or the merry time or feast.

Rongmei – A group belonging to Zeliangrong community (also known as *Kabui* by Meitei while other tribes call them as *Meirong*).

Rotcham – Bagpipe, refers to indigenously made bagpipe musical instrument.

Rui – Lit. Comrade/Fellowship.Young followers of the village council (also called as Changrui or as Changloi).

Ruicham/Ruisem – The bagpiper or the wind blower.

Ruihong – Lit. Bring in the comrade/friends. A term use for the first political initiation ceremony among the members of unit.

Ruishang or *Loishang* – Refers to the bachelor's house or the youth's dormitory. (All kinds of training are given to the youths by seniors and elders in this bachelor's house, besides the deities' caretakers also stayed with the youths.

Ruikai or *Luikai* – Refers to the Tug-of-war game, played in ancient days by youths.

Ruipi lam – Lit. The Python's dance. It refers to the criss-cross circular movement dance carried out at the end of *Innampei* festival symbolising the twisting of Dragon-Python.

Ruipi – Lit. Adult/matured python. But refers to Dragon-python.

Ru kokna lethoi–Lit. Rain invoking rite.

Ruu/Aruu – Lit. Trapped net. Often refers to any kind of fishing trap net.

Saam – Hair.

Saamtharnu/Saamthanu – Lit. A lady with a beautiful hair.

Sachou – The otter. The totem of the *Thao's* clan.

Sae-kupkonjai – The divination of small coins.

Sakma – The cucumber.

Sakma lethoi – The rite of cucumber (A rite performed when a child falls sick due to the influence of an evil-eye or witchcraft act).

Sakting – Northern side.

Sala-atheirrin – The dead invocation ritual.

Salam sari – The seven meat shares.

Samtrok or *samtok* – A shrub thorny plant with small bitter fruits (*Spe. Solanum Kurjii*).

Sana – Gold.

Sanamahi – The god of wealth.

Santai – Lit. Like a red basket. Refers to the Dragon's fire balls.

Sanpan-lei – A tropical thorny shrub plant with tiny flowers.

Saphei – Lit. The slope side of veranda.

Sapu – A person in-charge for decoration.

Sarrnu/sheinu/chanu – The biological younger sister.

Saram-ngaram – The socio-religious custom of preparing the meat/ fish and sharing equally in accordance to the norm among the exclusive seven elders of village council.

Sataipa – The act of hunting.

Sawai-zu – The husk rice beer (prepared by mixing some paddy husk and dry yeast bark).

Selungpa or *Keirung-noupong* – The junior rice treasurer or accountant.

Sentreng or *Konjin Tuthokpa* – The Meitei mythical name for *Pakhangpa*.

Shamla ming-shang – Refers to the ritual to signify that the child's hair has grown and his name has been cleanse.

Shang/ Shaang – The paddy, in Chothe.

Shanghong lethoi – A ritual performed to the paddy's god, to have a good harvest.

Shang-jaire – Lit. The paddy/rice of good health.

Shangjek – A taboo, prohibiting rice plantation on *lamleh lethoipa* ritualistic day.

Shang-koinu – Lit. The curve paddy (refers to a variety of paddy with curved tip).

Shang kokpa (Sabuhung) – Lit. Calling the paddy. Refers to the rite for plentiful harvest.

Shang-likte – The tiny paddy/rice.

Shang-maichamnu – The wrinkle paddy/rice.

Shang-ningshiton – The sweet fragrance/oily paddy.

Shang-phou laa – The song of drying paddy.

Shang-rung – The talisman of paddy. Lit. Paddy stone. Believed to bring wealth and riches by this paddy stone talisman.

Shapa/Chapa – The young unmarried boy/male. Lit. Bachelor/ youth.

Sharu sipa – Lit. The bone washing ceremony. Refers to the complete assimilation ceremony to become a valid permanent citizen of Chothe community.

Shawai-zu – The fermented husk rice beer.

Shei – The spear.

Shiam lethoi – Rite for malnutrition child.

Shimleinu – The supreme queen of mother earth.

Shirsim – A kind of wild vegetable grown in forest. Considered the totem of Parpa's clan.

Shomareng – The locust. Refers to the big and huge locust king.

Shuk – The pasta. Refers to the indigenous made huge pasta for pounding paddy.

Shuk/ Shei junpa – Lit. The javelin throw. In olden days this huge pasta is used as javelin when youth play games and sports.

Shuksoi – The snail (the edible small varieties).

Shuum/Shum – The gong (made of brass or tin often used in festival, death and emergency).

Shunglung – The gods of four directions of a village. The Rongmei call it as *Bambu*.

Si or *waie* – The decay or death, or left side or even number.

Sire or *Leikoi lam* – The hand twisting dance of the boys normally around a bon-fire.

Sikan chei – Lit. The baton. Refers to a special cane stick use to punish and beat the disobedient youth.

Sikang laa – Lit.The punishment song. A song sung to remind and encourage the culprits.

Sikan-ongpa – Lit. The official report and thanksgiving ceremony to the higher authority. It refers to the act where three boys made formal report by showing their gratitude (*thoukeipa*) to the elders and the host for the good time they had on behalf of the youths at the end of the festival.

Siki – The animal's horn (the horn of bison or buffalo).

Siki lam – The bison or mithun horn dance. The dance performed during *Shanghong* festival.

Sora – The lion king.

Soraren – Refers to the Sky or Sun god, symbolising like the ferocious lion that decide the fate of man.

Soknoudon/Anphui – An edible shrub plant with heart shape leaf (*Spe.Clerodendrum colebrookianum,* common name is bleeding heart).

Sumphai adon – Lit. Cloud shoots or the dew.

Sunu/saarnu/chanu – The maiden or young girl.

Sunurembi/pi – The Pakhangpa's wife, addressed by the Moirang people.

Sutrai – Lit. The crazy vagina. Refers to the spirits of a woman or a child who died during child birth.

Tabun – Wrestling.

Tai – Basket (any storage basket).

Tai-don – The plinth basket.

Tairen – (*Spe. Toona ciliate,* common name is *Toon*). Some Chothe called it as '*Ateithing*' (the firewood plant) where the leaf is often used in religious purposes.

Tai-ten – It means a 'farm hut or tent', derives from the ancient practice of making a basket (*tai*) in such farm huts.

Tai-wang – Large holes basket.

Taibelou Pukphat Sapeilou – The Pakhangpa's treaty place near Bishnupur town in the south-western region with Thokchao the eldest Angom prince.

Tanghung-chang – A leader among the leibaks who is in charge of sports.

Tangkip – The mythical first chief (*Hulak*) of Chothe and also the eldest son of *Zurung/Yuhlungpu.*

Tanglai-chang – The leader of junior soldiers (*leibaks*) in charge of decoration.

Tang-ngarinta bungkung – Lit. The matured-adults. Refers to the second highest unit/house of the village council.

Tangsha – The senior leader of the *Tang-ngarinta bungkung* (matured-adults unit).

Ta-shan – The bamboo strap divination.

Tastepata – *Spe.Cinnamomum tamala* plant leaf.

Tenyimis/Tinyimia/Tenyidie – Refers to an ethnic group believed to have common origin, comprising of Chakhesang, Angami, Mao, Poumei, Maram, Zeliangrong (Zeliang, Liangmei, Rongmei), etc. inhabiting in Nagaland and Manipur. Some called themselves as *Tenidii.*

Thamoilempi – The name of Pakhangpa's mother, known after her marriage by the Moirang people instead of calling her as Khamlangtaopi.

Thanidam – Lit. 'The moon and the sun are alright'. The mythical wife of *Kachokte/Kachoite* and the first woman of Chothe.

Thangwai atengba – Lit. 'The aided man of King Thangwai Kongding of Moirang. A popular name given to Pakhangpa by Moirang people as 'the faithful assistant' of Kongding before Pakhangpa succeeded him as the sovereign king of Moirang Principality.

Thangvan-rengpa – The heavenly King/God.

Thangting – The south or back side (*Kha/santhong* in Meitei).

Thangvan lam – The land of God, signifying the heavenly abode.

Thawai – The soul or spirit of the death.

Thawai kokpa – The ritual of calling of the soul/spirit.

Tha/thla tepa – The counting of the months (Counting of the lunar calendar).

Thakna – The tobacco leaf (lit. Scratchy/allergy).

Thangting or *Hute shunglung* (*Bambu*) – The village deity of the southern gate direction.

Tha/thla-pa – The Moon (Mythically considered as a male).

Thao – A major clan of Chothe (lit. Fats or oily).

Thao-lum – The oil manufacturer.

Theel-hongpa – The merit feast thrown by a rich villager in order to attain social position and status in the society by erecting monolith as a sign of posterity and God's blessing (Lit. *Theel* = erection of stone, especially before a person is dead).

Theichang – The fig tree or fruit.

Thei-chura or*Shuru* – The goose-berry.

Theinompa – The ghost who hurl granule or shakes fruit trees, especially at night.

Theinou – The mango fruit.

Theipi (*mashipoi*) – (bot. *Meyna laxiflora/Muyna*) a kind of wild fruit that looks like apple. The fresh leaf served as delicacy when prepared as chutney.

Theipong – The jack fruit.

Theiru – The red beads of a rare fruit seed wore as necklace in olden days.

Thirang ampa – Gastric or gastritis symptom of sickness.

Theirupok – An extremely sour fruit like orange with thick covering. A piece of the dried covering is added in meat and fish curry for its pleasant flavour.

Theithui – The lemon fruit.

Theithum – The mandarin orange.

Thi-duh – The dead anniversary.

Thiemrui – Followers of the priest.

Thiempi – Priestess.

Thiempu/Thiampu – The priest.

Think – The stick (any small stick).

Think-bompa – Lit. 'The assemblage of the scrolls or sticks' held before the main festivals.

Think keirui tamae – Lit. 'Shall we roll up the scroll sticks back'. A proposal term used by the barn secretary (*Keirungpa*) to the council of elders after the counting of the scroll sticks and assigning the portfolios ceremony is completed.

Think-tumpathink-tepa – A term to denote the ceremony of taking down and counting the scroll sticks and re-distribute the political portfolios of the village council.

Thirsu – The blacksmith.

Thla/Thaa – The moon.

Thlan – The cemetery.

Thoipithoi (*Thi-duh*) – The purification ritual done when a woman or child dies in child birth.

Thong-git – The ceremony of piercing the spinal cord, done among the council of elders (*Urinta bungkung*) members to obtain status in society and enable to occupy chieftainship in future. A ceremony performed after the '*Kui-git*' (ear-piercing).

Thoukeipa – The formal report to the village higher authority and the thanksgiving ceremony, carried out by three members from each unit of village council at the end of festival.

Tingpa – The act of shocking something in water or to ferment like rice beer (e.g. *Zu-ting*).

Tingtricknu – The elf or a kind of female spirit that live around thick bushes or stream areas.

Tlaan-chom neilah – The marriage by elopement.

Tokana(*Asheim*) – Lit. Gift in kindness. Refers to the fees paid to the priest/priestess for the service (ritual) rendered.

Tolaihong – Carrying of the palanquin to the new appointed king or chief.

Tongjei Maril – Lit. The straight mounted passes. Refers to the old-Cachar road that passes from Bishnupur to Tripura, Bangladesh (Sylhet) via Cachar (Assam) valley.

Tongkaipa – Lit. Stretch/pull the word. Refers to the simple short offertory prayer.

Tong-theina – Refers to the part of child naming ceremony meaning 'to develop speaking'.

Tongthi – The special bamboo wine pipes, 2½ feet long.

Tongthi gitpa – The ceremony of inserting the bamboo wine pipes for the festival to begin.

Tongthi-lashukpa – Removing the bamboo wine or pipes from the jar/pot after the festivals.

Toukhamlei – The beautiful red flower of Kharam tribe originally known as *Sunurembi Toukhamlei* ('The queen's forbidden flower' in Meitei) after a decree was proclaimed by Pakhangpa prohibiting any commoner from wearing it in honour of his lover Sunurembi.

Tui – Water.

Tuichum – Lit. The process of filtering water or any liquid.

Tuichum loipa – Here *tuichum* refers to the precipitation process of fermented husk rice-beer, since it is collected in droplets from the inserted small bamboo pipe to small earthen pots. Therefore, *tuichum loipa* signifies the custom of visiting each council member's houses during *Innampei* festival to relish and taste their filtered rice-beers and wine, and thereby acknowledge the best wine of the year.

Tuihumpa lethoi – The water purification ritual. A ritual performed when a person died unnaturally.

Tui laihu – The water gods/ any spirits.

Tui-patheing – The water God.

Tuishak-changlai – The leader among the *leibaks* in-charge of water.

Tui-thoipa (*Tuikuk-thingkuk*) – The rite for the water/river and forest gods.

Tuituk lethoi – The ritual commemorating the discovery of perennial water source.

U-chikte – A kind of small brown bird. Considered the totem of Yuhlung's clan.

Ulin/Urin – The aged elders (senior citizens).

Umang lai – Literally it means 'the forest god' in Meitei.

U-marok – Refers to the king chilly, in Meitei. Some called it *Naga mircha* or *Raja mircha*.

Ui-chup lethoi – Lit. The ritual of dog pillar sacrifice. Refers to the dog sacrificial ritual for children suffering from physical retardation.

Uiathin jan – The divination of dog's liver.

Urinta (*Ulinta*) *bungkung* – The council of Elders' unit around the banyan tree.

U-sil lethoi – The ritual is performed for the exchange of soul with a fish (*ngamu*=dog fish) by releasing the fish in the water. It is performed for children suffering from certain water borne diseases.

U-tang – A kind of bamboo plant species (Lit. matured wood).

Utong – The long hollow bamboo pipe. Also means a hollow bamboo cup.

U-um – The bottle gourd, often used as (water) container in olden days.

Wai-wang – The loosely knitted winnow made of bamboo straps.

Wanchei – Vernacular term for Meitei referred by Chothe in ancient days. It is used even today amongst themselves to refer the Meitei or valley people.

Wari – The story or folktales.

Yaifuna laa – The glorification song of the clan or lineage (eg. *Meebo laa/ Innku laa*).

Yairitha rin – The post-harvest festival. Also known as *Achui rin* or *chultuk rin* or *butoi rin*.

Yangpalkung – The cactus plant.

Yangle – A climber yeast plant, in Meitei (*Yangzu* in Chothe).

Yangle zu – Liquor brewed from *yangle* dry yeast bark.

Yang-zu – The dry yeast bark (*Spe.Albizia myriophylla*) used in fermenting and brewing rice-beers and liquor by Chothe and other tribes. The dry bark of the yeast plant is crash and pounded together with dry paddy sprouts and is made into yeast cake known as *Achoi*. The Meitei called it as *yangle*.

Yulung/Yuhlung/Zurung/Zulung – A major clan of Chothe (Lit. intoxicated with wine).

Zu/Yu – The wine. Refers to any kind of beverages like rice-beers, wine or liquor.

Zuchom – The bottle gourd used for storing wine.

Zuchom leizu – The bottle gourd used for storing liqour.

Zuchom lakpa – The game of snatching the wine bottle from a pole.

Zujong ulin – The senior wine in-charge.

Zujong noupong – The junior wine in-charge.

Zu-ngou – The white rice-beer.

Zurung/Zulung/Yulung/Yuhlung – A major clan of Chothe (see Yulung).

Zurum – The tradition of serving wine after each simple offertory prayer (*Tongkaipa*).

Zupai – The wine manager.

Zu-ting – The fermented cook rice-beer.

Zutui shutpa – The process of wine extraction ceremony.

CHAPTER - 1

Introduction

The Study of Religion: Definition

Religion, a matter of belief and practice, is a universal social phenomenon that seriously concerns almost every living man. Generally, religion is understood by many as a belief in the Supernatural power or the Supreme Being and in their inter-relationship with the nature that surrounds them. Man, being a social animal, is also therefore, considered a religious being. Religion is also accepted as one of the strongest sources and means of social control. It is considered as one of the earliest institutions of mankind and is found in all societies of the past and present. Scholars from different disciplines of Sociology, Anthropology, Ethnology, Theology and Philosophy conceptualise the elements of religion in their own context; as a result there is no single uniform theory or definition on religion. Besides, religion being one of the earliest institutions is also one of the oldest subjects in the human history that is taught and is most widely spread and universally discussed at many levels. Numerous scholars have explained the origin of religion from different perspectives and some of their concepts, definitions and approaches are herein discussed below.

The term religion carries a different meaning for different people. Ronald L. Johnstone puts it in this way, "The English word 'Religion' has a Latin root i.e. *'Religare'* meaning *'to bind together'* (suggesting the concept of a group or fellowship)", (1961: 7). Therefore, because of the richness and variety of the subject matter, opinion and understanding differs in theoretical conceptualisation.

Emile Durkheim in, *The Elementary Forms of the Religious Life* (1915) conceptualised religion as a dichotomy on the basis of social facts by studying of the indigenous Aborigines of Australia and arrives saying that "religious phenomena are naturally arranged in two fundamental categories of beliefs and practices", the first being the 'states of opinion' in the representation of the mind; the second 'determined modes of action' which is the practical side of life" (1915: 36). Durkheim's religious concept focuses on the importance of the Aborigine's 'totem', a symbolic representation of their clan or society where he sees nothing in the practical meaning of the rites and rituals; rather he believes that it is in the sacredness of the totem that the rites and rituals are practiced to reinforce their group cohesion and solidarity which is seen to be the expression of collective consciousness (*ibid.*: 37). Accordingly he states that "religious representations are collective representations which express collective realities" (*ibid*: 10). Therefore, he claims that, all known religious belief systems, whether simple or complex, presents one common characteristic that presupposes a classification of all the things as 'real and ideal', into two classes or opposed groups designated by two distinct terms or words — 'profane' and 'sacred' (*ibid*: 37). Thus, Durkheim gives one of the most convincing definitions of religion as:

> "*A unified system of beliefs and practices relative to sacred things, that is to say, things set apart and forbidden, beliefs and practices which unite into one single moral community called a church, all those who adhere to them*" (1915: 47).

Durkheim's religion is focused on the dichotomy of beliefs and practices (rites) embodied in the objects of the sacred and profane which is generally accepted as the essence of all religion, irrespective of whether being a simple or complex society. Universally, belief is an aspect of a powerful conviction upon something, a conviction that has the potential and capacity to create a strong faith. Hence, belief is understood to be the manifestation of conviction; faith and values consecrated in the sacredness of the object that is revered and honoured with adoration. For example, the Arc of the Covenant, sacred texts like the Gita, Quran, Bible, etc., besides these, there are also some objects considered to have endowed with certain power and having certain indispensable values for an individual or society, that have been conceived as sacred, like totems: bear, crow, tiger, beaver, etc. According to Durkheim, anything which is not sacred is 'profane'. So, we see that no society or culture is completely free from the elements of sacred and profane. Hence, the treatment of sacred things differs from one culture to another but generally honouring sacred things or objects may involve simple to complex religious activities or rites and rituals, for some they may be an obligation carried out in the form of certain socio-religious norms or moral principles.

According to James G. Frazer, "Religion is a belief in a power superior to man, which is believed to direct and control the course and nature of human life" (quoted from Rao 1990: 446). Elizabeth H. Nottingham, on the other hand defines it from the perspective of emotional and sentimental attachment of the traditional practices of the past as the determining criteria for religious belief. She says, "Religion is for many people so much an affair of the heart, so often inexplicable even to themselves, so coloured by their own special feeling for the particular belief and ceremonies that have become sacred to them through long association" (1971: 4). Another view closer to the above definition given by Malcolm Hamilton is that "Religion is seen to be the product of psychological factors inherent in all human beings and on the other it is seen as providing support for social values and social stability" (2001: 133). He believes that religion originates from the mind out of fear and security for the group cohesion guided by the moral principles of social values to stabilise the social system. Considering the above given definitions and many others that are excluded here shows there is no consensus among them. As Lucy Mair states, "anthropologists have always agreed on the importance of the practice, but their treatment of the beliefs has been very different at different times" (1972: 211). Therefore, on the above statements Roger A. Johnson combines all the elements of religion into one aspect and states that "Religion is an extremely complex phenomenon. It encompasses beliefs and doctrines, myths and rituals, sacred scriptures and cultic objects, and the manifestation of transcendence in this many aspects" (1973: 9).

On the other hand, religious practices are all aspects of religious behaviour which is characterised by peculiars acts or practices, observances and performances executed under the umbrella of religion, such as moral principles or morality, socio-religious norms, ceremonies, magic, rites and rituals, taboos, superstition, etc., where the believers consider it an obligation or feel indebted to it for their life as they have faith in it.

In this study, the term "indigenous" and "tribe" are used as interlinked conceptual terms for identification and description as both the terms in application are argued as true for the Chothe. The most cited description on the concept of the indigenous is given by Jose R. Martinez Cobo, the Special Rapporteur of the Sub-Commission on "Prevention of Discrimination and Protection of Minorities" of the UN.[1] On the basis of this, B.K. Roy Burman says that there are two definitions widely accepted in the international parlance on 'Indigenous and Tribal Peoples' that are contained in ILO Convention 107 of 1957 and ILO Convention 169 of 1989 (1994:15-16). However, the recent "Workshop on Data Collection and Disaggregation for Indigenous Peoples" organised by United Nations (UN) in New York, from 19th - 21st January 2004, presented one of the most simplified working definitions of the indigenous, which reads as:

> *"Indigenous communities, peoples and nations are those which, having a historical continuity with pre-invasion and pre-colonial societies that developed on their territories, consider themselves distinct from other*

sectors of the societies now prevailing on those territories, or parts of them. They form at present non-dominant sectors of society and are determined to preserve, develop and transmit to future generations their ancestral territories, and their ethnic identity, as the basis of their continued existence as peoples, in accordance with their own cultural patterns, social institutions and legal system".[2]

So, some equivalent terms used for indigenous peoples are: aborigines or aboriginal peoples, native peoples, scheduled castes, scheduled tribes, first peoples, first nations and autochthones. The confusion between the terms of 'tribes' and 'indigenous' is well explained by Virginius Xaxa, who says tribes are groups of communities living outside civilisation free from the administrative socio-political organisation, so also the indigenous. But the indigenous are considered more a native or aboriginal tribes of the place (1999: 1393).

Brief Profile of the Chothe Tribe

Chothe is an indigenous tribe inhabiting in the state of Manipur having its own distinctive indigenous religion, socio-cultural, economic and political institutions.[3] The Chothe have been classified as an *Old-Kuki Tribe* by the British Political Agents like J. Shakespeare (1912), McCulloch (1859), R. Brown (1873), T.C. Hodson (1904), and Greirson (1904) in the Linguistic Survey of India (L.S.I.) on account of their "early migration to Manipur" (Ansari, 1991:14). The Chothe have been notified as one of the 29 recognised *Scheduled Tribes* of Manipur by the Government of India on 29th October, 1956. Ansari has categorised the Chothe as a *very small tribe* of Manipur comprising of only 0.58 per cent of the total tribal population in the state (*Ibid.:*58). The Census of India, 2011 gives the total population of the Chothe as 3585, with a literacy rate of 69.79 per cent. They are concentrated in two districts of Manipur i.e. Bishnupur and Chandel respectively. However, they are divided into three groups or zones based on their village agglomeration viz.; (a) Western, (b) Central Clusters and (c) Eastern groups (Basu, 1985:38). According to K.S. Singh, there are only 2.85 per cent of the Chothe total population who still follow their indigenous religion and 8.59 per cent have not stated their religion as opposed to 88.50 per cent who are all Christians now (1994: 225).

They speak Chothe language and have no script of their own. They commonly use Bengali-Manipuri and Roman scripts in writing. The community in study has many distinctive features in religion, kinship, marriage, political and socio-economic systems. The distinctiveness is obvious from anthropological and sociological perspectives with their typical 'Marriage Alliance System' brought into the anthropological map of the world, initially provided by the empirical data of T.C. Das' (1945) '*The Purums: An Old-Kuki Tribe of Manipur*'.[4] Whereby, Claude Levi Strauss (1949) used Das' data in his '*Elementary Structuralism*' for his 'Alliance Theory'. Thereafter, this particular theory was seriously propagated by Rodney Needham as 'Matrilateral Connubium' in many of his writings from 1958-1964. Gogoi also asserts Needham's theory is against the protagonist of the 'Descend Theory' and that Chothe practice 'prescriptive marriage rule' (1989: 9).

Statement of the Problem of the Study

The Chothe since time immemorial believes that they are the descendants of *Pu Lungchungpa* or *Ruipi Santai* or *Pu Pakhangpa* the mythical Dragon-Python God as their Supreme Principal Guardian God.[5] They also believed in the cosmic Heavenly and Earthly Gods i.e. *Thangvan rengpa* and *Shimlei rengnu*. They considered that *Pu Pakhangpa* is the avatar or Divine-incarnate of *Pu Lungchungpa* and therefore revered and worshipped Him. It is believed that the God *Pakhangpa* is a horned serpent possessing a supernatural power to transform himself into anything like, stone, tiger, dog, human being and even take human birth at any time and place (Naorem 1991: 104). British political agents like McCulloch, Hodson, Shakespeare and other scholars have stated in their ethnographies and books that the Chothe worship several gods like *Lungchungpa, Pakhangpa, Soraren, Sanamahi, Leima, Chungthieng* and *Tuipathin* in addition to a host of other gods and goddesses. Among the above deities *Thangvan rengpa* or *Chungthieng* or *Soraren* have been treated as Heavenly God, while *Pu Lungchungpa* or *Pakhangpa* as God on earth (Yuhlung, 2002: 6). They also believe in life after death and reincarnation, besides being riddled by myth, legends, superstitions, omens, taboos, magic, rites and rituals, folklores, animistic beliefs and practices. These factors contribute to the making of Chothe indigenous religion which is considered as polytheism; constituted by several animistic and cosmologic beliefs and practices. It can also be considered as a pre-literate religion, since they have no written scriptures of their own like many other tribal religions of North-East India (Sen, 1993: 23).

The Chothe indigenous or pre-literate religion is now on the verge of extinction because majority of them have converted to Christianity and just a handful of Lamlanghupi Chothe still practiced their indigenous faith. Despite, being very small in number, they are seen to perform many of their socio-religious activities accordingly. But some of their beliefs and practices are seen symbolically represented and being observed for the sake of observance due to multiple factors. The crux here is that there is not much work done on this subject matter for which reason this research work was undertaken to explore and examine and document the age old indigenous religion.

Some scholars have written on different subjects on this community but there has not been any in-depth and comprehensive work undertaken on this aspect. On the other hand, the reason why this study is felt to be necessary is because when most of the tribal of Manipur or North-East are said to have lost or are losing their indigenous religion, it is significant that the Chothe still retain their indigenous religion although confined to just a minority of the population. The significance is that along with this religion, traditional features still find relevance in their continuity despite considerable changes within the system. Therefore, there is a dire need to re-construct and record the Chothe indigenous religious beliefs and their socio-religious practices of the past from the existing system that is enduring even today before it completely disappears. Moreover, there seems to be a close similarity and connection between the Chothe and Meitei belief system which is obscure, this has also been somehow reflected in this study. All these factors and the dynamics of change pose a challenge and generated a strong fascination and an academic interest to study this community intensively and extensively.

Objective of the Study

The basic objective is primarily devoted to the study and documenting the Chothe indigenous religion in relation to their belief and practices. It also aims at understanding the phenomenon of their indigenous religion by examining their myths, legends, rituals, festivals, superstitions, social and religious taboos, folklore and folk culture, etc., which are in practice even today. On the other hand, the study also focuses on some factors and influences that are responsible in the weakening of their indigenous religion. The study is basically exploratory and descriptive in nature, which is expected to bring out further details about the Chothe indigenous religious belief and practices over and above existing information, whereby this effort, it is hoped, will serve as a future reference and benefit those interested in cultural and religious studies.

The basic objective is therefore, to study the gamut of the Chothe indigenous religion from the contemporary perspective.

Research Methodology

The study is basically exploratory and descriptive in nature, and is based on qualitative data. Therefore, the bulk of the data is the empirical findings gathered by participatory observation, extensive interviews and interview scheduled techniques carried out both in the forms of a structured and an unstructured manner among 200 individuals consisting of religious heads, village elders, senior citizens, youth leaders and lay members during field work. The universe of research consists of twelve villages confined to Bishnupur and Chandel districts of Manipur, over which the Chothe population is spread out into the three village agglomerations as given above. Since, the followers of the indigenous faith are less in number, the extensive interviews and interview scheduled are also conducted among the Christian group of people who are mostly recent converts i.e. especially among the village elders, senior citizens and lay members who still have vast knowledge about their indigenous beliefs and practices.

For comparative analysis, we also refer to various secondary data in published and unpublished books, manuscripts, journals, newspapers, thesis, dissertations, village and church souvenirs, booklets, etc., which immensely provide deeper insight in understanding the Chothe indigenous socio-religious history from the perspective of their belief and practice which have helped to direct and shape the development of the present study.

A brief profile of the respondents' backgrounds may also be summarised. The Table 1(i) shows that out of a total of 200 Chothe respondents interviewed, both followers of indigenous faith and Christians, there are exclusively 40 (i.e. 20 per cent) respondents of the indigenous faith with 24 males and 16 females, and 160 (i.e. 80 per cent) are Christian with 134 males and 26 females belonging to different Christian denominations from different Chothe villages. The table 1(i) shows that the majority of the Chothe respondents are Christians, irrespective of denomination, indicating that majority of the Chothe population already has been converted to Christianity, and only a handful of them continue to cling on to their age-old indigenous faith at the present time. These Christian respondents were taken into consideration because many of them still have the traditional knowledge as many are recent converts. The 200 respondents comprise of different age-groups who are religious heads, village elders, village leaders, senior citizens, youth leaders and lay members, both male and female, irrespective of religion. Their responses vary from the simple to the complex depending on the questions asked, where some could provide good answers while others could not. It is also found that individuals of similar age groups shared similar opinions because of their experiences.

In considering the distribution of male/female respondents of both, the followers of the Indigenous faith and Christians there are a total of 158 (i.e. 79 per cent) males and 42 (i.e. 21 per cent) females that indicates the male ratio is almost triple to the female respondents [Table 1(ii)].

Table 1 (i): Distribution of Chothe Respondents by Faith

Religion	Male	Female	Total	Percentage
Followers of the Indigenous faith	24	16	40	20
Followers of the Christian faith	134	26	160	80
Total	**158**	**42**	**200**	**100**

Table 1 (ii): Distribution of Chothe Respondents by Gender
(Male/Female, Both Followers of Indigenous Faith and Christians)

Category	Followers of the Indigenous faith	Followers of the Christian faith	Total	Percentage
Male	24	134	158	79
Female	16	26	42	21
Total	40	160	200	100

On the criteria of the Chothe socio-political structural system or classification as shown in Chapter 3 under *Political Institutions*, the researcher has broadly divided the respondents into three age-groups viz.; (1) Youths (*Nungak-luthei/ luther*), (2) Matured Adults (*Tang-ngarinta*) and, (3) Village Elders (*Urinta*) by taking their average socio-political standard age-groups as 20-40, 40-60 and 60-100 years respectively. According to the Chothe socio-political and structural system the youth (*Nungak-luther*) generally falls within the age-group of 15-40 years and are generally considered unmarried individuals comprising of mostly students and youth leaders. The second group is generally taken by them as matured adults or married individuals within the age-group of 40-60 years that have had already certain experiences in their lives and are called *Tang-ngarinta* (matured adults) comprising of village leaders, political leaders, senior citizens and lay members. They are the intermediate group between youths and village-elders as they form the bridge of social bonding between the two polar groups of the young and old. The third group called *Urinta* or village elders consist mostly of village elders, religious heads, senior citizens, retired or aged political leaders and old lay members of the community.

Although the initiation age of Chothe youth starts from 14-15 years, for this study the researcher has taken the minimum age of the respondents as 20 years since they are accountable to the questions asked. An interval of five years has been used from 20-25 onwards till 100 years [see Table 2(i)].

Table 1.2(i) shows that out of 40 exclusive respondents of followers of the Indigenous faith; 18 (i.e. 45 per cent) belong to the youths (*Nungak-luthei or luther*) with ten males and eight females, 12 (i.e. 30 per cent) are matured adults (*Tang-ngarinta*) with six males and six females, and the third group of village elders (*Urinta*) comprises 10 (i.e. 25 per cent) respondents with eight males and two females respectively. The data indicates that there are more youth respondents than matured adults and village elders.

In considering the male/female distribution of the followers of the indigenous faith only, there are more males 24 (i.e. 60 per cent) and females 16 (i.e. 40 per cent) with males exceeding by 20 per cent [see Table 2(ii)].

Table 2(i): Distribution of Respondents of Indigenous Faith Followers by Age-group

Age-groups	Frequency		Category	Indigenous faith		Total	Percentage
	male	female		male	female		
20-25	2	5	Youths (*Nungak-luther*)	10	8	18	**45**
25-30	7	3					
30-35	-	-					
35-40	1	-					
40-45	1	-	Matured adults (*Tang-ngarinta*)	6	6	12	**30**
45-50	-	-					
50-55	2	3					
55-60	3	3					
60-65	3	-	Village elders (*Urinta*)	8	2	10	**25**
65-70	-	1					
70-75	2	-					
75-80	1	-					
80-85	-	-					
85-90	-	1					
90-95	1	-					
95-100	1	-					
Total	**24**	**16**		**24**	**16**	**40**	**100**

In considering their age-groups, both followers of the Indigenous faith and Christians of Lamlanghupi, out of a total of 62 respondents there are 30 (i.e. 48.38 per cent) who belong to the youth group, 17 (i.e. 27.41 per cent) matured adults and 15 (i.e. 24.19 per cent) village elders. Table 3(i) show there are more youths compared to the other two age-groups.

In the distribution of male/female of Lamlanghupi respondents only the [Table 3(ii)] indicates that there are more males with 38 (i.e. 61.29 per cent) than the female respondents with 24 (i.e. 38.70 per cent) as the males were more responsive to questions.

Table 2 (ii): Distribution of Indigenous Faith Followers by Male/Female

Category	Followers of the Indigenous faith	Percentage
Male	24	60
Female	16	40
Total	**40**	**100**

Table 3 (i): Distribution of Lamlanghupi Respondents by Age-group (Both Followers of Indigenous Faith and Christians)

Age-groups	Indigenous faith		Christians		Total	Percentage
	male	female	male	female		
Youths (*Nungak-luther*) between 20-40 years	10	8	9	3	30	48.38
Matured adults (*Tang-ngarinta*) between 40-60 years	6	6	2	3	17	27.41
Village elders (*Urinta*) above 60 years	8	2	3	2	15	24.19
	24	16	14	08	62	100
Total	**40**	**22**	**62**			

The Chothe began converting to Christianity in 1938, the first village being Leininghu. Ever since, the process of evangelisation has gained momentum among the people and continues in the region even today. Out of a total of 2675 Chothe (COI-2001), more than 88.50 per cent are now Christian while the rest are Hindus and followers of the indigenous faith. The Christians have various denominations and as a result a tribe or a village may have more than one denomination at a time. There are four denominations among the Chothe viz. Chothe Baptist Church Association (ChBCA), Roman Catholic (RC), Evangelical Free Church of Independent (EFCI) and Independent Church of India (ICI). Distributing 160 Christian respondents by denomination, there are 88 (i.e. 55 per cent) who belong to ChBCA, 35 (i.e. 21.87 per cent) Catholic, 34 (i.e. 21.25 per cent) EFCI, and 4 (i.e. 2.5 per cent) ICI respectively. The data indicates that the number of Baptist respondents is more than the other three denominations because Baptist churches exist in almost all the Chothe villages [see Table 1.4].

Table 3(ii): Distribution of Lamlanghupi Respondents by Male/Female (Both Followers of Indigenous Faith and Christians)

Category	Followers of indigenous faith	Followers of Christian faith	Total	Percentage
Male	24	14	38	61.29
Female	16	08	24	38.70
Total	40	22	62	100

Table 4: Distribution of Chothe Christian Respondents by Denomination

Denominations	Youths (20-40) years		Matured adults (40-60) years		Vill. elders above 60 years		Total	Percentage
	M	F	M	F	M	F		
Chothe Baptist Church Association (ChBCA)	23	10	32	4	18	1	88	55
Catholic (RC)	12	4	7	4	6	1	35	21.87
Evangelical Free Church of Independent (EFCI)	9	-	17	-	7	1	34	21.25
Independent Church of India (ICI)	2	-	1	-	-	1	4	2.5
	46	14	57	8	31	4	160	100
Total	60		65		35		160	100

The Table 5(i) the village-wise distribution of all the Chothe respondents by age-groups irrespective of their faith; both followers of the indigenous faith and Christianity shows there are 78 (i.e. 39 per cent) youths (*Nungak-luther*), and 77 (i.e. 38.5 per cent) matured adults (*Tang-ngarinta*), and 45 (i.e. 22.5 per cent) as village elders (*Urinta*) respectively. This table gives more detailed information about the number of respondents according to their village.

Table 5(ii) shows the distribution of male/female ratio of the Christian respondents only on the basis of their age-groups in which there are 134 (i.e. 67 per cent) males and only 26 (i.e. 13 per cent) females indicating the high ratio of male to female respondents. The reason why more male respondents are considered is because the researcher finds them more accountable to the questions asked as most of the females shy away due to ignorance.

Table 5(i): Village-wise Distribution of Chothe Respondents by Age-group (Both Followers of Indigenous Faith and Christians)

Age-groups	Lamlangkupi (Indigenous faith)	Lamlangkupi (Christians)	Ajouhu	Tampakhu	Old-Wangparal	New-Wangparal	Chumbang (Purum)	Khongkhang	Chandrapolo (Phunu)	Zionlung	Leininghu	Chothe Khunou	Chandonopokpi	Salemthar	Lunghu	Lungleh	Total	Percentage
Youths between 20-40 years	18	12	2	5	2	3	5	6	2	5	4	1	-	10	-	3	78	39
Matured adults between 40-60 years	12	5	5	5	7	3	8	10	3	5	3	1	3	3	2	2	77	38.5
Village elders above 60 years	10	5	3	6	3	3	2	2	2	1	2	1	-	3	2	-	45	22.5
Total	40	22	10	16	12	09	15	18	07	11	09	03	03	16	04	05	200	100

**Table 5(ii): Distribution of Chothe Christian
Respondents by Male/Female**

Category	Youths (20- 40) years	Matured adults (40-60) years	Vill. elders above 60 years	Total	Percentage
Male	46	57	31	134	67
Female	14	8	4	26	13
Total	60	65	35	160	100

Table 6, distribution of educational qualification of Chothe respondents, shows that out of 200 respondents the number of under-matriculation or drop-outs comprises the maximum number with 66 (i.e. 33 per cent) among the literate groups. This is followed by Matriculate individuals with 45 (i.e. 22.5 per cent), Pre-university or class-XII passed with 41 (i.e. 20.5 per cent) and 31 (i.e. 15.5 per cent) Graduates, and only One (i.e. 0.5 per cent) Masters Degree holder from Lamlanghupi village. The number of illiterate respondents comprises only 16 (i.e. 8 per cent). Looking at the overall figure, indicates that the literacy rate of Chothe is high but the percentage with higher education declines as the degree goes higher. The reason is probably because of social or economic backwardness and other factors.

Table 7, the village-wise distribution of occupation of 200 Chothe respondents both followers of the indigenous faith and Christians shows that the number of farmers comprises maximum respondents with 70 (i.e. 35 per cent) signifying they are mainly agriculturists followed by students with 40 (i.e. 20 per cent). The third in rank belongs to the self-employed (Business and other allied activities) individuals who stay at home with 26 (i.e. 13 per cent), followed by government employees (both state and central) with 25 (i.e. 12.5 per cent), and housewives comprise 24 (i.e. 12 per cent). The rest of the respondents were pastors and reverends with 10 (i.e. 5 per cent), and the private-school teachers 5 (i.e. 2.5 per cent).

Chapterisation and Key Issues of the Study

The whole thesis comprises nine chapters, broadly divided into three sections. Chapter One, Two and Three introduces the objective of the thesis, the tribe "Chothe" in the study and its institutions. Chapter Four, Five and Six describes; Chothe mythology, belief systems and their practices. Chapter Seven and Eight constitute the subordinate description related to the core of the thesis like; festival and its folk culture, and factors responsible for the declined of their indigenous religion, while Chapter Nine formed the Summary.

Chapter One: discusses the definitions of religion, statement of the problem, objective of the study, research methodology, chapterisation and

Table 6: Distribution of Education Qualification of Chothe Respondents (Both Followers of the Indigenous Faith and Christians)

Education qualification	Lamsingkupi (Indigenous faith)	Lamlangkupi (Christians)	Ajouhu	Tampakhu	Old-Wangparal	New-Wangparal	Chumbang (Purum)	Khongkhang	Chandrapoto (Phuntu)	Zionltang	Leitinghu	Chothe Khunou	Chandonpokpi	Salemthar	Lungthu	Lungteh	Total	Percentage
Illiterate	3	2	-	3	1	-	-	2	2	-	1	-	-	1	1	-	16	8
Under-matric	8	7	4	7	7	6	1	7	1	1	2	1	1	9	1	3	66	33
Matric	6	2	1	3	1	1	6	8	2	5	3	-	1	4	1	1	45	22.5
Pre-univ XII std	13	7	3	1	1	1	5	-	1	4	1	1	-	1	1	1	41	20.5
Graduate	9	4	2	2	2	1	3	1	1	1	2	1	1	1	-	-	31	15.5
PG/Master degree	1	-	-	-	-	-	-	-	-	-	-	-	-	-	-	-	01	0.5
Total	40	22	10	16	12	09	15	18	07	11	09	03	03	16	04	05	200	100

Table 7: Village-wise Distribution of Occupation of Chothe Respondents (both followers of the Indigenous faith and Christians)

Occupation	Lamlangkhupi (Indigenous faith)	Lamlangkhupi (Christians)	Ajounu	Tumpakhu	Old-Wangparal	New-Wangparal	Chumbang (Purum)	Khongkhang	Chandrapoto (Phuntu)	Ziontlang	Leitingphu	Chothe Khunou	Chandonpokpi	Salemhar	Lungshu	Lungleh	Total	Percentage
Farmers	5	7	4	8	7	5	5	6	2	4	2	1	2	5	3	4	70	35
Govt. employees	7	4	3	2	-	-	3	2	2	-	1	-	-	1	-	-	25	12.5
Private-teachers	2	2	-	-	-	-	1	-	-	-	-	-	-	-	-	-	05	2.5
Self-employed	3	1	-	1	2	1	3	4	-	1	4	1	1	3	1	-	26	13
Pastors	-	-	1	3	2	3	-	1	-	-	-	-	-	-	-	-	10	5
Students	15	3	2	-	1	-	3	4	2	4	2	1	-	2	-	1	40	20
Housewife	8	5	-	2	-	-	-	1	1	2	-	-	-	5	-	-	24	12
Total	40	22	10	16	12	09	15	18	07	11	09	03	03	16	04	05	200	100

key issues, the confusion of the Chothe and Purum tribes, theoretical formulation, and a general view on religion and culture.

Chapter Two: introduces the Chothe in brief. It begins by describing the geographical location of the Chothe Viz: Western Chothe, the Central cluster Chothe and the Eastern Chothe. Their historical background like the genesis of the Chothe, migration, demography (Factors and consequences leading to de-population; assimilation, natural calamities, wars and battles, low selection potential of mates) are also discussed. Wars and battles involved in the past, literacy and the influence of neighbouring tribes to the Chothe are briefly stated.

Chapter Three: discusses the Chothe institutions of kinship and marriage; political and economy that have changed from simple to complex over the past hundreds of years. It describes how the Chothe endogamous prescriptive matrilateral cross-cousin marriage system is being slowly replaced with the modern exogamous cross-cultural or inter-tribal marriage system as people prefer to marry girls from outside their community. It discusses the Chothe political system in which the age-old traditional gerontocratic form of government is practiced in the Lamlanghupi village only and how the rest of the Chothe villages follow an elective democratic forms of village administration. It also explains how agriculture, the main occupation and the primary source of their economy is changing from the traditional to modern mode, since many are now found employed in government services serving either in the secondary or tertiary sectors, while others engaged themselves in private entrepreneurships.

Chapter Four: which is the core of the study, discusses the Chothe mythology in relation to the Chothe genealogical myth and the legend of Chothe Thangwai/Thangmei Pakhangpa. The Chothe genealogical myth describes their world view, its creation and the origin of their religion and the development of their socio-cultural systems in an evolutionary manner. The Chothe indigenous religion like many other religions of the world describes that Chothe Thangwai Pakhangpa is the avatar or Divine-incarnate of their Supreme Guardian-God *Pu Lungchungpa* who is regarded as the mythical Dragon-Python God that represents the Almighty God on earth according to the traditional belief.[6]

For this analysis various manuscripts like the sacred manuscript *Chothe Thangwai (Thangmei) Pakhangpa* and several other literatures like *Cheitharol Kumpaba, Moirang Ningthourol Lambupa* are being referred besides the Chothe oral history. It suggests that Chothe Thangwai Pakhangpa and Nongda Leiren Pakhangpa the first historical king of Manipur is one and the same person born of a Chothe girl. The confusion about Pakhangpa's identity and his genealogy is prevalent even today because of the inferences in the later historical writing by various local scholars and also because of the naming system of the people of Manipur inhabiting the state. To substantiate the evidence of the above statement various analytical issues are discussed in the chapter like Pakhangpa's mother's identity, his romantic relationship with his wife Sunurempi (Laisna/ Leima) and his political relationship with other great leaders of his time like Khongding, Puleiromba, Luwang Langmaiba, etc.

Chapter Five: describes the Chothe religious belief system that is considered as polytheistic, comprising elements of cosmologic, naturalistic, animistic and totemic, although they acknowledged the existence of one Supreme God. It discusses that they also believe in a host of other lower gods and goddesses. They also emphasise in the believed in the re-incarnation (re-birth) and consider that every animate object has a soul. It also discusses about the concept of three worlds: the Land of God, the Land of the Dead and the Middle or the temporal world. It also describes about their relationship with various totemic objects like some of the American Indians, as each Chothe clan is associated with a specific totem like an animal, an insect or a plant. It also describes various types of superstitions and taboos.

Chapter Six: discusses about the Chothe religious practices. It focuses on the whole procedure of the "rites-de-passage" that comprises of various rites and rituals and ceremonies from birth to death. Special emphasis is also given on death and other death-related ceremonies which has deep socio-religious significance.

Since the Chothe rites and rituals are of varying degree and types which are performed with simple to complex or minor to major ceremonies, in this regard an attempt has been made to classify into three types on the basis of its importance and seriousness.

The Chothe practices different types of magic like - imitative magic (*Doi-ai*) and contagious magic (*Pot-sem* or *Kut-sem*). They consider that unlike today, magic was commonly practiced in olden days. However, the influence it has had on the society has been discussed in this chapter. The type of witch and witchcraft are also stressed. Since the Chothe believes in a variety of talismans, amulets and fetishes the manner of usages are discussed. The Chothe performed various types of divinations (*Tasanpa*) in almost every minor or major rites and rituals according to the severity problem or sickness. The various aspects on the nature and its significance are discussion in this chapter.

Chapter Seven: elaborates the two types of Chothe festivals, and the merit feast. Festivals being an indispensable component of the socio-cultural and religious aspects of a community are celebrated once or twice almost every month in olden days. But now the Chothe in a year celebrates only two major festivals viz. (1) *Innampei rhin* and (2) *Achui rhin*. These festivals are important because they presents and portrayed their cultural identity, community's belief systems, socio-religious and cultural practices. It manifests their past resplendent days. The Chothe now seldom perform merit feast (*lohchou-maichou*) unlike in the past that was once commonly organised in order to gain social status, respect and prestige in the society due to various reasons. Some of the merit feasts are discussed in the chapter. The interface between the Chothe culture and tradition with that of the so called modern culture is discussed too.

Chapter Eight: brief describes folk culture of the Chothe that includes-folktales, folksongs, folkdance, folkmusic, folk games and sports played in the past. Some of the folk music and dance and even games and sports are rarely seen practice by them now.

Chapter Nine: discusses the various factors responsible for the declined of the Chothe indigenous religion. The indigenous religion of the Chothe that was followed by the entire community or tribe for many centuries is now practiced by just a handful of them. Investigations by means of interview and scheduled are carried out in order to find out the factors responsible for the declined of the age-old socio-cultural and religious institutions.

The last Chapter Ten: summarised the discussion and the findings of the study.

The Confusion of the Chothe and Purum tribes

There are only five published books available on the Chothe. T.C. Das's '*The Purums: An Old Kuki Tribe of Manipur* (1945)', Biman K. Das Gupta's (ed.), '*Proceeding of the Symposium on: Purum (Chote) Revisited*'(1985), Yuhlung Standhope's '*Chothe Athouna*'(1986), Lai Imo's '*Chothegee Kunung Eshee*' (2002) and Hidam Brojen Singh's '*Chothe Grammar*' (2008). Apart from these books there are some critical informative articles found in different journals by, J.K. Bose's '*Current Science*' (1933), R.C. Roy's '*Man in India*' (1936), while Rodney Needham (1958, 1960, 1964, 1967), Claude Levi-Strauss (1949), Floyd. G. Lounsbury (1962), Charles Ackerman (1964), G.L. Cowgill (1964), F.B. Livingstone (1964), E.W. Muller (1964, 1966), W. Wilder (1964), Geogheagan and Kay (1964) all debated in the '*American Anthropologist*' on the Chothe Marriage Alliance System. The articles by Bose and Roy are, however, based on brief notes and ethnographic contents of the community collected during their field work. However, the articles in *American Anthropologist* basically deal with the arguments and discussions on the Chothe (Purum of T.C. Das) prescriptive marriage system based on the matrilateral alliance or connubium theory. Although they are of exceptional quality, the articles do not have much of an implication to the present study but those interested in the subject for argument, may find a continuation in *Sociological Bulletin* journal written by Cheithou Charles Yuhlung (author).

The name Chothe has been confused with Purum for another tribe by the operating Census officials of India, Manipur; thereby confusing many scholars of the world. The so called Purum, who distinguish themselves socially and culturally from Chothe, live in the North-east of Imphal in Senapati district of Manipur (Gupta, 1985: 26). The propaganda with the paradox of ethnic identity began with the publication of the T.C. Das's classical monograph titled '*The Purums: An Old Kuki Tribe of Manipur*' (1945), in which he apparently studied the Chothe of "Central cluster group" under the name '*Purum*' because their village names bear the prefix '*Purum*' as commonly referred to by the neighbouring plain peoples, in spite of having their own indigenous local names. The name Purum took a centre stage in the academic world, especially among the anthropologists, because of the theoretical debate on the marriage alliance system. Rodney Needham attempted to find out whether the Purum with a population of 305 people still exists or has become extinct, and also to prove his alliance theory against the descent theory of marriage. Further, the confusion of identity was exposed in the 1971 Census, reporting the Purum population as '*Nil*' or '*Unspecified*' while the Chothe population substantially increased to 1905 souls in the same year because the Census Operators identified them, i.e. the Purums of T.C. Das or the Central cluster groups as a unit of "Chothe" (Ansari, 1991: 67; Gupta, 1985: 52), (see Table 8).

However, on the above confused basis, a symposium "*Proceeding of the Symposium on Purum (Chote) Revisited*" was organised at Calcutta in 1983 by the Anthropological Survey of India (ASI). Thereafter, the paradox or confusion was clarified at the national and international level in the *Amrita Bazar Patrika,* a daily newspaper from Calcutta on 10th March 1983, stating that Das' Purums are the Chothe who were mis-understood by a generic term derived from i.e. "Purum Khullen" (Ajouhu) the place of their settlement. Accordingly the newspaper states "the correct name of the tribe Purum is the character of the geography of this area, which is added as a prefix to the name of their villages". Biman Kumar Das Gupta, who headed the ASI-revisit team pronounced "We were sure that we were among the group who called themselves as Chothe whom Das had described as Purum" (1985: 53). There are also clear remarks given by some scholars who attended the symposium. They are T.S. Wilkinson, B.B. Goswami, R.K. Das, Dipali Danda, H.K. Rakshit, Surajit C. Sinha, etc. Individuals still not satisfied with these scholars' positive remarks may read the 'eight point' explanation of S. Jibonkumar Singh and H. Vokendor Singh on the misnomer of Chothe-Purum identity in which the last point suffices to clear all the historical confusion and confirms that "as one of the sources of history, folksongs of the people serves as a valuable source. Nowhere in the folk-songs of the people, the word Purum, is found. But the word Chote (the original word for Chothe) is frequently found" (2005: 232). Therefore, on the above explanations we shall use the name "Chothe" for all purposes under this study in the context of the Purum of T.C. Das or the Central-cluster groups of Chothe.

Table 8: Chothe Population Census of Manipur,
India from 1931-2011 (Scheduled Tribe)

Year	1931	1951	1961	1971	1981	1991	2001	2011
Chothe	250	695	1033	1905	1687	2571	2675	3585
Purum	305	43	82	*Nil*	447	388	503	254

Theoretical Formulation

Belief is understood as the manifestation of conviction, faith and values consecrated in the sacredness of the symbol or object by showing reverence and veneration. They believe it is endowed with some kind of Supernatural powers. But this philosophy of human thought with respect to religion changes from time to time. Evolutionists, like Auguste Comte in *Positive Philosophy* (1830) assert that as the human knowledge gradually develops from time to time, it directly corresponds to the development of human society. He propagated the concept of "Law of Three Stages", (1) theological, (2) metaphysical and (3) positivist. According to him, the theological stage is predominated by irrational thought and behaviour and that any phenomena or experience are treated as supernatural. The metaphysical stage is a transitional period marked by reasoning and logic and the third, positive stage is all about human reasoning scientifically. He believes his positive religion is the 'religion of humanity' in which the positivist priests are the new intellectual officials of banking and industry, etc., whose interest is the welfare of the state from the economic standpoint for the betterment of the society (Martineau, 2000). When talking about the origin of religion, John Lubbock in *The Origin of Civilisation and the Primitive Condition of Man* (1870) says "fetishism" is the foundation of all religion where man can compel some divine power to carry out his designs which he calls a phase of "magic" subsequently followed by nature worship or totemism, shamanism, idolatry and finally the ethics of religion through morality.

On the other hand, Charles Darwin one of the most outstanding evolutionists of the world, asserted in his illustrative book, *The Origin of Species* (1859) that every creature was the outcome of natural selection or survival of fittest in its environment, and his denial to accept the mythical belief of human history that everything on this earth was the creation of the Divine God or the Creator, produced universal speculation. His assertion is that any change in the physical structure of any species was the result of gradual change over millions and thousands of years, and that the changes were unnoticed because the species had undergone a tremendous change from its originality, consequently he claim that even man had evolved from primates. This proposition speculated worldwide controversy as it is considered a contradiction, and threatens all existing religious beliefs, doctrines and practices, especially the Christian faith.

Despite the arguments of many evolutionists, E.B. Tylor propounded another new theory in his classical work *Primitive Culture* (1873, 1958), that "animism" or the belief in the existence of a "soul" or "spirit" is the base of all the philosophy of religion in every society and believes that the concept continues to hold even in modern spiritualism. He is of the opinion that most of the primitive societies of the world have the doctrine of soul or life or spirit endowed in all the living beings either plants or animals and this notion was carried on till the medieval period, and has undergone an extreme modification in the course of cultural evolution with the advancement of societies. Tylor disagrees with Lubbock's proposition and firmly asserts that despite multiple alterations in the fundamental animistic belief, the theory of the soul is one principal part of system of religious philosophy, which unites, in an unbroken line of mental connection, the savage fetish-worshipper and the civilised Christian (1972: 19). Therefore, he explains from the common phenomena of mankind: sleep, ecstasy, sickness, and death and most importantly dreams and hallucinations as the base to support his theory on origin of religion, with the view that fetishism provides evidence of the existence of souls and spirits, and that sacrifice (rite) is the symbolic expression of the relationship between man and spirits. Another strong advocate of the evolutionary theory is Herbert Spencer, who, in *Principles of Sociology* (1896) supplements the above proposition at the juncture between fetish and spirit and assumes that the veneration of the dead out of "fear" is the immediate outcome in the development of ancestor worship among primitive societies as they believe in the existence of the "ghost" or "spirit" of a dead man and the supernatural phenomena they experience. Such fear in ghosts is further induced to conviction when they happen to dream of the person or relate the dream with an event. Accordingly, he opines that the notion first evolved from the cult of plants and animals, and nature worship in general.

J.G. Frazer disagreed with the above evolutionary propositions of fetish, soul or spirit, fear and ghost theories. According to him, "magic" was ahead of religion and that religion is the outcome of magical practices. He describes in his masterpiece *The Golden Bough: A Study in Magic and Religion* (1911-15) that magic as an art is comparable to science because both involve mental operation. His ethnological theory on the origin of religion is based on the principle of a dichotomy that magic and religion are two different entities. Thus, he classified his "Sympathetic Magic" into two type viz.; homeopathic or imitative magic and contagious magic (1972: 416). He said that homeopathic magic function according to the law of similarity - *like produce like* - which means, a doll like image or figure of a targeted person when invoked with a spell and is inflicted on it by something sharp needle/stick can directly or indirectly affect the concerned person. While the contagious magic or law of contact is said to have a direct effect on the person when a magical charm is spell on any body parts like hair, nails or clothing of the concerned person (*ibid.:* 425). Therefore, Frazer believes that when such sacred magic practices were affected, and its cause became known to the members of the society, such able magicians were, in due course, looked upon with fear by the common man for their awesome powers. Subsequently, the people begin to revere them for their skills and magical powers to communicate with the supernatural forces. Then, when society slowly accepted the practice and regularise it into customary law for certain positive benefits, it thus, gives rise to the magico-religious system.

Magic is a powerful mental or psychological medium between man and the supernatural forces that have the potential to transform certain particular words into action, but one wonders where such powers were derived from and how religion originated. So, for naturalists like Max Muller, the cosmic phenomena served as the point of departure for religious evolution.[7] Muller said, "Nature was the greatest surprise, a terror, a marvel, a standing miracle, and it was only on account of their permanence, constancy, and regular recurrence that certain features of that standing miracle were called natural..." (quoted from Durkheim, 1915: 74-75). The natural elements are the sun, the moon, the stars, the earth, the fire, the sky, water or rivers, trees, the wind, etc. These sensuous experiences of natural forces provoked the human mind to transform into a concept of something through language or word, and he believed that these standing miracles made men awesome; fearing this, he later began to revere and worship these infinite forces and the mysterious power that surrounded him.

Unlike the evolutionists, ethnologists and the naturalists, the functionalists like Emile Durkheim, Bronislaw Malinowski, A.R. Radcliffe Brown, Max Weber, Talcott Parsons give a totally a different version. They assumed that since religion is found universally in all societies it has a vital function in maintaining the social system as a whole, and the main social requirement that religion is deemed to fulfil is the necessity of ideological, sentimental, cohesion or solidarity and the biological needs. Bronislaw Malinowski, one of the most prolific and outspoken functionalists, explained that every socio-religious act and deed has its own functions that ends in itself in the "biological needs of human beings" (1948: 90). He claimed that "the function of magic is to ritualise man's optimism, to enhance his faith in the victory of hope over fear. Magic expresses the greater value for man of confidence over doubt, of steadfastness over vacillation, of optimism over pessimism" (*ibid.:*90). Further he explicates that the naming and initiation ceremonies of a child, the marriage ceremony, etc., all have their own functional means and ends. Malinowski, like Frazer believes that magic came first, and then the science of reasoning entered to foster the development of religion.

Another modern functionalist is A.R. Radcliffe Brown who has similar views like Durkheim and stresses on the importance of rites in any religious system in *Structure and Function in Primitive Society* (1964), that rites are the consequence of beliefs which determine the elements of the social functions in society. He also suggest several points in the study of religion and how one should specifically focus on religious action and discover the sentiment developed in the individual in a particular religious cult.

E.E. Evans-Pritchard also makes a distinctive contribution in the study of religion as he specifically focuses on some elements of religion like witchcraft, oracles, magic and other related aspects from the perspective of Azande's culture and Nuer. His articles, *The Notion of Witchcraft among the Azande* and *Oracle among the Azande,* describes how the Azande accept and relate any unfortunate or misfortune as the act of witchcraft, the essence of an oracle when a serious aspect arises out of the event and the need for magic and its application for the consequences are well elaborated. His book, *Nuer Religion* (1956) also describes the various intrinsic aspects of the Nuer religious beliefs and practices.

However, Max Weber's view on religion is quite different from Karl Marx, Emile Durkheim and many others as his study is based on rationality. In fact, his thesis is a counter-attack to disprove Karl Marx's epitome statement that "Religion is the opium of the masses". Marx in his effort for a communist society sees that the bureaucrats had seized religion as an instrument and had poisoned the minds of the proletariat by convincing them that their condition of suffering would be rewarded in heaven. On the above basis, Marx inferred religion to be a powerful conservative and oppressive force that denies the freedom and liberty of an individual by suppressing the masses, since majority of the people have accepted their suffering as their destiny without reasoning. He propagated the above statement in, *The Capital (Das Kapital),* (1867).

Max Weber, contrary to Karl Marx's theory, argues that religion does not suppress all societies; rather it uplifts some societies economically. He justifies his proposition in his famous and classic work, *The Protestant Ethic and the Spirit of Capitalism* (1930). Before this book he had already analysed different types of world religions. He sought his main justification from the Calvinist doctrine, asserting that religion helps define the motivation which finally gave raise to modern capitalism. He says the Calvinist doctrine exhorts every member of the Church to work hard, where to work is to glorify God, which is a calling of God and that the hard earned money should be properly spent for the greater glory of God and should not be spent lavishly or unnecessarily. Thus, the spirit of motivation for the pursuit of salvation became the motivation for the pursuit of wealth, which resulted in the spirit of capitalism and the accumulation of wealth.

There are also innumerable scholars like Claude Levi-Strauss, Clifford Geertz, E.E. Pritchard, Andre Beteille, M.N. Srinivas, T.N. Madan, etc., to name a few, who have immensely contributed to the discipline of sociology, especially in the area of religious study. Their keynotes are highlighted: Claude Levi-Strauss whose specialisation is structuralism, was perplexed to find out in his work *The Structural Study of Myth* (1955, 1963) that most of the mythical stories of the world are fantastic and unpredictable, and sometimes the content of the myth seems to be completely arbitrary, but interestingly on the other hand, he sees the paradox that myths of different cultures from one part of the world are surprisingly similar to the myths of cultures from another side of the world. This intrigued him to develop a basic theory of human thought that universal laws govern all areas of human thought, by examining the underlying structure of the relationships between the elements of the story rather than by focusing on the content of the story itself. Thus, he says that "myth exhibits a 'slated' structure which seeps to the surface…through the repetitive process" (1972: 301). He also asserts that every word in a language is the condensed form of a story, object, or a concept of a thing, where each word has a conceptualised structure of itself when de-constructed.

A new concept introduced in the study of religion by Clifford Geertz, sees *Religion as a Cultural System*, in the meaning of "symbol" where sets of symbols establish powerful pervasive motivation in men by formulating a concept of existence, which is induced into the mind of people and become cultural patterns in society. These cultural patterns are "models" in relation to the other entities, according to him, which shape into a religious system (1972: 168-169). Clifford Geertz's cultural patterns may be seen in T.B. Bottomore's concept of "morality" as described in his book, *Sociology* (1962). He stressed on the development of the origin of religion and religious institutions and also morality based on three distinctive methodological characteristics i.e., Evolutionist, Positivist and Psychologistic. Bottomore, unlike Levi-Strauss, who studied myth from the structural point, rather looks into the content of the myths in which the morality found in myths serves as the guiding principle for the development of religion. Brian Morris too has unravelled many theoretical strategies in his work, *Anthropological Studies of Religion* (1987) that have been developed and explored by many anthropologists.

Many exceptional Indian scholars have also immensely contributed in theoretical formulations of religious study. M.N. Srinivas in *Religion and Society among the Coorgs of South India* (2003) describes various aspects of the Hindu religious beliefs and practices, particularly the cultural patterns or the caste system by taking the Coorg community of Karnataka (south-India) as a model for the whole Hindu society. Karl Marx's perception of religion as a suppressive mechanism is perfectly perceived by M.N. Srinivas among the Coorgs, although Marx's society is divided into two social groups of the 'haves' and 'have-nots', Srinivas' Coorgs are broadly divided into four hierarchical castes viz., Brahmins, Kshatriyas, Vaishavas and Sudras. One very significant observation he makes among the Hindu believers that is deeply rooted is the change in the cultural and belief systems but not the structural change. The change is that many lower caste groups like the Sudras and the Untouchables began to imitate the Brahmins or Upper Caste groups in the manner of eating, drinking, dressing, etc., which were strictly prohibited.

M. Kirti Singh has compiled various folklores in *Folk Culture of Manipur* (1993) some of it is believed to have already disappeared. He devotes one chapter particularly on the, *'Python Lore of Manipur'* where he describes the origin myth and legend of the God *Pakhangba* the first historical King of Manipur. The book is indispensable for this study.

O.L. Snaitang's *Christianity and Social Change in North East India* (1993) described the role of social change among the Khasi-Jaintia people of Meghalaya, with respect to the influence of Christianity beginning in 1840 with the advent of the British rule in India. He discusses how Christian missionaries have positively contributed to the process of social change and modernisation especially among the Khasi-Jaintia people and also among the North-east tribals in general. Similarly M.C. Behera's (ed.) *Tribal Religion: Change and Continuity* (2000) contains numerous papers on various aspects of religion. It focuses on the syncretic religions of various tribal communities that emphasis on syncretic characteristics, that have emerged over time in spite of the influences of propaganda and other dominant religions on tribal religious traditions, either by the process of symbiosis or acculturation (as Hinduism on tribal religions), or in superposition (as Christianity on tribal religions).

Whatever the predicament involved in defining religion, the basic study of religion of any society, whether primitive or not, is to have an understanding on the belief and practice systems of that particular society on the criteria of the desired focused objectives. Andre Beteille's paper *Religion as a Subject for Sociology* (2005) emphasises the importance of how religious study should be approached. He says there are two important features, both common to sociology and social anthropology, "the first is the extensive use of the comparative method, and the second is the investigation of religious beliefs, practices, and institutions in relation to other aspects of society and culture" (Gupta, 2005: 56). Therefore, he claims that "the comparative method is central to the discipline of sociology and, as such, to the sociology of religion" (*ibid:* 56). In this way, for theoretical conceptualisation, many sociologists, anthropologists, ethnologists and philosophers have taken primitive societies for comparative study as obsessed by the belief that life on earth, biological and spiritual, had evolved from the simplest forms, and being the oldest form aroused the greatest interest of study (De Vries, 1967: 220). Primitive society is regarded to exist in the crudest form and is looked at as the most reliable source for such studies. Though simple it is believed to have contained almost all the basic elements of a religious system that could establish the base of a religion. Subsequently, various scholars have propounded the notions of pre-animism, fetishism, animism, and totemism each took a turn as the oldest form of religion, which was welcomed, and finally religion was dissolved in magic as a twin issue later.

In this particular study of the Chothe Indigenous religion, Andre Beteille's second approach has been adopted because investigation and recording of the Chothe indigenous religious beliefs and practices is considered more important at the moment. Since what little remnants are left is also vanishing rapidly and might disappeared completely. As the religious value systems of most tribal societies are gradually undergoing a dynamic change through various agents of Change like proselytisation from one religion to another, the Chothe society is no exception to it. On the contrary, there are also societies that somehow retained their traditional cultural value system in some way or the other like the economic or political systems. Despite the advent of Christianity and other powerful modern external forces of change, the Chothe indigenous religion, kinship and political institutions are systems that continued to exist even today, although practiced by just a handful of the Chothe population.

A General View on Religion

Since, no man is a perfect being, but strives for perfectionism; therefore no scholar's have escaped their writings from the blade of criticism. Roger A. Johnson says that the criticism of belief developed along two levels: a rejection of particular beliefs, and a critique of belief itself as dishonest, debilitating, and dehumanising (1973: 3). For instance, the first level, a rejection of particular beliefs is seen in the critical proposition of David Hume to a Calvinist Church for its orthodoxy doctrine, Rudolf Bultmann, speaking against the Lutheran Christian Church and Teilhard disagreement with the notion of the divine creation of the world in the Catholic faith. Similarly, Malinowski, an influential functionalist criticised E.B. Tylor and many others in his book *Magic, Science and Religion* (1948) says that Tylor's view on primitive religion was "based on too narrow a range of facts, which made early man too contemplative and rational" and also for over emphasising the primitive culture in the development of his animistic theory because he saw that the Trobriand Islanders "were rather interested in their fishing and gardens, in tribal events and festivities than brooding over dreams and visions, or explaining 'double' and cataleptic fits" (1948:18), argued that the primitive people in their early stage of life would not have developed such a critical mind to think about dreams and the souls or spirits rationally and scientifically as assumed by Tylor. Such are the critical comments on Tylor, despite appreciation for his earnest work. However, Malinowski gives overall credit to J.G. Frazer for his outstanding contribution to the scientific study of religion and his classifications. Durkheim argues that the origin of religion is neither Tylor's animism nor Frazer's magic but began with the belief in "totem" and that the essence of religious beliefs and practices derived from sacred and profane concepts.

Clyde Kluckhohn said that scholars like Durkheim, Radcliffe Brown and Malinowski, despite their immense contribution to religious study and particularly the relationship between myths and rituals, are so interested in formulating the relations between conceptual elements they have lost the sight of the concrete human organism and fail to present the description or base of their specific arguments of their analysis (1972: 98). Kluckhohn feels that a functionalist should begin with the description of some particular ritualistic behaviour to relate the myth but such specific detailed information is lacking in all of them as a result their discussions on the subject are generalised, which he condemns. Lévi-Strauss' also does not escape from criticism as his theory on the origin of the "Trickster" has been criticised on number of points by several anthropologists. For example, Stanley Diamond (1974), strongly disagrees Lévi-Strauss' for suggesting that the Trickster is a "mediator" and for assuming that the secular civilised often considers the concepts of life and death to be polar but primitive cultures often view it as an aspect of a single condition, the condition of existence.

Although at the second level, a critique that belief itself is dehumanising, as seen in Charles Darwin's evolutionary theory of natural selection, Karl Marx's epitome remark on religion as "the opium of the masses", and Freud's "illusion" a regression to infantile dependency in a self-defeating effort to overcome anxiety and fear, like consoling a child by protective parents are some few examples. It is considered sometimes that the criticism of belief itself is more fundamental than the rejection of particular beliefs. Most of these critics are humanists. Thus, they attack and preach against religious attitudes as dehumanising; their views on religious belief are regressive, exacting the high price of perpetual immaturity and psychic suffering. When examined by the light of reason; rather the very posture of believing was thoroughly dysfunctional and destructive as preventing the realisation of rationality, social justice, and psychological maturity. So, several critics contended that religion has no independent reality in itself because it is vague and considers merely the by-product of some elements more basic in the human process. Some claim that religion is nothing but a distorted expression of psychic dynamics, a reflection of underlying social factors, while others argue that it is only a primitive antecedent of scientific thinking. Thus, due to unexplained phenomenon criticism on the writings of any religious study does not end even today, despite a relaxation. Since, people are more inclined towards science and technological exploration. Whatever religious belief one may practice; firstly, what matter most with many people is to believe in himself, and act according to his/her heart's decision (developed self-consciousness to attain spiritualism). Secondly, develop trust and have faith in the One God whom he/she believe that he derives some kind of inner strength, protection and mental calmness. Thirdly, to experience such feelings one has to learn listening to himself, especially when his soul is weak or confronted with unseen forces. Imagine, our life compared with an inanimate object like a vehicle/car; the engine with a human heart, the driver with the mind and the fuel (spirit) with the soul. Thus, the personality of a person is defined by these three basic elements where the strength of his heart lies upon his faith, the mental power with his knowledge and wisdom, and the tranquillity of his soul lies in the purity of the spirit/ fuel.

Notes

1. Indigenous definition. (http://en.wikipedia.org/the free encyclopaedia/indigenous definition) Accessed on : 20/4/07.

2. Indigenous definition. (http://en.wikipedia.org/the free encyclopaedia/Indigenous definition/United Nation concept on Indigenous 2004 WS.1 3.htm). Accessed on : 24/06/07.

3. *Manipur*: The name Manipur was popularly used only in the later 20th century A.D. Before it was known by different names like Casey, Kangleipak, Meiteileipak, Sanaleibak, Manipur and so on.

4. *Purum*: The term Purum and Chothe tribes have been in confusion since 1945 with the publication of a monograph by T. C. Das (1945) *"The Purum: An old Kuki tribe of Manipur"*. Shakespeare and Wainel says that, the Purum claim to be the descendant from Tonring and Tonshu, (The first man and women according to their mythical belief) who issued from the earth. Wainel said that "Pu-rum"

mean "hide from Tiger", which closely connects them with the Lamkang legend (Shakespeare, 1912:150, Wainel, K. N. 2002: 156). The other version is that 'Purum' means 'hide with a shawl', referring to cognatic group of Chothe who tried to escape from a quarrel. These brethren's because of their past behaviour subsequently came to be popularly known as 'Purum'. However, presently the people who claimed as 'Purum' are the Purum Likli inhabiting in Senapati district of Manipur, a closed cognatic group of Koireng.

5. *Lungchungpa/ Pakhangpa*: The name *Lungchungpa* is believed to be an ancient Chothe term which literally means 'the Rain God' or 'the God from the above', identified with the 'Dragon-Python King'. In Chothe laymen term the Dragon-Python is also called as '*Ruipi-Santai (Shantai) Rengpa*' which means 'the red adult python'. Similarly the Meitei refer this Dragon-Python as "Nong-ta Leiren pakhangpa" literally 'Python the Rain God' (Nong=Rain; Leiren=Python, *khangpa*=one who frightened). So, the early Meitei or Plain people like the *Chothe Genealogical Myth* and the legend of *Chothe Thangwai Pakhangpa* of Chothe considered this *Pakhangpa* as the Avatar of *Lungchungpa* the Guardian God of earth because of Pakhangpa's varied powers and mysticisms displayed (See Chapter Four for more detail).

6. Dragon-Python = In ancient Chothe this semi-Dragon-Python or adult Python as '*Ruipi Shantai*' lit. *Ruipi*- mother/ adult python, and *Shantai* lit.it means 'Deep red stripes'.

7. Max Muller. 1890. *Physical Religion* (pp.119-120).

CHAPTER - 2

Introducing the Chothe

Introduction: Geographical Location

Manipur is located in the North-eastern region of India. The state lies between 23" 50' to 25"41' North latitudes and 93"2' to 94"47' East longitudes. The state is surrounded by Myanmar (Burma) in the east, Nagaland in the north, Assam in the west, Mizoram and Tripura in the south. The State has a geographical area of about 22,327 sq.km. The man-land ratio of the state is varied with regards to the hills and valley. The hill area covers about 20,089 sq.km (i.e. about 3/4th) of the total land area and inhabited by various tribal ethnic groups, while about 2,238 sq.km (about 1/4th) of the land comprises of the valley, predominantly inhabited by the Meitei.

As per the Census of India (COI) 2011, the state Manipur has 9 districts, 38 Sub-districts, 51 towns (Statutory towns 28, Census town 23) and 2582 villages. Out of nine districts five are Hill districts and four Valley districts. The Census 2011 indicates no specific increased in Districts, Sub-districts and Statutory towns but shows an increase of 18 Census towns and 191 villages as compared to 2001. Senapati is the largest and Thoubal the smallest districts by size. Imphal-west the most densely populated and Tamenglong the least populated districts. The Census of India (COI) 2011 indicates the total population of Manipur at 0.00 hours on 1st March 2011 is 25,70,390 (compared to 23,88,634 of 2001). The total Scheduled Tribe population is 9,02,740 (i.e. 35.1 per cent of the total population), while the total Scheduled Caste population is 97,042 (i.e. 3.8 per cent). The average density of population (persons per sq.km) is 115, an increase of 18 points from 107 per sq.km. The sex ratio is 992, an increase of 14 points. The total literacy rate is 85.4 per cent as compared to 68.87 per cent of 2001.

The Manipur state has 60 seats in the legislative assembly, out of which 19 are reserved for Scheduled (Castes or Tribes). There are three MPs in the parliament; two MPs in the Lok Sabha and one MP in the Rajya Sabha. As per the Constitution of India under 1956 Act of Part-X, the State has highest number of indigenous communities in India with thirty-three (33) recognised Scheduled Tribes. In the early phase of the survey on 29th October, 1951 as per the Constituency Act the Chothe was acknowledged and notified as one of the Scheduled Tribes of Manipur.

The Manipur land mass is considered part of the Purvachal or Assam-Burma geological structure and the hills are part of the Eastern Himalaya mountain chain. The Mt. Tenipu (*Isii*) about 2,994 metres is the highest peak in Manipur located at Mao area, Senapati district. The Manipur hills are largely made up of sedimentary and tertiary rocks which belong to two series viz. Disang in the eastern and Barail in the western part (Laiba, 1992:95). The soil is mostly alluvial. The climate of the State is of sub-tropical monsoon to temperate, which depends upon the elevation with varying temperature from $0°$ - $40°$ centigrade. The average annual rainfall is about 207.77 cm or 1467.5 mm (*ibid:* 95). Some of the important rivers of Manipur are: Barak, Irang, Leimatak, Makru, Tipaimuk, Imphal, Nambul, Iril, Thoubal, Khuga, Lokchao, Maha, Thongjoulok and others.

Historical Background: Genesis of the Chothe

The Chothe history is obscured as they have no written records of their own and all that is known has been passed down from one generation to another through oral narratives. Since, there are only five books on Chothe, their historical background has been elaborated for a better understanding of the tribe in study. There is no certainty and reliability on human memory for long and explicit narration of complete folklores. But one has to accept that it contains significant value in the narrated history in many ways about the society.

The Chothe is an indigenous tribe and a highly cultured people of Manipur. They are consider one of the oldest tribes amongst the Chin-Kuki-Mizo speakers on account of their early migration and most advanced group to occupy the southern region of the State (Ansari, 1991:14; Roy, 1936:135). They belong to the Mongoloid racial stock and speaks the Sino-Tibetan language of Tibeto-Burman family under the category of Chin-Kuki and Naga-Kuki linguistic group or as 'Old-Kuki' speakers (Grierson, 1904; Shakespeare, 1912).

According to Chothe mythology, they believe that the origin of the word '*Chawte - Shote - Zote - Chote – Chothe*' is derived from the word "Kachokte" or "Kachoite" literally it means 'The child that I hold/ stirred with'. Mythically, he is considered as the first Chothe person. The second person is known as "Thanidam" lit. 'The moon and the sun are alright', who became *Kachoite's* wife. They lived inside the cave and their progeny multiplied year after year protected by their Guardian God called *Pu Lungchungpa* the Dragon-Python. The cave or hole where the *Kachoite* and *Thanidam* lived is called as *Khul/ Khurpi/ Hurpi/ 'Hurpithouranga'* lit. 'The cave in which five men sprang/ came out'. The exact location is unknown but believed to be somewhere in southern China (Maipak, 1985). The cave in which the Chothe men and women lived is said to be covered with a huge flat rock. When the time came, their Heavenly God (*Thangvan Rengpa*) sent a monkey to remove the rock and opened the cave. John Shakespeare says, "The Chawte told me the tale of peopling of the world out of a hole in the ground, adding the graphic touch that an inquisitive monkey lifted up a stone which lay over the opening, and thus allowed their ancestors to emerge" (1912:151).

So, the first Chothe man to come out of the cave is from the 'Makan' clan, who outwitted the ferocious tiger with the *Awa-ampi* shawl waiting outside to devour them. Thus, the Chothe men and women came out of the cave and began to live on the earth's surface. Henceforth, they have been migrating from place to place, far and wide from Huipithoranga to Lungleh-Waishu to Lungsukbung and ultimately to the present areas (Their myth and history related with the development of their religion and culture is discussed in Chapter 4 and 5).

The Three Regional Chothes

There are a total of eighteen Chothe villages. However, the Census of India recognised twelves villages only and the other six are new settlements, yet to be included in the Census as they have registered at their district Headquarters. The Census of India 2011 gives the entire Chothe population as 3585 with a literacy rate of 69.79 per cent (see Table). The Chothe are mainly confined to two districts of Manipur viz.: Bishnupur and Chandel. However, Arabinda Basu on the basis of the village agglomeration and geographical settings has divided it into three regional zones of groupings viz.: (I) Western group, (II) Central-cluster group, and (III) Eastern group (1985:38).

(i) The Western Chothe

The Western Chothe is known as "Lamlanghupi" (*Ram/Lam*- land/area, *lang*- bright, *hu*- village, *pi*- main), which literally means 'the main/ parent village on a bright land'. It is located behind Bishnupur Police Station or near the Tiddim/ Churachandpur State Highway.[1]

Based on the Chothe oral history, the early Chothe migrated from Mizoram side to the south-western region of Manipur and established many villages in and around Lungsukbung area (Behind Thangching/Thangjing peak). However, after the devastated annexation war by the Moirang king the Chothe and other cognatic tribes like Koireng, Kharam villages fled from the region and migrated as far as north of Imphal. Some Chothe claimed to settle around Chainapung near Loktak Project while others near Moirang and later many separation occurred due to internal conflict and battles with the advancing tribes. In the process, some Chothe moved north toward Wainem (near Oinam), then Imphal and then moved south-east.

However, Lamlanghupi the Western group is considered as the 'Parent Village' of all the Chothe villages. Since, they are consider the last original inhabitants to migrate from the *Ahu Lungsuk-bung/ Nungsuk ching* settlement area (now known as *Chothe-Munpi* near Henglep named by the migrant New-Kuki who occupied the area).[2] They said that the Lamlanghupians are the last dominant migrant group from Lungsukbung, who after successive migration settled at Lamlanglon/Lamlangtong (lit. bright mound) probably by 18th cc. The *Lamlanglon* was an open elevated mound located at the foothill of Laimaton peak of south-western (Loiching) hill range of Manipur that overlook the valley and the Loktak Lake. The Meitei (especially Bishnupriyas) called this abandoned area as 'Lamlangtong' (an inference term of Chothe and Bishnupriya) instead of calling Lamlanglon. The Vishnu Temple, Bishnupur Police Station, Bishnupur Higher Secondary School and the Magistrate Court Office are all located around this mount. Thambaljao said that probably by nineteenth century (i.e. during 1857-1880), about 130 years ago the *Lamlanglon* Chothe people shifted (from Khuman area) to the interior place and renamed the village as 'Lamlanghupi'. They shifted the village because of the severe epidemic of plaques where 5-10 people died every day (Parratt 2005:127, 147, 158). The new village is about 2 km from Bishnupur town or 1½ km south-west of Bishnupur Police Station or 30 km from Imphal, State Capital. The western Chothe is now divided into two villages, viz.: Lamlanghupi and Lamlanglon (as new village).

Historically, the Chothe are well known older indigenous tribe as seen with Moirang people from the event when settled at *Ahu Lungsukbung/ Nungsuk* area in Henglep, Churachandpur district interior of Leimatak river basin (see Chapter 19 of *MNL*). Mr. Khailet Haokip said the New-Kuki (Khongsai, Haokip and Kipgen) occupied the *Lungsukbung* (*Chote-Munpi*) settlement in 1717 A.D.[3]

However, the Lamlanghupi Chothe since 1983 has incorporated to the *Municipal Council of Bishnupur District* under *Ward No.12,* jointly with Makha Leikai after they shifted successively from Lungsukbung, yet they have not completely parted. Although, the Lamlanghupi Chothe comes under one of a polling centre as 'Chothe-Munpi' of Henglep Constituency (No. 57) under the Hill District of Churachandpur, North Sub-Division. Therefore, the Census of India still records 'Lamlanghupi' the western Chothe as 'Chote-Munpi' (lit. Chothe settlement, referring to the Lungsukbung settlement), although now inhabited by Haokips. Thus, the Census Operators failed to identify the people's relocation. This indicates that the original people of Chothe-Munpi now inhabits in a different place under a new village name i.e. '*Lamlanghupi*' near Bishnupur town and the chief is Mr Hiyang Thambaljao, while the old settlement Nungsukbung or '*Chothe-Munpi*' occupied by Haokip and Kipgen still exist at the same spot, and the chief being *Pu* Gilkhomang Kipgen.

The Neighbouring Tribes: The Lamlanghupi Chothe is surrounded by various ethnic tribes; the Meitei in the north, east and south-east, the Rongmei (Kabui/ Meirong/ Marong) and Chiru in the west and north-west; the Kom, Aimol and other Chin-Kuki in the south and south-west respectively.[4] Inter-marriages with these neighbouring ethnic groups are common but marriage with Rongmei is the highest with 32 girls followed by 17 Tangkhul girls compared to other tribes (Yuhlung 2015:53-54).

Occupation: Agriculture is the main occupation of the Lamlanghupi. But another important source of their income is brewing the wine/ liquor (*Leizu*), especially sold to the neighbouring Meitei community, while some depend on the secondary and tertiary modes of occupations.

Migration: In early days, the Chothe being the most advanced migrant group in the region occupied the Tipaimuk, Henglep, Thangching (Thangjing) and Leimatak river basins. And also on the lofty Laimaton (Loiching) hill range and at the foothill of Laimaton peak (present Lamlanghupi settlement) before other migrants inhabited the region (Singh, 1986:150). Loiching hill extends from Thangching peak in the south to Nungshai-Wainem hills in the north beyond Laimaton peak, and extends east-west from the bank of Loktak Lake to the Tipaimuk river basin. This shows the suzerainty of Chothe in the past, how they controlled almost the entire south-western region of Manipur, especially the entire Henglep constituency of Churachandpur (Hiyang, 1985:26).

W. Ibohal Singh said that "By far the Marims (Mareem) were one of the most important tribes in naming different places. It appears they were a cultural group of people" (1986:150).[5] According to Chothe oral history, when they occupied the Tipaimuk and Thangching region (Nungsukbung/ Chote-munpi settlement) they had constant conflicts and battles with various new advancing groups like Lushai, Moirang, Cacharis, New-Kuki, Rongmei and other neighbouring tribes. Later, when they cannot withstand such expensive brutal and frequent wars, they moved eastwards and occupied around Laimaton hills. Then, later settled at *Lamlanglon* because of matrimonial connection and a confederate partner with Meitei kings.

Geographically, this lofty Laimaton hill range is consider as one of the best location in the state due to many advantages like the magnificent view of the entire valley: its closeness to the Loktak Lake; as the best strategic position of war; the availability of many perennial river sources and the dense forest that covered the whole western region. The Loktak Lake is the largest fresh water lake in North-east region. The Laimaton peak serves better strategic check-point position than Thangching peak against the invading Kege-Moirang principality on the south, Imphal principality on the north, and the Tripuris and Bengalese on the west.[6] Many perennial rivers and streams in the area supply the best fresh water. In the past, the incessant dense forest of western mountain ranges extending up to Jiribam boundary supports their domestic economy being rich in natural vegetation and wild life. Thus, the peak serves as a grandiose view of entire Manipur valley from south-west.

Two Passes: There are two very important passes known as *Tongjei Maril* (Old-Cachar road via Bishnupur) and *Ngapurum-Chingjin* (New-Cachar road via Kangpokpi) both passes leads to Tripura (Tipperah/ Takhel) and Bangladesh (Sylhet) via Cachar town passing through Nungba sub-town of Tamenglong district and Jiribum.[7] The Chothe oral history says that in olden days, the elevated semi-plateau area at the foothill of Laimaton peak was called "Lamlanglon" by Chothe. But later it became known to some as *Poireiton Chingkhong* a prominent Princedom of the Meitei (Poireiton group).[8] Then, a little later by fifteenth-sixteenth century probably during Kyampa (1467-1508) or Khagemba (1597-1652) the place became an important military cantonment in the south-western region to defend against the Moirang uprising and to check the Cacharis/ Bengalese immigrants. Subsequently, this military cantonment developed into a major centre, and the original name "Lamlanglon" became known to outsiders as 'Lamlangtong' while others call it as 'Lamangdong'. Owing to certain advantages the area became very important centre in ancient days next to Imphal (Kangla) and Moirang principalities.

It is believed that the Chothe first gave a temporary asylum to the immigrants around Lamlanglon area and later lived side by side. However, the name Lamlanglon was subdued when the Bodo-Cachari, Bengalese (*Mayang*), Bishnupriya and Muslims migrated in large number through *Tongjei Maril* by 1606 AD and invaded Manipur (Kabui, 2003:214). Subsequently, the early eighteenth century marked the arrival of religious leaders like Goswami, Gopal Das and Shanti Das an adherent of Ramanandi Sect of Vaishnavism (Hindu) through this Tongjei Maril route and introduces the new religion in the state.[9] However, by latter eighteenth century when King Chingthang Khompa made Lamangtong as his capital in 1775-1779 AD for four years around C.I. College, Bishnupur (Kabui, 2003:281). Thereafter, by latter twentieth century instead of calling Lamlanglon or Lamangtong or Lamangdong the place was renamed as Bishnupur (being the earliest settlement of Bishnupriya derived from 'Vishnu').[10]

Maipak a respondent said "As a young boy I knew my grandfathers and uncles like Y. Chaothoi going to Jiribum or Cachar valley via Tongjei Maril pass on foot for trading, which is a day and night journey for a strong person. They took with them bundles of tobacco leaves and sold them there, while they brought salt, lighter, brass items, coins, etc. The villagers were very excited to see what they brought whenever they returned home".

The Chothe claimed that severe plaques and scarcity of water forced them to move to the present Lamlanghupi settlement about 130 years ago from Lamlanglon (Khuman area) probably during King Chandrakriti. The huge splendid country (Henglep zone) from Chothe-Munpi to Khawrakpan (Bishnupur canal terminal) that once belonged to Chothe no longer belongs to them. The Chothe having greatly reduced their population to few thousands due to frequent wars, battles and plaques various neighbouring ethnic groups like the Meitei (Bishnupriya), Rongmei, Chiru, Kom have continuously infringed into their territory posing a serious threat to their indigenous territorial rights, religion, economy, socio-culture and political systems.

Lamlanghupi Chiefs: Historically, various ancient texts of Manipur like ChK, MNL have mentioned many great Chothe chiefs and warriors of different Chothe villages like Natoi Nachaopa, Naharam, Neitangpu, Luihom, Tareng, Tanglung, Parirangpa, Chingthang, Mangthang, Sidan, Punem and others associated with politics, economic and kinships and marriages in the past (Hiyang, 1985). However, according to H. Yaikal (98/M) the subsequent prominent (assumed) leaders of western Chothe when settled around Lamlanglon are like Thokmun, Paihutha, Kangchungpa Hoitai Ngaithangpu and Shumhai. To provide them chronologically in succession is not possible because no specific written record is maintain nor any fully knowledgeable person exist today to verify this account besides other reasons.

According to Yaikal and Maipak, there are already eleven Lamlanghupi chiefs after they shifted probably around 1870-90 from Lamlanglon (Khuman village) starting with (1) Yuhlung Juhong, (2) Maipa, (3) Haoba, and (4) H. Marasing S/o Haoba. However, Thambaljao and H. Birensing claim as seven chiefs beginning with (in succession order): (1), Rukung Chongdam S/o Sumthai, (2) Thao Tonchao S/o Luithang, (3) Hiyang Tonlei S/o Boi, (4) Hiyang Mangolchao S/o Tuinem, (5) Mareem Pouhon-glung F/o Merachao, (6) Hiyang Thambaljao S/o Thaning/Thangte (renounced in 2014), and (7) Yuhlung Tomalsing S/o Linhoi, till date.

(ii) The Central-cluster Chothe

The Chothe Central-cluster comprises fifteen villages; including five new settlements, all located in the eastern Hirok hill range of Chandel District, Manipur. They can be further classified into two sub-zones of Eastern Central-cluster and Western Central-cluster, since the villages are divided by a ridge located on either sides of the south-east western Hirok hill range. Ajouhu (Zouhuring) also known as Purum Khullen is the parent village of all the Central-cluster villages. The dominant villages like Chumpang, Tampak-hu, Old-Wangparal, and Chandrapoto were initially separated from Ajouhu while the rest of the villages were the branches of the dominant villages too.

The villages lying on the western hill slopes are: Ajouhu (Purum-Khullen), Tampakhu (Purum-Tampak), Leininghu, Chandropoto (Phantu) and Chothe Khunou. These villages are located about 2-3 km east of Kakching-Sugnu road. The people does their marketing and selling of their forest and handicraft products in Waikhong, Thongnoujam and Kakching town. The villages on eastern hill slopes are: Chumbang, Old-Wangparal, New-Wangparal, Chandonpokpi (Phaipi) and Ziontlang, besides the new five small settlements: Lunghu, Salemthar, Leirungtabi, Lungleh and Bethel. All these villages are located on both sides of Pallel-Chandel road and does their marketing at Pallel, Kakching and Chandel towns.

Tarak Chandra Das (1945) the renowned Indian anthropologist describes the panoramic and the magnificent view of the valley from the abandoned settlement of Ajouhu (Purum Khullen), situated on the top of the hill about 4,500 ft. above the sea level as;

"The scenery of the surrounding country from this village is superb. Towards the east, range after range of hills rise higher and higher in successive tiers till they lose themselves behind the clouds. The dense jungle which covers them assumes a blue colour under the mid-day sun and one finds it extremely difficult to take his eyes away from such a magnificent sight. Towards the west the paddy fields extend far into the annually flooded area which ultimately merges into the calm waters of the Loktak Lake, studded with small but precipitous hillocks, in some of which the fisher-folk have built their houses. Beyond the lake, towards the west, the Laimaton range followed by six others one after another, holds sway up to the border of the Cachar plains. The north and the south are blocked by the two peaks which rise immediately beyond the village. In the south-west a few grass-covered straggling hillocks stumble here and there till we reach the more regular ranges which guard the southern boundary of the valley. Looking towards the direction of the capital of the State some may see the road which connects Imphal with Sugnu up to a great distance passing through villages hidden under the clumps of bamboos. This panoramic view is practically the monopoly of the Purums of Khullen, the three villages do not enjoy this privilege owing to their situation at a lower level" (1945:16-17).

Only some sixty years ago the Ajouhu abandoned their old village during the Second World War who relocated themselves at the foothill on the western slope. True to Das' word the panoramic view was their monopoly from the village location.

The main occupation of central-cluster is agriculture. During the off-season they engaged in selling firewood and handicraft products like bamboo baskets, winnows of different shapes and sizes to neighbouring Meiteis. In case of transport and communication with Chandel the district Headquarter, the eastern slope villages enjoys better advantage than those on the western slope whose expenditure is higher, since they have to travel an extra miles by crossing Kakching and Pallel sub-towns. There is no road that cuts across the hill ridge though they dwell just adjacent. The neighbouring tribes of Chothe central-cluster comprises of Moyon, Monshang, Tarao, Maring, Lamkang, Anal, and Meitei.[11]

Table 9: Chiefs of Ajouhu (Purum Khullen)

Sl.No.	Name of Ajouhu Chiefs	Sl.no	Name of Ajouhu Chiefs
1	Makan Sahompu	21	Khiyang Tute
2	Yuhlung Musan	22	Makan Louril
3	Khiyang Ramngir (Purum Tampak-hu/ Phaihu was split)	23	Rangsai Atonchao
		24	Makan Churamani
4	Marim Routam	25	Makan Darkhrok
5	Rungkung Amu	26	Chillangam
6	Parpa Lungpu	27	Thao Roungam
7	Marim Palshang	28	Marim Bunghong
8	Makan Lungshem	29	Makan Purnoching
9	Makan Angakpa	30	Khiyang Hamunchao *(village relocated to the foothill)*
10	Rimkung Thanil		
11	Makan Tomba	31	Marim Champu
12	Marim Hrungngir	32	Marim Chongdin
13	Khiyang Thatshel	33	Yuhlung Hongpa
14	Yuhlung Kungthang	34	Teching
15	Thao Thotpa	35	Makan Abershing
16	Khiyang Kasin	36	Khiyang Peter
17	Makan Kangngir	37	Thao AG
18	Pilling Jurou	38	Marim Khamba
19	Rangsai Jaipu	39	Thao Jacob
20	Shangkaichao	40	

Source: Ajouhu village secretary 2007. The Ajouhu (Purum Khullen) village in Chandel was established probably around 1847 during force Hinduism. They migrated successively from the south-western region (Lungsukbung country), then settled around Imphal, Moirangkhom and Waithou pat hill near Thoubal district before finally making a permanent settlement in western Chandel district.

The central-cluster Chothe claimed that when they arrived in the region more than three hundred years ago, much ahead of other tribes, the whole forest area on the western side of the Maha river belongs to them (The Maha River is one of the largest tributary in Chandel that originates from the south-west hill). But now, even their preserved community's forest approximately about 15 sq. km. in area has been diminished to small holdings after the Naga-Kuki ethnic crisis of 1987-1999. Some of the neighbouring villages of Moyon, Mongshang, Lamkang and Maring tribes who earlier settled interior of Tengnoupal hill ranges bordering Myanmar came down as refugees (leaving their ancestral places) and have occupied permanently around the Maha river valley along the Imphal-Chandel road as flushed out by the New-Kuki of Moreh region. So, the once dense forest area is now replaced with new pine trees due to continuous felling. This has pose serious threat to various endangered indigenous renewable plants and animals. Therefore, the eco-system of the region is in grave danger since the various food-chain and food-web of flora and fauna is greatly affected.

The New-Wangparal village though established in 1973 was officially recognised on March 1974, after separated from Old-Wangparal (1950). Their chiefs in succession order so far are: (1) Yuhlung Sonpu, (2) Parpa Shirhoi, (3) Makan Wilson, (4) Yuhlung Songpu, (6) Parpa Ngamthang, (7) Yuhlung Jonathan, (8) Parpa Ngamthang, (9) Marim Kulla, till 2004.

The Ziontlang village was established on 3rd October 1983, separated from New-Wangparal. The name of their chiefs are: (1) Makan Lungshem, (2) Thao Ngampa, (3) Rungkung Lukangam, (4) Makan Ibobi, (5) Parpa Nongthon.

(iii) The Eastern Chothe

The Eastern Chothe comprises only the Khongkhang village (derived from the word *Khongkap*) situated on the south-east of the Tengnoupal hill range of the Indo-Myanmar National Highway (NH-39). The village is about 72 km from Imphal; 35 km south-east of Pallel and about 35 km to Moreh town in the east.

In olden days, the Eastern Chothe was known as "Mouhulon" (lit. village of *Moupi*, derived from the term *Moupi* a variety of bamboo grown abundantly in the area). According to them, long time ago the Queen (Maharani) of Manipur visited their village when she came down to await the king who went to Kabaw valley (Myanmar). And when the villagers heard about her coming to their village area they immediately prepared a footpath for her like a ladder along the slope of the village. She was overwhelmed to see her old Chothe relatives living peacefully in a remote area. Since, the people gave her warm reception she had forgotten all her tiredness and exhaustion.

So, as a sign of her gratitude she gave her own gold ear-rings (*Sana-leirum*) to the village Chief and requested to continue on the bond of friendship and loyalty with the king (see Pic.17). Henceforth, after her visit the village was known as "Khongkap" (lit. Foot-pace) after she expressed the footpath was like ladder steps. Subsequently, *Khongkap* later generates to be known as "Khongkhang" Chothe.

According to H. Thambaljao a respondent said, the queen in reference could be either Charairongpa's daughter, or one of the wife's of Pamheiba/ Garibniwaz (1709-1748), while Laishram Imoba said the queen is the wife Maharaj Bhaigya Chandra (1769-1798). The queen/ princess gave her earrings to Chothe Khongkhang chief being closely related or being their granddaughter or daughter-in-law during one of their journey to Myanmar (Burma/Awa). Pamheiba's mother is said to be a Chothe lady called Shorha while the Meitei knows her as Nungthil Chaibi. This statement is supported by the Chothe folklore '*Thaowon Saamtharnu*' and H Bhuban Singh's article '*Whither Manipur*' (2007).[12] [Believed that the Meitei prince (King Charairongpa 1697-1709) captured her because of her beauty and immediately married her informally when a section of Chothe settled around Imphal].

The topography of the region is such that the eastern blue-mountains run successively in almost parallel high up to the north Kabaw valley of Myanmar (Burma) and one can endlessly enjoy the perfect beauty throughout the seasons from the village. Another breath taking sight of the area is the clear white fog that completely envelops the deep gorges and low-lying areas in winter. The sight is so captivating that one would not like to leave such a beautiful scene. On bright sunny days one can get a good glimpse of Tamu town of Myanmar from one particular angle in the south-east. But the west and north-west is blocked by the Tengnoupal hill range the highest peak in the region. There are still some big trees growing in the deep forest though it has been somewhat disturbed now by the influx of the New-Kuki from the east and by their jhum cultivation.

Khongkhang village, though located on the top of the mountain is very rich in natural resources like forest produced like timber, bamboo, various citrus fruits, and wildlife like tigers, leopards, wild-boars, monkeys, foxes, jackals, deer, and some varieties of jungle fowls. The rivers and streams between these mountains abundantly provide a variety of fishes. The climate is moderately hot in summer and cold in winter and it usually remains foggy on rainy days. The rainfall is also moderate. Unfortunately there is no immediate neighbouring tribe. The nearest are the Maring on the north and north-east, Lamkang on the south-west and the Thadou-Kuki villages on the north-west of Tengnoupal sub-division. All these neighbouring villages are located beyond 6-15 km from Khongkang village. The villagers depending

Table 10: Khongkhang Chothe Group: Their Villages and its Chiefs

Sl.No.	Village Name	Name of Chief	Sl. No.	Village Name	Name of Chief
1	Lamlanglon (Bishnupur)	Pu Punem	19	Khongkhang	Yuhlung Daithun
2	Yangpalkung (Near Koubru hill, Imphal)	Khiang/ Khiyang Paihutha	20	"	Marim Rimthou
3	Thampuilai	Marim Lenti	21		Makan Hutai
4	Hongchangjeilon	Damri	22	"	Yuhlung Teiri
5	Jouhulon	Yuhlung Sungnu	23	"	Marim Wonchung
6	Paitanglon	Khiang Eithou	24	"	Khiang Rangsakun
7	Hungtunlon	Marim Limathang	25	"	Yuhlung Paihuhoi
8	Yokkuilon	Thao Jaibunhoi	26	"	Yuhlung Tomphung
9	Makanlon	Khiang Hushub	27	"	Yuhlung Souba
10	Tengnoulon	Khiang Lamshu	28	"	Thao Ningthemchao
11	Chingkeilon	Makan Wonchoiwai	29	"	Khiang Kamen
12	"	Marim Kangla	30	"	Makan Chikungpa
13	Mouhulon	Makan Stairum	31	"	Yuhlung Hoichong
14	Khongkhang	Khiang Paithun	32	"	Khiang Khetrichao
15	Khongkhang (Present settlement)	Khiang Thimsut	33	"	Makan Chandra Kumar
16	"	Yuhlung Buring	34	"	Yuhlung Tarik
17	"	YuhlungChonghai	35		
18	Khongkhang	Makan Janghoi	36		

Source: Khongkhang Baptist Church: Golden Jubilee Souvenir (1941-1997).

Notes: The chiefs from Sl.No. 1-26 have all expired, while the rest still survives.

on the necessities of requirement do their marketing in three towns: Moreh, Pallel and Kakching. But to sell their forest produced they go to Pallel or Kakching. However, the transport and communication system is poor in this sparsely populated region.

Migration

Migration is a natural process. The Chothe, since early days, like any other indigenous people of the world have been constantly on move from one place to another due to various explained and unexplained reasons, generally at a slower pace. Some common reasonable explanation for their migrations in the past are like constant internal feuds and conflicts, wars and battles, expulsion, economic motives, scarcity of food, droughts and famines, population explosion, search for fertile land, epidemic diseases like plagues, smallpox, cholera and better geographical location for village sites. But with the advance in science and technology, economy, better transport and communication systems the rate and frequency of people's movement and migration have tremendously increased as compared to the past. The number and volume of people migrating from one village to another, from one town to another; one city to another; and from one country to another, is much larger and greater now than before.

The various tribes and communities living in Northeast India and Manipur have migrated to the region and state phased by phase from different directions since early days till the time of latter eighteenth century, the latest tribal immigrant groups being the New-Kuki group. Since, no written records were maintained by the early migrant groups their chronological dating could not be ascertain, except depend on their oral tradition, which makes difficult for historians to date chronologically their entry. The indigenous tribes like Chothe, Kharam, Koireng, Liangmei, Maring, Anal, etc. (Old-Kukis) claimed to have entered Manipur from south and south-east phase by phase.[13] Similarly, the *Tenyimis* (*Tenyidie* = Mao-Poumei speakers) and Tangkhul entered from North-eastern region phase after phased. Then, the Thai-Ahom from east and Bodo-Cacharis from west, and finally the Chin-Kuki-Mizo speakers entered Manipur from Myanmar from south-east phase by phase and spread far and wide upto Nagaland. In the social discourse, the old and new immigrants still continued their inter-migration and intra-migration till nineteenth century some move far while others move nearby their habitats. Since, there was no strict political boundary amongst these people there was always land disputes and inter-tribal feuds, until Manipur became part of Indian Union. Likewise, tribes like Biate, Jaintia, Khasi of Mongoloid origin entered Meghalaya from Manipur crossing the Cachar valley probably prior to eleventh century, while section of Bodo (Boro) who crossed the Brahmaputra River are known as Garo (see L.S. Gassah, *The War-Jaintia*).[14]

The Early Phase from Mythical Cave *Huipithoranga* to *Lungleh-Waishu*: The actual time and place when the Chothe began their migration to reach the present settlement is obscure. But from the oral and historical point of view, it is most probable they have migrated from the southern region of China during the mass expulsion and exodus, and occupied the Chin-hills of Upper-Myanmar (Burma) from the mythical cave *Huipithoranga*.

According to S.A. Ansari, "The Mongoloid race reached North-east India following two routes; one route passed through Tibet and another through Yunnan province of China. Those following the routes through Yunnan and eastern China moved southward to Vietnam, Laos, Cambodia, Thailand, Malaysia, Burma and further westward to hill regions on the Indo-Burma frontier tract. Important among these passes are Patkai, Chaukan, Aimol, Taungup and An" (1991:10).[15]

This remark is supported by the linguistic background. Since, the Chothe have been classified under the family of Sino-Tibetan language of Tibeto-Burman sub-branch of all Indian tribes categorised under the sub-sub branch of Chin-Kuki-Mizo and Naga-Kuki speakers (see the chart in Sl. No. 152 of S. Bharati 2005: 431). Maipak Yuhlung (64/M) of Lamlanghupi and Vincent (Babu) Parpa (56/M) of Tampakhu base on their legends and folktales said that "The Chothe and other Chin-Kuki groups could have migrated after the construction of the first Great Wall of China". If so, this period occurred after Qin Shi Huang dynasty, the first Emperor of China around 200-220 B.C.[16] Consequently, they believed after occupying for many years around Upper-Myanmar (Kachin kingdom) they moved down south either following the Chin-Win or the Irrawaddy Rivers and inhabited the southern of *Khyan* or *Khampat* (Shan and Pong kingdom) located on the north-western region of Myanmar extending the whole eastern part of Mizoram (earlier known as Lushai hills).

One very important facet, according to my Chothe respondents; H. Thambaljao and Y. Maipak about the direction of their migration as told by their great forefathers is found in their common vernacular, which they all claim to have migrated from the east, in the direction where the sun rises. It reads as -

"*Ani Chote ngei shu Nasu, Ni shukna kena wa-a ta, ani pu-pi na liphui-a*" (We the Chothe came from the east, in the direction where the sun rises, this is what our great grandfather and grandmother told us).

J.K. Bose also claimed that 'the Chothe are believed to have migrated extensively far and wide till the extreme south of Yangon (Rangoon) towards the sea and made a movement towards the north-west again' (1933). Hongpa Yuhlung a respondent also stated "My great forefather had the tradition of using variety of huge seashells (*Moipung*) in early days".[17] According to R.C. Roy, who first studied the Chothe said that "The Chawte clan is a branch of the 'Old Kukis', as the earliest immigrants in Manipur are called. Competent authorities tell us that the 'Old Kuki' clans came down from the Chhindwin valley generations ago and proceeded southwards toward the sea and turned northwards again up the hills. But my informants knew nothing of the seaward migrations of their forefathers. They possessed only a vague tradition of their migration to the present home from the south" (1936: 135).

Thus, it shows that they were pushed out from southern China (Kansu region) to Tibet (Kham) and later settled around Kachin in Upper-Myanmar, who later move down southwest and occupied Shan kingdom. And much later, they were forced to settle on the lofty mountain peak of Lungleh or Champai area (districts in Mizoram/ Lushai hills) before they finally entered the present south-western hills of Manipur in the successionist movements.

The Chothe assumed to settle at "Lungleh-Waishu" meaning 'Let the rock shine' (lit. *Lungleh* means plenty of rocks/stones; *Warshu* or *Waishu* means let it shine/bright or prosper) in Mizoram.[18] Historically, this period could be around seventh or eleventh century. The name suggest a beautiful elevated rocky area and is considered as one of the earliest and most important historical settlement in the Chothe history. Their folktales highly glorifies about their culture and long existence describing the climax of their society out there before it was driven out by another new invading group.

The Phase from *Lungleh-Waishu* to *Lungsukbung*: The Chothe at *Lungleh-Waishu* probably ends when the Shan or Khyan dynasty or another powerful (Lushai=Long head) group emerged and began their territorial expansion. According to Maipak as told by his grandfather, the Chothe made a strong resistance against the new invading forces in the battle but they were finally compelled out of *Lungleh-Waishu* because of the massive devastation causing hundreds of lives in the event. Historically, they were separated into different directions in this event that led the entire *Chothe/Chawte/ Shote/ Zote* population to be scattered. They left behind (the *Chawhte* of Mizoram), while some fled towards Tripura (Tipperah/Selyet) in the west and northwest (believed to be Rangkhol, Darlong, Halam groups), while the majority marched north towards the south-western region of Manipur crossing *Tuiva* River (supported by their *Achui laa* folksong).

Another version is that a quarrel broke out between two brothers: '*Thanghung and Shidang*' over jhum cultivation, in which Thanghung (Chothe of Manipur) the elder defeated his younger brother Shidang group. Now they are uncertain about Shidang group assumed to have returned to south (Hiyang, 1985:24). Lalsangnunga Hmar of Mizoram a friend in discussion also said that Shidang and Sailo to be a very close kins, and claiming Sailo as the eldest clan among the Mizo. Thus, suggesting the Chothe migrated from Mizoram side.

Based on the Chothe oral history, some of their most early settlements prior to entry of Lungleh-Waishu are: *Ahu-mul Huipithoranga…, Ahu Lungleh-Waishu, Ahu Tarik Jampebung, Ahu Thingtin Aishanlon (Tamilon), Ahu Toujanglon (Tamalon), Ahu Tumpokpi, Ahu Katokpi, Ahu Shimnudung (Tuirung), Ahu Wainudung,…* (CLAM, Souvenir 2000:2).

After the battle at *Lungleh-Waishu*, they made a permanent settlement at *Ahu Wainudung* near *Tuiva* River a place bordering the present Manipur and Mizoram states. Then, they moved north-west and lived at *Ahu Tuisarung* (lit. hot running water) believed to be near the Barak river or around Jiribum (Cachar), and then at *Ahu Tuilungsau* and *Ahu Tuiwaisu* where three rivers conjoined (Yuhlung, 1985:27). They kept migrating towards east, looking for suitable places and settled at *Ahu Nachangjoi,* then at *Ahu Saikhupai* believed to be around Tipaimuk area. Subsequently, they marched north-east from the earlier place and established permanent settlements at *Ahu Lungsukbung* behind Thangching peak near Henglep as described in the *Moirang Ningthourol Lambuba* (*MNL*). Thus, the subsequent few early settlements of Chothes in the south-western region behind Thangching peak are: *Ahu Lungsukbung* (*Nungsuk or Chothe-Munpi*), *Ahu Taipiruk, Ahu Ramudol, Ahu Surouthil, Ahu Lamngente* (Ngente-Leikentha), *Ahu Tuipi* (Leimatak area), *Ahu Chainapung, Ahu Kumpibung* (South of Moirang near Chura-chandpur), etc. (CLAM, 2000:3).

So far, the exact period when the Chothe entered in the south-western region of Manipur is unknown, despite *Moirang Ningthourol Lambuba* (*MNL*) one of the oldest historical texts of Manipur mentioned about the Chothe Kingdom on two important accounts, without referring to any periods in any part of the book. Historically, in the constant wars and battles the first valley group of Manipur to come into frequent conflict with the Chothe and other ethnic tribes was the Kege-Moirang as recorded in MNL and their folktales. The text described that *Ura Ngangoiba* or *Ura Khundaba* the fourth king of Moirang (Kege) "fought with the Chothe of Naharam of the western hills. The Chothe king was defeated and taken prisoner. The king himself participated in the battle and showed his dexterity in the use of weapons" (Kabui, 2003:178). The second account describes at length how the eighth king of Moirang *Kongting Hanba* (*Chothe Thangwai Atengba*) invaded the cluster of Chothe villages around *Lungsukbung* settlement in his campaign for confederacy (*ibid.:* 181-182).

The MNL described beautifully the aerial view of the early Chothes' country, how they inhabit the peaks of the five mountain ranges, where four rivers meet, formed by the gorges of those five mountain ridges, in which the country was ultimately destroyed in the devastating battle by the Moirang. The four rivers are; (1) *Tusamphai* (2) *Tukhaileng* (3) *Tuisareng* and (4) *Changbe Yemmathei*, and the name of five mountain ranges where the four rivers met are: (1) *Lungsuk ching* (2) *Thangkhong-Tanglou ching* (3) *Makan-Turu ching* (4) *Houpal-Thaba ching* and (5) *Lallum-Sagontak meina khubi ching,* and the five main Chothe villages that settled on the top of these five mountain ranges are; (1) *Thongnang-Kampa* (2) *Thangkhong* (3) *Tanglei* (4) *Makan* and (5) *Tuntha* (Singh 1982:92-93). The Chothe people have a story for each settlements. Some have similar historical accounts with tribes like Kharam, Tarao, Koireng, Chiru, Aimol, Kom, and Hmar of Manipur as they lived nearby. Locating the exact settlements and systematically re-constructing their history is a major predicament for well knowledgeable elders exist anymore.

The above accounts indicates that the Chothes in the early days enjoyed the political hegemony as a powerful tribe in the south-western region till the event at *Ahu Lungsukbung,* before the Kege-Moirang destroyed their civilisation and political dominance (Kabui, 2003: 176). There are also superstitious beliefs that prohibit intermarriages between the two communities (Chothe and Moirang) on reasons of history and religious connection. Religiously, any Chothe girl that marry a Moirang man is believed will not live long after their marriage. Konsam Manik-chand said that the Chothe especially, Mareem clan (*Khuman* in Meitei) and Ningthoujas of Meitei are not allow to marry each other considering a cognate, by linking with Pakhangba's foster father Kongding.[19]

In connection to the above, W.I. Singh mentions how the Pong or Shan came in contact with the Poirei and how Samlungfa after conquering Basa (Bengal/Sylhet), finally arrived at *Ngaprum Chingjeng* (New Cachar route) after crossing the river Gwai and Khebu Chingjeng by 1220 A.D. (1986:14-15). It is most probable that the Poireiton are immigrants group who originally came from the south-east (Tai-Chinese-Myanmar origin). It is believed that the early Poirei migrants in their entourage to the interior of south-western hills sought asylum in the Chothe territory. The Chothe as part of the custom granted them asylum probably at the foothill of Laimaton peak which few early Meitei called it as *Poireiton Chingkhong* (see endnotes 7). It is believed that few Poirei gradually moved north-wards and subsequently established a principality near Kangla-Tongbi. Later a section of the faction moved down south beyond Moirang area and occupied the Ewaitha-Sugnu region. After many years, Chothe Thangwai Pakhangba (Nongda Leiren Pakhangba) before establishing the Imphal (Kangla) principality made truce with Poireiton of south to form confederation. Then, Pakhangpa as head of Moirang principality and the south-western kingdoms (like Chothe, Kharam and Koireng) along with Angom Puleiromba (the absconding Tangkhul prince) jointly ousted the Khaba-nganba (Poi/ Poirei/ Falum/ Khoibu-Maring and Maram tribes) from Kangla-Tongbi areas (Imphal) Kingdom.[20]

Since, the inception of Kangleipak (Manipur kingdom) the Chothes and Meiteis have been living side by side harmoniously and peacefully assisting the Meitei king politically in war campaigns, economically and socially till nineteenth century. Although, the socio-political relationships got estranged due to various socio-political reasons at certain times. It is believed to have strengthened during King Kyampa (1467-1508) being a political allied partner before and the relationship got matured during the reign of King Khakempa again (1597-1652). Thambaljao said that this loyal political ties with various Manipuri kings continued till the time of Maharaj Chandrakriti (1850-1886/ 98) and Gambhir (1825-34), even after the *Seven Years Dissertation of War* (1819-1825) devastated by Burmese invasion (After these kings died the history of Manipur completely altered especially, with the hill tribes like Chothe due to secessionist issues among the Manipur royal family members).

However, the Chothes do not know their exact or direct ethnic descends connected with other southeast ethnic groups of the world. One may speculate whether they and other early cognate tribes could be part of the early Pong or Khyan group of the Proto-Tai-Sino-Tibetan group who reached Manipur with Prince Samlong (Samlungpha) a prince of Pong kingdom in 678 A.D. or, Could they be part of the Chinese general Ko-lo-feng's of Nan Chao who conquered Upper Burma, Assam and Manipur in 760 A.D, or Are they part of the early Kachin group who moved towards the south of Shan Kingdom in Myanmar?[21]

This proposition is based on *Cheitharol Kumpaba* and the Pong chronicles 777 A.D. mentioned by Pemberton (see Laiba 1992: 5; Parratt 2005: 6; Singh 1986: 16). The reason being some of the early historical kings of Manipur like, Samlungpha, Sukanpa, Taothingmang, Sameireng, Aayangpa, Loiyumpa, Chingthang, Tapungpa, Puranthapa, Punsipa etc. bears true tribal indigene names as mentioned in their folklores as claimed by Mrs. Tharaklei (87/F) of Tampakhu. Since, the Chothe do not have any written records of their own, therefore it is difficult to establish the nearest kin or ethnic group of proto-Sino-Tibetan family they actually connect. Only ancient language, genome and other peculiar cultural affinity will support the genealogical connection as claimed (Gupta, 1985:34).

The Medieval Phase after *Lungsukbung*: After this phase, three splits occurred within the region. The Central-cluster Chothe claim they were separated from the parent western Chothe probably during the reign of King Kyampa or Khakempa after a 'Tug-of-war' was organised in honour of their jubilant war celebration. According to them, the defeated group in the tug-of-war became the followers of the Queen and lived near the Palace (Imphal). The Chothe claimed the present Manipur Governor's campus opposite Kangla Fort as their old settlement called *Ahu Sishakung* (lit. Cowherd centre) and the decaying banyan tree existing with some stones near the Treasury Office around the Laison Office as their abandoned *Laimang* (Deity's sacred ground). Later with the Vaishnavism religious movement this Chothe group shifted to *Ahu Yangpalkung*. This place is mentioned by W.I. Singh that "The rest of the Mareems moved towards the north of their settlement. In the fifteenth century A.D. more precisely in the period from c.1403 to c.1415 A.D they were found to have inhabited the Koubru hills at a place known as 'Yangpham Chaklikpok" (1986: 150). Roushi opines, "It was during the reign of *Pu* Punem Mareem (a Chothe chief) that the split occur and who was later succeeded by *Pu* Lentih and *Pu* Damli in their sojourn. This Chothe left that place because of the political-religious turmoil and marched north towards the south-east hill ranges and settled at various places like *Ahu Thampuilai, Ahu Makan, Ahu Punkang, Ahu Langmeiching,* near Langthabal, Sandangsengba Maring, Waithou-Thoubal, Pallel, etc. until they reached the present Chandel region".

The *Ahu Lungsukbung* (*Chote-Munpi*) settlement is still remembered because of major defensive battles with Moirang in early days and also with the Chin-Kuki-Lushai group during later eighteenth century (before 1717 A.D, the occupation of Lungsukbung villages by New-Kuki). The latter event is said to have occurred after some brave Chothe men like Parirangpa, Neitangpu and other great warriors expired. The battle is consider very destructive like the *Lungsuk* (*Nungsuk*) battle fought with the Moirang in the past. After the event, many scattered and resettled in places like *Ahu Kumpibung, Ahu Kanwai* and *Ahu Oksongbung* around Moirang and Churachandpur border (Hiyang, 1985: 26). Then, the Kamhau the Sukte Chin group soon followed the Khongsai (New-Kukis) migrants and fought several defensive wars with Chothe before they could re-established their villages. The *Cheitharon Kumpapa* (*ChK*) records that 'nine *haos* were abducted from Chothe Paya by the Khongsais' (Parratt, 2005: 151).[22] There are many similar accounts recorded in *ChK* where the Chothe encountered many defensive battles against the Rongmei (Kabui) in the southern region around Khoupum valley (*ibid:* 160). The Rongmei of Manipur origin seems to connect with *Tinyimia* (*Mao-Poumei*) and the Thai of Thailand as suggested by their culture and language.

According to the Chothe oral history, the second major split occurred at the village of *Ahu Chainapung* (south of Loktak Project) in which one section of Chothe group headed towards the north and temporarily occupy *Ahu Purumkhong* (near Wainem village). These group further moved north around

Imphal and later migrated down south-east of Chandel (see ChK). The event at *Ahu Chainapung* occurred during latter Khongsai (New-Kuki) aggression and probably much before the reign of King Chingthang Khompa (1759-60, 63-74).

According to Kamei "on 20th December (Wakching) 1786, Chingthang Khomba went in an expedition against the Kukis. He marched to *Lamlangtong* where he spent a night; spent another night at *Chainapung*, then proceed to the Laimatak base, spent a day at Nungshai" (Kamei, 2004:64). There is a confusion to ascertain this period. According to P.S. Haokip "during the reign of King Chandrakriti, Kamhau the Sukte Chin king declared war on the Meitei Kingdom and captured the King, taking him away to Chin land" (1998:27). This indicates that another major war with the New-Kuki occurred during the reigned of Maharaj Gambhir Singh (1825-34) or Chandrakriti (1850-86). The Chothe elders claimed that earlier their great forefathers jointly fought many battles with Chandrakriti in the territorial expansion and so Chandrakriti used to visit certain Chothe villages (Singh, 1995:103). The loyalty and political alliance between Chothe and Chandrakriti (Manipuri king) is proven by a decree/ edict in metallic plate and other valuable ornamental personal assets given to Chothe, Many of such ornamental artefacts of various kings of Manipur obtained during their relationships are still preserved and treated as sacred items by the Lamlanghupi Village Council (see Pic. 7, 8, 9, 10, 11, 12, 13 and 14).

It does not necessarily mean for the Chothe, the process of migration and territorial expansion ended at *Ahu Chainapung*. The second and third Chothe migrant groups (i.e. Eastern group and Central-cluster) kept changing their places and continued splitting, depending on the situation. The Lamlanghupi the western Chothe settled around Laimaton peak and later moved down at the foothill and named the village as 'Lamlanglon or Lamangtong' by nineteenth century (i.e. during 1857-1880). As described above, although some moved north and settled around Imphal for certain period, later they migrated to south-east along the eastern mountain range towards Waithou-pat (Thoubal) and finally confine themselves to the present Chandel region. This exodus from Manipur valley occurred during forced Hindunisation and those group of people like Loi, Andro, Chothe, Koireng, Kom, Karam, etc who refused to embraced the new religion moved to countrysides. The Central-cluster group has many stories to tell about themselves. Roushi and Neilut claimed that earlier they attacked and snatched *Ahu Sumpum* a Kom village located between Pallel and Kakching hillocks and temporarily occupied it, before they further move down south and settled at *Ahu Chipi'*.[23] Both asserted that the confusion of identity between 'Chothe and Purum' began from this incident, which need further research.

Parpa Roushi (76/M) of Ajouhu said there is one folksong to prove that the Chothe Central-cluster group settled at *Ahu Chipi* composed by Pu Theipu (village chief) in dedication to the Banyan (*Bung*) tree which he had planted. It is said to be their tradition and custom to plant banyan trees at new settlements. The title of the song is "Chipi-laa", and the first stanza in free translation is given below:

> *"Keina sakting Chipi zaija-o,*
> *Suva bungpi phunche,*
> *Kolvai lamna - o hoisa ae".*

> > (*I will witness the Chipi's prosperity,*
> > *When this Banyan tree grows big,*
> > *Dancing around would be delightful to see*).

Some settlements that followed after *Ahu Chipi* are *Ahu Belhuring, Ahu Louhar, Ahu Lunghu, Ahu Phaihu, Ahu Ajouhu* (Purum Khullen), *Ahu Waipu-Inlon* (Tampakhu), *Ahu Chumbang,* etc. Subsequently, the rest of the Central Cluster villages bifurcated from these three principal villages. They also tell a mysterious event when settled at *Ahu Louhar* that all the roofs of the Makan families were blown off on one stormy night. Believe to be because of a false promise made by a Makan man to the village authority, after a quarrel broke out with a fellow friend. The story is discussed in Chapter four.

The Lamlanghupi (Western group) and Khongkhang (Eastern group) also kept changing their settlements from time to time around the area due to religious and environmental factors. Lamlanghupi village is said to have changed at least four times from seventeenth century onwards within a radius of 5-10 kilometres. The first one was said because their god augured them to change their Sacred-grove from Laimaton peak through divination. The second due to the epidemic of cholera and smallpox, while the third because of scarcity of water source as it was too far from their habitat. So, the present settlement is said to be more than one hundred years old after shifted from Lamlanglon (Khuman) village.

On the above description, it is significant to note that since early days, the Chothe and other cognatic indigenous tribes like: Kharam, Koireng, etc. have migrated and colonised the whole south-western region of Manipur. But it is unfortunate that we cannot ascertain the exact period of their entry in the region, except that the two historical texts describing only about their early presence and later subjugated by Kege-Moirang. The *MNL* text states 'The conquest of Kharam village of Langte was the beginning of the Moirang invasion on the hill tribes on the western hills', and subsequently the other surrounding sub-groups too fought bravely against the Kege-Moirang (Kabui, 2003: 176).

John Shakespeare, a British political agent has classified the indigenous groups of Manipur into "Old and New-Kuki" clans/ tribes based on the entry period, direction of migration from the southern region, cultural traits, language, dress, food habits compared with the new-influx or New-Kuki clans/ groups of Chin-Kuki-Mizo. Shakespeare's Old-Kuki clans are: Aimol, Anal, Chawte (Chothe), Chiru, Kolhen (Koireng), Kom, Lamkang, Purum, Tikhup and Vaiphei (1912:149).[24] S.N. Ansari in support states that 'the Chin-Kuki tribes, on the basis of their arrival are divided into 'Old-Kuki Clans' and the 'New-Kuki Clans', thereby resulting in the generic usage by many scholars of today' (1991:14).

Shakespeare made a serious statement about Chothe's history in a nutshell that, "Though the chronology of the Chronicle is not beyond suspicion, I think this may be taken as proof that these clans appeared in Manipur a good deal earlier than their relations the Bete and Rhangkhol entered Cachar" (1912:148). There seems to be no doubt about Shakespeare's remark as far as the Chothe oral history is concerned, since the Chothe and other Old-Kuki groups claimed they had a large population and controlled huge tract of land in the early days. Finally, they were reduced to minority because of numerous factors like bloody and frequent defensive wars and battles, succession, famines, plagues, invasion and assimilation.

McCulloch, in connection similarly substantiated the above remarks that "All these tribes were much more numerous than they are at present, and not further back than thirty years ago, some of them who are now represented by but one or two small villages in position far removed from their former ones, occupied large tracts, but though reduced in numbers they retain all their particular customs, speak their separate languages, and are objects of much interest" and that "they are now but small remnants" (1857:42, 65). Truly these indigenous/ Old-Kuki tribes of Manipur are still small remnants like the Native Americans who were almost exterminated by colonialist in the frequent wars and battles, internal feuds and natural calamities. Broadly these indigenous tribes show common origin and similar cultural traits but since the early ethnographers could not identify and club them together, they are listed under *Scheduled-Tribes* category by the Govt. of India as separated entity.

Many of the so called 'Old-Kuki' tribes classified by Shakespeare strongly disagree with the usage of "Old-Kuki" as suffix or prefix to their ethnic identity. Marim Rimril of Lunghu (my Chothe informant) said the word 'Kuki' is irrelevant while referring to them, being a generic term coined by the British Colonialists and all of these classified tribes living in Chandel prefer to identify themselves with their own historical ethnic/ indigenous names' because earlier they were never known as Kuki, being a recent generic term.

This grievance can be contended with the writings of William Shaw who says that, "The origin of this word 'Kuki' is not known, but it first appears in Bengal in Rawlings' writings of the "Cucis or Mountainers of Tipra" in Asiatic Researches (II, xii) in 1792. And he discovers in the works of Lewin (Exercises in the Lushai Dialect, p. 1) a derivation for 'Kuki' from DZO (Lushai) word, 'Tui-Kuk', for the Tipperah (Sakchip) Tribe (1929:11). While some scholars opine that it was the name of the first Thadou village around Cachar. So, the term 'Kuki' is a generic word derived from 'Tui-kuk' during the British colonial period, and became widely popular because of the frequent usage and references made in various discussions and writings. Similarly, names like Maring (Poi/ Falam), Meitei (Loi), Moirang (Kege), Chiru (Chi-ru), Purum (Pun-rum), and Kom (pit) are also considered as generic terms derived from certain peculiar characters, behaviour or event in identifying among themselves in their relationship, despite having their own original ethnic names.

Demography: Factors and Consequences Leading to De-population

The Census of India 2011 shows the total Chothe household of 791 with a total population of 3585 (1706-M/ 1879-F). However, the previous 2001 Census of India gave the entire Chothe population as 2675, while the first Indian census report of 1931 shows only 250 souls, which excludes the "Purum" (Chothe) of T.C. Das with 305 souls (see Table 8). The exclusion was because of the internal confusion in the survey between the Census enumerators and the people living in the State due to nature of nomenclature they used. The most intriguing question is, why the Chothe population remains so thin even today despite absence of wars and battles unlike in the past? Could it be due to high mortality and low fertility rates? Or could there be other reasons like ancestors' cursed, as they believed?

According to Chothe, there are certain explained and unexplained reasons for their slow and low population rates, such as: frequent devastating wars and battles in the past; natural calamities such as plagues, smallpox, cholera and typhoid; low selection potential of mates; assimilation into Meitei through matrimonial and political relationships, etc. Similar factors are also explained by McCulloch (1857:42, 65) and Shangkham (2006:2-3).

Assimilation: The process of acculturation and assimilation cannot be denied in the history of Manipur, since Meitei culture is a blend of various ethnic communities, though they may have their own distinctive original identity. Imphal (Kangla) the capital of Manipur is a melting pot of numerous ethnic groups from the surrounding hill tribes. This fact is pointed out by R.K. Ranjit who writes, "Instances of the hill people coming down to the plains and identifying themselves with the plains people had been a common

Table 11: Chothe Population by Village: Census of India 2001 and Personal Data 2004

Census SL. No.	Census of India (2001)	No. of household	Total pop.	Male	Female	Common indigenous village names (Estt. year)	No. of household	Personal data Sept.2004
79	Chandonpokpi (Phaipi)	8	41	19	22	Phaipi (1977)	19	91
121	Khongkhang	47	256	133	123	Khongkhang (1936)	49	296
154	Purum Tampak	88	387	195	192	Tampakhu or Phaihu (1856)	72	332
155	Purum Khullen	26	126	53	73	Ajouhu (1821)	38	164
157	Purum Lainingkhul	37	200	95	105	Laininghu (1937)	35	204
158	Chothe Khunou	14	66	37	29	Chothe Khunou (1972)	14	67
159	Chandrapoto	53	243	117	126	Phantu (1947)	54	260
197	Ziontlang	34	178	81	97	Ziontlang (1983)	31	186
198	New-Wangparal	33	158	68	90	New-Wangparal (1973)	25	138
199	Old-Wangparal	29	127	56	71	Old-Wangparal (1949)	21	111
203	Purum Chumbang #	154	800	402	398	Chumbang (1847)	72	336
177	Chothe Munpi @ (Lamlanghupi)	54	306	170	136	Lamlanghupi (1887, Shifted from Lamlanglon 1700's)	53	291
						Lamlanglon* (1997)	13	42
						Bethel Happy land* (2003)	04	13
						Lungleh* (1996)	10	50
						Salemthar* (1982)	10	42
						Leirungtabi* (1986)	05	27
						Lunghu* 1986	06	39
		577	2888	1426	1362		531	2689
	Total		2675					

Note: The asterisk * marked villages are new settlements which are not yet recognised by the Census of India (COI). While @ mark, indicates the abandon settlement of Lamlanghupi in Churachandpur district (Henglep sub-division). The total population of the Chothe tribe is given as 2675 by the Census of India 2001, almost equivalent with the personal data collected. But the village wise Census data gives the total population as 2888, an error is occurred with the Purum Chumbang village.

occurrence... the period was characterised by a type of relation where the various tribal villages became either the subjects or the allies of the Meitei kings only due to the latter's military supremacy" (1988: 86). Ranjit's view point is confirmed by *Cheitharol Kumpaba* that most of the *haos* (hill tribes) were made to pledge to become blood brothers especially during King Chandrakriti King Garib Niwaz's period on the basis of Hindu religious movement (Parratt, 2005:110).

In connection to this origin of Meitei, many Chothe too claimed that those who were left behind around Imphal like: *Ahu Yangpalkung, Ahu Sarouthil* (near new Checkon), *Ahu Saishakung* (the Manipur Governor's campus, opposite Kangla Fort), *Ahu Makan* (near Moirang-khom), *Ahu Langmeiching* (Langthabal hills), around *Ahu Waithou-pat* of Thoubal etc., were assimilated long ago with the Meitei. No doubt, there is a place called *Haobam Leikai* an old tribal colony in Imphal, these inhabitants are believed to have assimilated by accepting the *Salam sagei* or clan of the Meitei.

Several literatures supports that indigenous/ hill tribes like the Chothe, Tangkhul, Maring, Kharam, Tarao, Koireng, Rongmei, Liangmei, Anal and the latter ethnic groups like Bengali-Muslim (Hindu/ Pangal), Cachari, Tripuri, etc. were also absorbed and amalgamated into Meitei culture by latter eighteenth century after being converted to Hinduism and live in different Imphal areas.

For example, few Muslim families who came and settled in Manipur by late eighteenth century as soldiers and traders from Cachar (Assam) had been assimilated and are now known as '*Meitei-Pangal*'. Most of the indigenous tribes and others assimilated to Meitei are by matrimony and politics subjugation; as war captives, domestic helpers, some are leaders holding high political portfolios, matrilineal kin members of the subsequent kings and queens, and his royal family members. Moirangthem (2008) mentions that 'Meitei are a conglomeration of migrant group's on the above basis.[25] One simple evident that suggest the present Meitei as the conglomeration of various old tribes is that many of this valley people still bears tribal indigene names, despite using Hindu names on account of being assimilated to Hinduism.

Natural Calamities (Epidemics) and Superstition: Natural calamities like epidemics, plagues, droughts and famines, wars and battles and also other superstitious beliefs are also considered the causes for their low demographic profile. The chronicle *ChK* records many events of wars and battles and some major epidemics that seriously affected the state. The first epidemic occurred in 1520, while the second, third and fourth occurred in 1720, 1737 and 1744 respectively, and all are related with the diseases of smallpox, cholera and typhoid, killing a great number of people (Parratt, 2005:46, 127, 145, and 158). It is mentioned that Khuraileima Mayampi one of the queens of Garib Niwaz too became a victim of the deadly smallpox in 1720 (*ibid:*127).

According to Chothe oral history, the epidemics were so devastated in their region that thousands of them perished. They claimed to have buried five to ten persons in one burial/ tomb as it was impossible to dig a tomb for all the deceased, since their tomb's design is very complicated. They also claimed that those seriously infected and died by the dreaded diseases were even burnt for fear of contamination and spreading it to the survivors. Such cremation is erroneously written by M.T. Laiba that "the Chothe-Wainem in earlier days burn their dead bodies" (1992:27). The fact is that, the Chothe traditionally buries their dead body accompanied by several rites and rituals.

The Chothe being superstitious, believes that the cause of the epidemics in 1520, 1720, 1737 and 1744 were cursed given to them by their hostile enemies like the Moirang, Maring, Khongsai and Rongmei for extensively using magic and witchcraft (*Doi-ai*) during the barbaric wars, battles and feuds (Parratt, 2005:46,127,147,158). According to H. Thambaljao and Y. Maipak of Lamlanghupi, "In olden days, Chothe were very famous for using powerful magical charms". They believed many powerful magical charms and spells were lost to the Meitei and Maring priests during acculturation process. Hiyang Gulapsing of Lamlanghupi opines according to their folktale that "The first plague was the cursed of an old widow (name unknown) married to a Moirang man". He said, 'the old widow visited her Chothe parents' village, and after her visit, she was dropped by some Chothe youth in a boat, who left her all alone on the south-eastern bank of the Loktak Lake and asking her to go on her on from there. Since, they refused to escort till her house, she out of her extreme anger and cursed the youth that their descendants should have a short life'. Y. Tomalsing also described a similar magical story that relates to the declined of Chothe power and population called '*Ruipi Loiyang*' (The Python's horizontal beam of a house).[26] He said the Python's shining beam of the chief's house was a very powerful magical talisman for all the Chothe, until it was taken away by the Moirang man who married a Chothe girl (name unknown) by tricking her and her father to give that golden shining Python's beam as dowry (*Mansum*). Thereafter, it is believed that the power and strength of the Chothe began to decline gradually.

Superstitiously, some Chothe believes that it was their forefathers' negligence or mistake to pay due reverence correctly to their Supreme Guardian God *Pu Lungchungpa*, wrong veneration or invocation of magical formulas and improper rites and rituals practiced that their population could not increase. For example, Lamlanghupi Chothe claimed to have had a large population more than 500 households at one point of time when occupied at *Ahu Lamlanglon* but was substantially reduced to few households in the natural epidemics. Considering all the above explanations, many Chothe still believes their depopulation was because of magical pride, ego and mistakes, malpractice of magic and rituals, and negligence.

Similarly, the *Ajouhu* of Central-cluster narrated a tragic incident at *Ahu Tuitrit* where half of their village population mysterious disappeared in a midnight landslide. They believed the tragedy was a cursed upon their village chief for his cruelty and wickedness for dividing the society into: the rich and poor, and celebrating the festivals separately. Accordingly, there was incessant heavy rainfall in one of their main festive. Then a mysterious landslide occurred at the elevated zone where the rich people were celebrating, who all perished that night. The Central-cluster group claimed that they are the descendants of those poor people who survived the tragedy as they celebrated on the narrow ridge.

War and Battle: The early history of Chothe is all about wars, battles, feuds and conflicts, from the mythical cave *Huipithoranga* till the latter part of eighteenth century in Manipur. The frequent destructive and expensive wars and battles, plundering and burning down of houses of the entire villages against the Moirang, Meitei, Maring, Kharam, Kamhao, Khongsai and Rongmei have cost them thousands of lives and heavy losses of property, since their arrival in the southern region which ultimately led them to their downfall and depopulation, as described and recorded in various historical texts of Manipur. It is described in detail below.

Low Selection Potential of Mates: Another theoretical explanation given for the reason of their low demographic profile is the high mortality rate and low fertility rate. Although their superstitious beliefs might not be necessarily true, but it is very convincing looking at the demographic profile of their slow population growth rate and the high mortality rate as indicated in Arabinda Basu's (1985) statistical data that the high mortality rate is especially found among the middle-age group rather than with the infants and to be more precise the percentage of men in the age group of above fifty-five years is very low compared to other ethnic neighbouring communities. Basu writes, "Infant mortality rate before reproduction (i.e. 15 years and below) seems to be very low in both the Purum isolates compared to other Indian tribes" (see his Table 13, supported by Table 3 and Table 5). Further, Basu states that "Purum display greater mortality than fertility components; the same ratio where mortality components exceeds fertility components by about two times" (1985:40, 43, 49).

Basu from the perspective of kinship and marriage, rather than from the superstitious point of view states that "The low selection potential among the Purum is the result of their lower pre-reproductive mortality as well as their lower mean and variance in number of offspring" (1985: 49). These statements reasonably support the Chothe (Purum) prescriptive marriage system. The selection of mates among Chothe is somehow limited and complicated because they have their own distinctive rigid endogamous marriage system confined within their own community, although now the rate of intermarriages with other ethnic groups have increased.

Wars and Battles Chothe Involved in the Past

The early history of Chothe is all about wars, battles, intra/ internal feuds and conflicts, subjugation and territorial issues against various aggressor ethnic groups from *Ahu Lungleh-Waishu* settlement in Mizoram to *Lungsukbung* and *Ahu Chainapung* in Manipur till the latter part of eighteenth century, which are defensive in nature. They claimed they had large population at *Ahu Lungleh-Waishu* in Mizoram before they were completely devastated in the battle against the new invading Chin-Kuki groups. Later they claimed to re-establish their supremacy and political hegemony in the southern region around the Leimatak (Henglep) but soon the abrupt attacked of the Kege-Moirang on Chothe *Ahu Lungsukbung* (*Nungsuk*) villages left them devastated. Subsequently, till the later part of the eighteenth century, similar wars and battles continued in the region especially with the Moirang and other neighbouring ethnic tribes like Kamhao (Sukte-Chin group), Khongsai (New-Kuki), Rongmei (Kabui/ Zeliangrong) which are all evidently supported by historical books like *Moirang Ningthourol Lambuba* (MNL) and *Cheitharon Kumpaba (ChK),* besides several local sources including folktales, folksongs, legends and myths that survives to tell even today.

Moirang Ningthourol Lambuba gives an account that the Chothe fought the first historical war with Moirang (Kege/ Keke) during the reign of King Ura Khundaba or Ngangoiba the fourth king, although the specific period is unknown (Kabui, 2003:178). Kabui writes "He fought with the Chothe of Naharam of the western hills. The Chothe chief was defeated and taken prisoner. The king himself participated in the battle and showed his dexterity in the use of weapons. The reference to the defeat of the Chothe is a historical confirmation, to the tradition of Chothe that they migrated to the present habitats of Manipur" (*Ibid.:*178). Much later, the Moirang for the second time invaded the Chothe country during King Khongding Ahangba (Thangwai Khongding) the eighth king of Moirang when Chothe settled at *Lungsukbung* (*Nungsuk*) interior of Thangching peak and forcefully brought all Chothe villages under his political confederation.

The text described that Thangwai Kongding (Pakhangpa) first attacked a Koireng village at Khunganching and defeated chief Nungnangchong, then he conquered the Chothes of *Nungsuk* country. The text elucidates the nature of war: 'In the land of Chothe conglomeration all the brave and courageous warriors of Kege-Moirang gathered together in the middle of the main village called Chothe, wearing all chest plates, spears in their hands, surrounded and attacked them. The Moirang soldiers led by the king fought a ferocious battle. Chothe villages were destroyed, and Kharam a neighbouring village too was completely shattered. The entire villages were completely destroyed. In that battle the Chothe King *Natoi Nachaoba* was defeated and captured' (Bhagashore, 1992:93). Thus, describing the types of warrior's uniform wore, the nature of wars, and the degree of destruction and devastation.

The *Cheitharon Kumpaba* chronicle gives an account of the Chothe involvement in wars and battles till the twentieth century. One probable early incident, as an evident, begins from King Thangpi Lanthapa in 1302 A.D. which is recorded as: "They also fought against the Loipi Hao at Seku hill in the south and were victorious. They captured in battle Tenkongbi and *Mareem Namngap*" (Mareem/ Marim is a major clan of Chothe). During the reign of King Kongyampa in 1324 A.D. it is recorded as: "They captured in battle Mayang Maipa Samloipa... Lakasumka Tao and Aaring Aarang Tao were detained and later fought against Chakpa, at Khurai Haora at Lamangtong".[27] During King Tenheipa's reign in 1335 it recorded as: "They also fought against (inhabitants of) *Loipi Mareem* and at Yangpham Chaklikpok in Koupa (Khoupum) mountain range. They were victorious. They captured *Mareem Sanlungpa*". In 1359, during King Tapungpa's reign it was written as: "They fought against the (inhabitants of) *Loipi Mareem* at Yangpham Chaklikpok". Then in 1404 during King Punsipa's reign, it recorded as: "They captured *Keihou* the king of the *Tangkhuls* and *Mareem Khamtingpa*. And in 1653 during the reign of Khunchaopa (1652-1666), it recorded as: "They attacked Makan village. Aachongnga, Maichampa and Chammaingang, these three and others totalling eighty people were captured in the battle" (Parratt, 2005:35, 36, 83).

It is believed that when Kyampa became king the relationship between Meitei and Chothes was strengthen again, and got matured during the reign of King Khakempa since the Chothe helped him defeat the Moirang uprising. Henceforth, the close relationship between the Chothe and the Meitei began to revive, not forgetting their loyalty and matrimonial friendship they had during Pakhangpa's time. Example of frequent inter-feuds and battles is given by G. Shangkham who states that 'the Kharam in the south fought with the Chothe during which many men lost their lives', and also in the north at "Kharam-pan" (Khwairamband bazaar), Imphal (2006: 2, 44-45). Shangkham said that the only world Women's market (Ima keithel) commonly known as 'Khwairam-ban bazaar' is derived from 'Kharam-pan' literally 'the blocking/ fencing from Kharam people' from the fight between the Chothe and Kharam, when settled around Kangla (Imphal).[28]

By eighteenth century the Moirang principality and other surrounding tribes were subjugated by the Imphal principality, and so the Chothe were relaxed without wars for some time. But soon, their attention was focused to the new immigrants like the Kamhao (Sukte Clans), the Khongsai (New-Kuki), the Cacharis (Maihang/ Mayang), Rongmei (Meirong). The war especially, with the Kamhao and Khongsai entered a new phase in their history. These wars are narrated even today because of the severity that caused massive destruction and resulting in constant change of settlements. H. Thambaljao and Y. Maipak said that many pitiable and tragic stories still survived even today but such stories are never recounted by the elders for its sensitiveness, who feels and feared it could arouse enmity again from the peaceful co-existence. It is believed the events occurred after the brave and courageous Chothe men like Parirangpa and Neitangpu expired (Hiyang, 1985:26). And the most probable period is seventeenth and eighteenth century, as similar accounts are recorded in *ChK* that in 1741 in the month of June-July (Yingen) on 3rd Saturday, "nine *haos* from Chothe paya had been abducted by the Khongjai (tribe)" (Parratt, 2005:151).

Then, in the mid-eighteenth century there were many minor battles with the Kabui who came down from the northwest. These minor wars were commonly referred as *Meirong/ Marong Lan* (Rongmei war) by the Chothe. One such incident is recorded in 1745 during the reigned of Garib Niwaz (1709-1748) in the month of Phairen (January/February) as: "On Thursday, Kabui Chothe were scattered and 105 Hao's were slain" (*ibid.* 2005:160). Y. Hongpa opines that the reference "Kabui Chothe" here should be read as "the Chothe and the Kabui", since both belong to different ethnic entity. Many serious territorial disputes and several defensive battles were fought in the past amongst them and many are believed to have died in such events after the *Khongsai Lan* (Kuki aggression). Similar disputes and minor battles over territorial rights with other ethnic groups continued till the time of Maharaj Chandrakriti (1850-86).

Therefore, the early history of Chothe is replete with wars, battles, feuds, territorial disputes and exodus starting from Chin-hills (Myanmar) to *Ahu Lungleh-Waishu* (Lushai hills/ Mizoram). The skirmishes continues upto the settlements of *Ahu Lungsukbung* and *Ahu Chainapung* in the south-western region of Manipur till the early nineteenth century. Although when a war and conflict finally ends with one group there seems to be another group waiting on the other side of the village boundary readied with spears and swords for the next battle. However, by late nineteenth century they appear to have grown tired and exhausted because of constant battles and the natural calamities of plagues that greatly reduced their population to mere thousands. The severe cause and effect of wars and battles have taught them the moral of human values much before others could learnt. Thereby, they refused in the later period to partake in any warfare or made any political alliances. Rather they were more concerned with the freedom of feasting, drinking and merrymaking away from the Kangla Kingdom. Therefore, T.C. Das (1945) described that 'Chothe appeared docile and submissive in nature', fed up with battles. Thus, the Manipur kingdom began weakening since the hills tribes who earlier supported in the territorial expansion left due to the politico-religious movement.

However, most of the tribal people, though politically subjugated by the Meitei kings, remains autonomous and functions independently. The concern of the Meitei king was manpower or soldiers to help him in the war campaigns and the tributes. It is said that people captured in wars and battles were treated as king's slaves or bonded labourers in Imphal, instead of killing them. The personal diaries and accounts of British Political administrators like Ethel St. Clair Grimwood's '*My Three Years in Manipur and Escape from the Recent Mutiny*' (1891) gives us clear picture of Manipur socio-political conditions of the past.

Human sacrifice or Head-hunting culture practiced by Naga tribes like the Ao, Konyak, Lotha, Tangkhul, Angami, etc. existed even among the Chothe. The Chothe claimed during *Zarr rhin* festival, captured humans were sacrificed. Later this tradition was abolished and symbolically replaced with rat sacrifice as *Aju-rhin* the ceremony initiated by Parpa clan. This shows that the Chothe in earlier days were once acknowledged as brutal and powerful tribe with large population, but later due to above known and unknown reasons they have become subservience to Manipuri's kings by alliance and treaties.

Literacy

The Census of India 2011, indicate the total literacy rate of Chothe is 69.79 per cent and 2010 as 72.35 per cent a remarkable achievement in the field of education with an increase of almost 10 per cent from 59.89 per cent from 1991. However, my personal survey conducted in September-October 2004 also shows 68.76 per cent (average is 70.79 per cent), (see Table 10). The variable is taken from Class V passed to Post-Graduates. The variable of the classification in percentage is given in Table 7, where the total number of under-matriculation or drop-outs from Classes V to IX is 1194 (44.40 per cent), Matriculation or Class X passed is 318 (11.82 per cent), Pre-university Class XII passed is 224 (8.33 per cent), Graduate is 100 (3.71 per cent) and post-graduate is 13 (0.48 per cent) respectively.

Table 10 indicates that the bulk of the literate populace belongs to the under-matriculate category while the percentage of graduates and post-graduates is extremely low in all villages, except Lamlanghupi which has the maximum number of graduates - 26. This indicates that majority of them attended high-school but did not continue further due to various socio-economic reasons. The following six villages viz.; Chumbang, Khongkhang, Phantu, Chandolpokpi, Old-Wangparal and New-Wangparal, one Govt. Lower Primary (LP) school each is found, and one Govt. Junior Board (JB) school each in the four villages Viz.; Lamlanghupi, Tampakhu, Laininghu and Ajouhu. Besides, Lamlanghupi, Ziontlang and Salemthar have one Private English School each. Each village has at least one Govt. Primary or High School but the enrollment of the students in these institutes is very low due to irregularity of teachers and very poor infrastructure, as a result most of these village children enrolled themselves in private schools as it offers them better modern education.

Pallel, Chandel and Loyola School (Estd. 1982) the Jesuit Catholic missionary school at Lamlanghupi, Bishnupur, besides these two schools, other private missionary schools have immensely helped Chothe society and its neighbouring communities, especially in the field of modern education and socio-cultural development. The high literacy rate among the Chothe and other tribal groups now in Manipur is attributable to the dedicated service render by priests, nuns, voluntary educationists and teachers of these private schools, rather than Govt. schools.

Relation with the Neighbouring Tribes and their Influence

The Chothes are immediately surrounded by various ethnic groups and they have been influencing one another through the ages in language, religion, economic, political, and other socio-cultural aspects like food habits, dress codes, moral code of conducts and behaviour. The Chothe of Lamlanghupi are closely surrounded by various ethnic groups like the Meitei, Rongmei (Meirong), Chiru, Kom and Khongsai. But the Central-cluster neighbours are encircled by Moyon, Monsang, Lamkang, Tarao, Anal, Aimol, Maring and Meitei (Scheduled Caste). The Khongkhang the Eastern Chothe neighbours are the Maring, Lamkang, and Kukis (Thadou, Haokip). All these ethnic groups have their own distinctive customs and traditions which are similar, yet different from the other in many cultural traits.

Interestingly, despite living side by side now they maintain a high status-quo without interfering in any internal or political affairs of others: rather they tend to appreciate the other's distinctive socio-cultural values. These indigenous groups are highly democratic and diplomatic in settling various disputes like land, marriage and political issues in traditional methods. Every village Chief or Head of the community expects equal respect from the other ethnic group. If one does not conform to such ethical formality the initiator/ defaulter is always blamed and charge for his incompetence and negligence, sometimes which may result to severe violence and conflict of mistrust.

Table 12: Chothe Literacy Rate: Census of India 2001 and Personal Data Sept.-Oct. 2004

Category	Ajoulu (Purum) Khullen	Bethel Happy land*	Chandonopdi	Chothe Khunou	Chumbang (Purum)	Khongkhang	Labhingu	LamnGanghupi	Landington*	Leirungtabi*	Lungnu*	Lungleh*	New-Wangparal	Old-Wangparal	Phanu (Chandrapolo)	Salemhar*	Tampakhu (Purum)	Ziontunlung	Total	Percentage
Illiterates (COI-2001)	35	-	-	08	19	75	09	17	02	04	-	01	06	05	29	01	53	23	287	10.67
Literacy rate COI-2001	88.6	-	77.0	67.2	84.4	47.6	76.6	74.32	-	-	-	-	85.9	77.1	75.5	-	71.0	74.0	-	72.35
Under-matric (CI: V-IX)	38	12	53	39	42	135	132	117	25	13	21	12	106	66	96	24	169	94	1194	44.40
Matriculation (CI-X)	09	-	13	07	64	21	30	32	02	-	07	-	06	16	28	02	47	34	318	11.82
Pre-university (CI-XII. Std)	14	-	10	04	52	19	11	42	02	02	04	-	03	07	09	03	26	16	224	8.33
Graduates	09	-	03	04	13	06	06	26	01	01	02	-	01	08	07	01	10	02	100	3.71
Post-graduates	01	-	-	-	02	-	01	04	-	-	-	-	-	-	02	-	03	-	13	0.48
Total	71	12	79	54	173	181	180	221	30	16	34	12	116	97	142	30	255	146	1849	68.76

Note: the asterisk * marked villages are new settlements which are not recognised by the Census of India (COI) yet.

Since each village/ community has its own traditional ethos; rules and regulations, any complication that arises is amicably resolved by mutual ethical understanding. Moreover, their rigid customary laws of tribes are becoming flexible due to various external forces influencing them. For example, intermarriage is encouraged by many, and the penalty for wrong doers is becoming lenient as compared to earlier days. Each community still maintains their own social ethos, moral code of conduct and lives harmoniously despite having enmity in the past.

R.C. Roy states about the Western Chothe that "The culture of the Chawte of Loktak Lake region in Manipur has been largely influenced by their Manipuri or Meitei neighbours" (1936:137). Truly, now the Chothe of Lamlanghupi speaks the Meitei language more fluently than other Chothes due to their geographical location and daily interaction with the Meitei of Bishnupur. From the historical point, in the past the early Meitei acculturated many Chothe and other tribal cultural elements, but now the reverse process of acculturation is happening amongst them due to reversed dominancy. For example, language, dress code, life style, folkways are some elements acquired by the Chothes from Meitei now. But Roy remarks are made from an external observation. Yet, intrinsically the Chothe still practice many of their rigid indigenous socio-cultural tradition being autonomous and functions independently without outside interferences. For example, their intrinsic customary laws like rites-de-passage; birth, youth initiation, marriage and death ceremonies, festivals, rituals, nature of worships and village administration system are completely different from the Meiteis.

Regarding the Central-cluster and Eastern Chothes there is so much cultural affinity with most of the neighbouring ethnic groups than with Meiteis since the degree of influence are very negligible, since the surrounding ethnic groups are mostly tribals who share similar cultural traits and developmental activities in the region. Moreover, intermarriage among them is very common. Many individuals who marry girls from other tribes are in most cases could speak their wife's language or dialect. But these groups of people never tried to impose their wife's custom and tradition upon their husband's society. The basic elements that influences are education, modernisation, liberalisation, globalisation, Government developmental policies and programmes, Annual Student's Conferences and Meetings, flexibility in the custom and tradition and most importantly the Advent of Christianity have brought vast changes to the entire Chothe society and Northeast from traditionalism to modernism.

From the historical perspective the earliest ethnic neighbours of Chothe who inhabit the south-western region are the Kharam, Tarao, Koireng, Funan, Maring, Moirang (Kege) and the Poirei (now Meitei). But significantly the

Chothe, Kharam, Koireng, Tarao, Kom, Aimol, Chiru, Purum are all believed to have originated from one common ancestor, based on the semantics of their language, cultural and historical backgrounds. The variation is probably developed because of the cross-cultural mixture and inter-marriage with the neighbouring tribes over the centuries. It is also said the Chothe, Kom, Koireng have a historical link with the Rangkhol and Darlong of Mizoram and Tripura while Aimol and Chiru shows close affinity with the Maring, though a cognate of the former tribes. According to ancient historical and religious texts of Manipur, the Chothe and the Meitei (Poireiton) close bond of relationship began with the matrimonial and political alliance since Nongda Leiren Pakhangpa who is claimed as the progeny of a Chothe girl (Daishin the daughter of a chief).

According to Y. Hongpa and Y. Chouyaima the respondents of Lamlanghupi said that,

"The people in olden days often claimed supremacy over others to identify themselves as distinctively as possible from others by keeping their reputation high. For example, the Chothe identified the Kharam for their virulent and bravery attitudes in war front with big swords and huge shields, the Maring for their powerful magical practice and peculiar hair style as they tied their hair knot (*Samtun*) in front near the forehead unlike other Chin-Kuki-Mizo groups who tied at the back of the head. The Moirang, earlier known as *Keke/Kege* (Chinese) derives the word from 'Mai-rang' (painted face/ striped dresses). They are also known to have 'wild and aggressive attitude' in battles recognised by their painted faces and striped dresses. The word Meitei is said to have originated from the word 'Mai-tai' meaning 'people who apply white paste' (*Tika* or *Chandon*) on their face/ forehead). The second connotation derives from the word 'Mee-atei' meaning 'stranger or foreigner or outsiders' that refers to Cacharis or Bengalese of Hindu/ Vaishnavite sect or Muslims who migrated to Manipur (by 17th-18th century) from the west by the Chothe and other cognatic groups. Besides, there are many other ethnic groups that distinguish themselves from other cultural groups and are known by their peculiar behaviour and cultural traits like Tangkhul, Anal and Kuki. On the other hand, some amalgamated old groups developed as sectionalist and successionist, and created a new group of their own with the natural situation designed like Purum, Thangal, Loi and so on".

***Cheitharol Kumpapa* Accounts on Chothe**: Various historical texts of Manipur mentions Chothe in several accounts. *Moirang Ningthourol Lambupupa* (MNL) in Chapter 19 the 'Chothe Thangwai Pakhangpa' describes well about Chothe and its people. Similarly, we also find thirteen direct accounts that mentioned Chothe and several related statements in *Cheitharol Kumpapa* (ChK). They are:

(1) The first record found mentioned is in 33 A.D. that 'Chothe Thangwai Pakhangpa' or Meingai alias 'Nongda Leiren Pakhangba' was the first sovereign ruler of Kangla (Imphal).

(2) Then, in 1597 it states that "Chothe made a racing barge named Meirongpa Naran phapa" probably during Mungyampa or Khakempa.

(3) In 1645 it states as "The land of Chothe was inspected".

(4) In 1646 "Yipungo Aahan Khongchompa inspected the Chothe village".

(5) In 1670 "The area of Chothe was inspected" probably Paikhompa.

(6) In 1687 "Loukrakpa Porou produced a boat named Yikhai Chaipa from the village of Chothe".

(7) In 1700 "Yiron Ngasingpa and others brought two boats from Chothe with curves sterner" during Charairongpa.

(8) In 1700 "All the haos (tribe men) of Nungshai (Chiru) were ask to stay with Namlon where Chothe lived".

(9) In1706 "The land of Chothe was inspected".

(10) In 1729 "Those who went to Chothe to drag the racing boat return" during Garibniwaz.

(11) In 1739 "Thangjam Chothe was murdered in the fish auction market".

(12) In 1741 "It was reported that nine haos from Chothe paya had been abducted by the Khongjai (Kuki)".

(13) In 1745 "Kabui Chothe were scattered and 105 haos were slain" (Parratt, 2005:64, 80, 89, 98, 110, 115, 136, 148, 151, 160).

However, the *Cheitharol Kumpapa* the Court Chronicles mentions the name 'Mareem' a major clan of Chothe as early as 1302 AD onwards that "They captured in battle Tengkongpa and Mareem Namngapa", and also in 1335, 1359, 1404… (Parratt, 2005:35, 36). Besides, the name Tao (Thao) another major clan of Chothe is also mentioned as early as 1324 AD stating that "Lakasumka Thao and Aaring Aarang Thao were detained. Also they fought against the Chakpa at Khurai Haora at Lamangtong" (*Ibid.*: 35). There are also numerous accounts of Chothe and its people associated with Manipuri kings and princes under various names and events like 'Pidonnu' a historic tragedy love story, although the relation began with Chothe Thangwai Pakhangpa (Nongda Leiren Pakhangba) in 33 AD.

Affinities with Other Cognatic Tribes: Linguistically, the tribes nearest with Chothe by degree in terms of syllable, phonetic, etc. are: Kharam< Tarao< Purum< Hmar< Aimol< Paite< Gangte< Simte< Zou< Rangkhol< Impui< Liangmei< Thadou (Kuki)< Koireng< Kom< Chiru< Vaiphei< Mizo< Moyon< Monshang< Anal< Lamkang< Maram< Thangal< Maring and so on (all belongs to Tibeto-Burman speakers).

Cognatic tribes that share similar myth and origin stories are: Kharam, Tarao, Koireng, Hmar, Kom, Maring, Aimol, Chiru, Lamkang, Moyon, Monshang, Anal and Kuki (*Hurr* or *Khulr and stories about the man eater tiger and dragon myth*).

Culturally, tribes showing similar customary laws and attires with Chothe are: Kharam, Tarao, Koireng, Kom, Aimol, Chiru, Thadou (Kuki), Rangkhol, Maring,...

It is found that the variation depends on the influences impacted by the dominant neighbouring groups in the process of acculturation and assimilation that had taken place over five centuries due to reasons of geographical location, matrimonial alliance and political subjugation particularly, besides other reasons.

Notes

1. *Ram* or *Lam*: It means land or area. Many original words sounding with *R* is interchanged with *L*. For instance, *Rung* or *Lung*, *Rui* as *Lui*, *Piring* as *Pilling*. Similarly *Chao/ Chou* as *Jao/Zou*; *Zu* as *Yu/ Ju* etc. indicating that many of their original words and vocabulary are diminishing each day.

2. *Chothe-Munpi*: Chothe-munpi settlement was originally known as *Lungsukbung* (*Nungsuk* by Meitei). *Lungsukbung* literally means 'the rock that sprang near the banyan tree' to mean 'the water that sprang from the rocks near the banyan tree' (see Chapter 9 MNL). This settlement was abandon four-five centuries ago but it was recognised by the New-Kuki migrants as the Chothe settlement. Therefore, Haokips and Kipgens who now occupied the area named it as 'Chothe-Munpi' (lit. Chothe settlement). Recently, a team of Chothe leaders headed by *Lamlanghupi Village Council* and *Chothe Literature Committee* visited Chothe-Munpi (Lungsukbung) on 18th-20th March 2013 guided by Mr. Khailet Haokip. Mr. Khailet said the New-Kuki occupied the area by 1717, which means that the Chothe left the place much before that period. The team captured pictures of the huge old magnificent Banyan tree that still survived the test of time, the small perennial spring water that sprang out from the rocks, the sacred sites of *hushapa/ bumboo*) and other historical places that were still preserved by the villagers (see pic no.: 108, 109, 110).

3. *Khongsai*: The term "Khongsai" is the name of a prominent Kuki clan. They are considered the first clan/ group of the New-Kuki or the Thadou speaking group that comes in contact with the so-called Old-Kuki groups and the valley people of Manipur in 18th century, which is why, generally the Meitei identifies to all

the Chin-Kuki-Mizo speaking groups as 'Khongjai' (instead of Khongsai), unable to distinguish culturally and linguistically the distinctive features of other cognatic groups due to close similarities.

4. *Meitei*: Kabui states that "The origin of the Meitei is shrouded in mystery and the study on the subject is greatly influenced by the religious faiths and the political ideologies of the Meities themselves. Thus, making the problem highly speculative and controversial", and that "B.H. Hodgson in the mid-nineteenth century thought, was a, combined appellate of Siamese 'Tai' and Kochin Chinese 'Moy' (Moy Tai= Moytai =Moitai = Meitei)", (2003:15). Still some local scholars attempt explaining differently the origin of the word "Meitei".

W.I. Singh states that "The *Mareems* gave names of other places associated with the word 'Moi' lying in the valley like Moi-chachinm, Moi-ching, Moi-tangpok… The *Mareems* used to call the Loi, Lai, Chakpa and other Tai by the name Tai. Hence, the Chothe *Mareems* probably game the name *Moi-Tai* to the tribes of Tai origin inhabiting in the *Loi-ching* foothills close to them. It is believed that subsequently other immigrants also call these tribes *Moi-Tai* as transferred from the *Mareems*" (1986:424). The Chothe oral history supports Singh's statement because earlier the south-western hills (North-Churachandpur district) was the country of the Chothe. Secondly, the new valley group they come in contact was the Kege-Moirang whose origin is traced to Tai-Chinese group while the Old-Kukis shows a cognate of Kachin group culturally and linguistically.

Y. Hongpa of Lamlanghupi Chothe in consonance with W.I. Singh stated that "The word 'Meitei' is derived from the Chothe term '*Maitei-ngei*' (*Mai* - face, *Tei* - apply, *ngei* - other people) meaning 'people who apply (white paste) on their face or forehead' (ticka/*Chandon* in Meitei). The white paste is a religious symbol signifying the Hindu/ Vaishnavite sect, while the term '*Mee-atei*' actually means 'outsider or foreigner'. It is a local coded term secretly used while communicating amongst themselves to indirectly refer the particular person/ group on the criteria of his/ their distinctive character and behaviour". This naming style or usage is still practice by the Chothe said Hongpa.

This could also suggest to those few Thai (Thai-Ahom origin) people who were left behind in the region while crossing the western Manipur hills before 14th - 15th century in search of Ayodhya the birth place of Buddha and other Hindu sacred places in India after they were influenced by Hinduism or Buddhism. Although these early Meiteis may have different genealogy but now the nomenclature applies to most people living in the valley. The reason being that the latter historical period suggest another new ethnic migrant groups like Bodo-Cacharis and Bengali-deshi of Vaishnavist faith and later the Muslim migrated to Manipur by 17th – 18th century A.D through Old-Cachar route. The last migrants/ foreigners were referred by the indigenous inhabitants like Chothe and other cognates as *Mai-tai* or *Mee-atei*, but later the pronunciation have developed in short form as '*Meetei*' or '*Meitei*', popularised by the local scholars.

It is learnt that in the early period the Poireiton group after being defeated by Pakhangpa at Ewaitha (Moirang) is believed to have settled at the foothill of Loiching/ Laimaton peak or *Poireiton chingkhong* or Lamangtong (Bishnupur). In connection to the Chothe oral history, the Maring tribe are originally known as "Poi or Falum" by others in the south. But after they (Poi) took refuge in the

Chothe territory (Henglep zone) and left, they were referred as '*Meiring lu-ngei*' (as Maring) for stealing live fire (see Assimilation/ Maring tribe or *Poireiton Chingkhong* below). There is a Maring folklore that speaks that once upon a time, the Maring people hired a Chothe widow's bull to let open their cave to enable them to come out on the surface of the earth, where they paid thirty silver coins. Henceforth, a section of the Poi-reiton group who first settled around the Laimaton foothill or Loiching hill range came to be known as "Loi" by themselves. Thus, the Chothe believed that "Poirei = Poi = Loi" (Maring) are the original/ early Meitei of Manipur. Their genealogical origin may be traced to Tai-Chinese like the Ahom of Assam. Captain Pemberton also reported that the Meitei originally came from Tartar Community (Kabui, 2003:28). This does not refer to the amalgamated Meitei/ Manipuris.

The present Meitei is considered a conglomeration or composites of various ancient indigenous surrounding tribes of Manipur valley like Poi/ Loi, Maring, Funan, Chenglei, Shelloy, Liangmei, Chothe, Kharam, Koireng, Tangkhul, Anal, etc. in the early days, later joined by the new Hindu sect (*Mai-tai*) immigrants of Bodo-Cacharis or Bengalese and Muslim from 18th century that amalgamates to form a new cultural group through acculturation and assimilation process till the early 20th century and subsequently began to identify themselves as "Meitei" along with the original valley Meitei (also known as Loi/ Poi/ Fhalam/ Maring/ Khaba-nganba) as they inhabit around the Loktak Lake. The conglomeration of various ethnic groups in valley first began after Chothe Thangwai Pakhangpa (the Moirang King) along with Angom (Tangkhul) group ousted the dominant Khaba (Maring) group from Kangla-Tongbi in the north, and thereafter founded the Kangla or Imphal Principality and introduced the seven *Salai*/ clan with the Ningthouja (Mangang) as the head clan. The numerous *Yek-Salai* (hundreds of sub-clans and seven clans) proved that Meitei is a conglomeration and inter-mixture of various hills tribes and latter migrants. Thus, the word *Meitei* originally derives from the generic tribal (Chothe Marim) terms of *Moi-tai/ Mai-tei/ Mee-atei* to refer to the conglomeration of valley inhabitants and latter migrants. Linguistically, the Meitei has close affinity with the Maring tribe while they owe their distinctive indigenous cultural costume including Lai-haraoba dresses to Kege-Moirang and their black warrior dress code to cognates of Chothe, and their Hindu religious-culture to the new migrants of Aryan origin.

5. *Marem* or *Marim Chothe*: The word 'Marem' (Mareem) often mentioned as tribe in various historical texts of Manipur probably refers to one of the major clans of Chothe called 'Mareem/ Marim' indicating to one of the old village of Chothe clusters headed by a Mareem/ Marim chief, located around Lungsukbung behind Thangjing hills on south western hills (See MNL Chapter 19). The mistake is the grammatical error in pronunciation. Kabui stated that "Mareem was a tribe who settled in the south western hills of Manipur" not tribe but major clan of Chothe (2003:169). W.I. Singh also identifies the Chothe people with a leader who belonged to Mareem/ Marim clan since in olden days it was the tradition to identify a village by a king's/ chief's name or by his title or with peculiar geographical/ landscape setting. So, we often found many old writings confused with vernacular and common (nick) names. For instance, *Makan Turuching* a Chothe village headed by a "Makan' chief was named after him, Makan being a major clan (see in page 13). Singh pointed out that "By far the Mareems were

one of the most important tribe in naming different places" (1986: 150). Singh describes that "A little later than the Loi another tribe of proto-Sino-Tibetan origin arrived and settled on the north-west of Lamangdong on the Loijing range. This particular Tibeto-Burman tribe of proto-Sino-Tibetan was called *Mareem*. The *Mareems* came to their habitat on the *Loi-jing* range by the southerly route" probably by 11th century A.D. (Singh, 1986: 150-153, 208-9, 423-4; Kabui, 2003: 169). The Chothe oral history supports Singh's remark. In the early stage of migration the Poireiton group first seeks shelter in Chothe territory when settled in the interior southwest around Henglep zone. But subsequently, much later due to internal-feuds, wars and battles the Chothe migrates time after time towards northwest around Laimaton foothills and settles at Lamlanglon (Lamangtong), Bishnupur.

6. *Moirang:* Though Moirang are originally known as 'Kege/ Keke' the Chinese-Tai stock, however they are also refer as '*Mai-rang*' literally 'aggressive face or attitude' in ancient days by Chothe Mareems which actually means the 'striped face/ people' as they wore stripe dresses. Kabui states that they belong to upper-Burma who moved into Manipur valley through chin-hills and Kabaw-valley. He said Moirang was derived from 'Mairan' called by the Mareem to mean the land of the sun. Mareem was a tribe who settled in the south western hills of Manipur (2003:169). In much later period they come to be identified with their dominant clan known as 'Khuman' by Imphal Meitei. Konsam Manikchand also described that "The Khumans were particularly famous for their wild and turbulent nature" (see in Naorem 1988:154). The term 'Moirang' is also believed to have derived from the word 'Moriya' king. Some still claimed the term 'Moirang' originate from '*Mui/Moi*' means hair or silk (fibre), because the Kege-Moirang are believed to be the first group to have introduced silk and silk-worm rearing in Manipur (Kabui 2003:14). In Chothe the indigenous cotton/ silk spinning machine is called as *Mui/ Moi* (hair/ thread like fibre) but the Meitei called it as *Tareng-Masha* and the silk cloth as *Mokka phei*.

7. *Tongjei Maril: Tongjei Maril* (lit. elongated pass) is an Old-Cachar road and *Nga-purum Chingjing* (lit. ell hill route) the New-Cachar route are two important ancient roads leading to west - Cachar/ Bengal/ Tripura (Selyet). The former located near the Laimaton peak of Bishnupur, and the latter near Kangpokpi passing through Tamei village of Tamenglong district. These are two important trading routes exist on the south-western region where the Poi-reiton group, Hindu and Muslims of Bengal, Tripura, Cachar (Silchar) migrated. Laiba describes the condition that "*Tongjei Maril* existed during the years 1837-44, in a bad shaped and peddles" (1992: 354).

8. *Poireiton chingkhong:* See the context of 'Meitei', 'Moirang' and 'Maring' above and 'Mayang' below too.

9. *Mayang*: The Chothe elders claimed that names like: Moirang, Maring, Mayang, Imphal, Chiru, etc. were also given to them because of their peculiar characters and behaviour. *Mayang* is probably derived from '*Mai-hang = Mayang*. In Chothe and Chin-Kuki it means 'black or dark face', that refers to the dark skin/ coloured people of Tripuris, Cacharis, Bengali-deshes of 17th century migrants or traders who came through *Tongjei Maril* and *Ngapurum Chingjing* routes. (See the *Chiru* tribe too below).

10. *Vishnu Temple:* This temple is now preserved as a cultural heritage protected by the state as historical monumental site. M.T. Laiba claimed that it was King Pamheiba or Garib Niwaz (1709-1748) and not King Kyamba who introduced the image of Vishnu and constructed the Vishnu temple at Lamangtong/ Bishnupur (1992: 43). This statement is undeniable as Pamheiba is believed to be son of Goswami and Nungthil Chaibi a Chothe lady. The Chothe knew Chaibi as Shorha or Thaowon Saamtharnu according to their folklore.

11. *Maring:* In ancient days, the 'Maring' tribe is originally known by some as Poi or Falum (Khaba-nganba) proved by their cultural character. They acquire the name as Maring (like Meitei/ Moirang/ Chiru) probably given by the Chothe, derived from '*Mei-ling ru-ngei = Meiring = Maring,* meaning 'people who steal live fire' (see Singh, 1986:15; see Pic. 104). The close affinity with Chothe is found in Maring's folklore stating that 'they came out of a cave after a Chothe widow's bull's horn open the cave, where they paid thirty silver coins'.

12. Singh, H. Bhuban Lt. Col. (Retd.) in *Whither Manipur* states that the mother of controversial King Garibniwaz is a tribal from Chothe community according to his reliable source of information. (Courtesy: The Imphal Free Press, www.e-pao.com. Accessed on 25/06/2007.

13. *Liangmei:* The Liangmei, Maram and Thangal tribes of Manipur are considered a cognate of Chothe (Chin-Kuki groups) proved by their linguistic and cultural affinity. They are considered advance migrants from south who moved northwards following upstream rivers and later acculturated by inter-marriages with the *Tenyime* (Mao-Poumei) and Rongmei (Kabui) Tamenglong group on the northwest, where they assimilated most culture.

14. Gassah, L.S. 'The War-Jaintias'. http://megartsculture.gov.in/herit_ vol.II.htm, Accessed on 18/10/2011.

15. *Aimol:* The term *Aimol* is a Chin-Kuki-Mizo word (*Ar/ Ai* = Cook, and *Mul/ Mol* = Mound/ hill) which refers to a settlement. It is probably derived from the nature and practice how a settlement is established by the old tribes. In olden days, a village is established by performing the egg divination or if a cook crows at the chosen site. Although, *Ai* also refers to a 'crab' in Chothe but here it probably means a fowl, not a crab.

16. *Great Wall of China:* (http://en.wikipedia.org/wiki/Great Wall of China). Dated: 15/ 9/08.

17. *Moipung:* Yuhlung Hongpa of Lamlanghupi claimed that in olden days his forefathers' used different shaped and sizes of huge colourful seashells (*Moipung*) for different purposes. He said such large sea-shells were used as a whistle to signal the people for the preparation of wars and battles along with drums and gongs. It was also used when the king and his party returned from wars and battles, or sometimes to acknowledge the arrival of important persons like the king or any royal members. The utility and function of such seashells become meaningless after their autocratic and feudalistic society was replaced by the democratic elective system. Thus, their grandparents retained it as a decorative ornamental assets. But most of it seems to have lost or disappeared during their course of migration, while many are believed to have buried along with their forefathers as it is the Chothe custom to bury such personnel assets when they died. Hongpa did not have any idea from where it came but believes that it must

have obtained during their process of migration or from foreign traders. The Chothe no longer used it, but some Meitei are seen using such seashells in certain religious ceremonies.

18. *Lungleh-Waishu*: Lalrammuana *Chawhte* of Durtlang, Leitan south, Mizoram-796025, presently pursuing his Ph.D degree in the Dept. of Anthropology, NEHU claimed they are part of the Chothe group who stayed behind during the early stage of migration. Being minority in the state they are being assimilated as one of the Mizo (Lushai) clans as "Chawhte" and comes under the aegis of Mizo Federation as one of the twelve dominant clans.

19. *Ningthoujas*: Dr. Konsam Manikchand said "The fact that the Ningthouja salai still do not marry these two sage is of Moirang is a living trace of what had occurred in early times" because when Pakhangba (N.L) took a refused at Moirang after a fight with the Khaba-Nganbas, he left two progenies *Mungyang Chaopa* and *Tangkhrum Limiyipa*, who were later absorbed into the Moirang salai (clans) and became two sageis (sub-clans), (Naorem 1988:152). Therefore, they believe that some of the dominant clans like Ningthouja and Khuman clans of Moirang are cognates of Meitei Ningthoujas, which applies to the Chothe Marim and Khiyang (Hiyang) clans too, since they believed that whosoever marries a Moirang girl did not survive long after their marriage. Hence, they claimed that the two clans are cognates, therefore the taboo is still observed even today.

20. *Imphal:* The original word for 'Imphal' is probably derived from the Chothe word "Inn-phai", which literally means "big house/ palace in the plain/ valley". Some seems to have pronounced as "Yum-phal" an inference of Maring and Bodo-Cacharis/Bengali phonology to mean the king's throne/ palace. Such phonology syllable variation between the hill tribals and valley people often confuses many in the context of its origin and etymology. It is very obvious that the latter migrants like Cacharis/ Bengalese had difficulty in pronouncing like the indigenous tribals. For example terms like 'Pa' is pronounce as 'ba', *Pi* = bi, *Chao*= jao, *Yai*= Jai, *Ram*= Lam, *Rui*= Lui, *Mai*= Moi, *Angam*= Angom, or Bengal= *Pangal*, *Tong*= dong, and so on.

21. Kachin: There is a reference of Kachin in the Chothe folksong of 'Shanghong rhin laa/ Shangkokna laa'.

22. *Hao*: It is a general term to mean 'tribes', often referred by Meitei to all the hill tribes/ tribal of the Manipur.

23. *Purum:* The word 'Purum' is believed to have derived from '*Pun-ruum*' meaning 'hiding themselves by covering with cloths', where *Pun* = shawl/ cloth, *Ruum*= hide. Mrs. Y. Tharaklei (92/F) said 'Purum', thus refers to those descendants who hide themselves covering with shawls during an inter-feud war. They are considered a cognate of Kom, who belonged to physically weak and meek category. No doubt, Kom, Koireng, Aimol, Chiru, Karam, Tarao all are cognatic groups of Chothe by origin.

24. *Chiru*: They are one of the indigenous scheduled tribes of Manipur. It is said even this tribe's name "Chiru'" or *Chi-ngu,* literally 'salt thief' is said to have given by the Chothe to those descendants who steal salt from their fellow brethrens Purum. P.S. Haokip based on the folktale said, a section of people

were involved in stealing salt from the Purum. Thus, landing themselves into a problem, so they asked Chothe to be their mediator. When the matter worsened and the Chothe asked them to swear, their denial on *hah* (by their teeth), they confessed their guilt and asked forgiveness. The mediator who intervened was so unsatisfied with the trial said, 'since you have been denying your guilt from now on you will be named 'Chiru' (Haokip, 1998:34).

25. Moirangthem Thawanthaba. *Manipur: A case study on migration*. Enet, Accessed on 12-june-8.

26. *Loiyang/ Loiching*: It is said that after a Moirang man married a Chothe girl and took away the shining beam (Python) from her parent's house as per her father's promised, the Chothe who were once prosperous with huge population in Lungsukbung area began to diminish in its wealth and population. Therefore, some Chothe attributes their depopulation to this incident. They believed the western hill range (*Loiching*) probably derives its name from *Loiyang* (i.e. the main horizontal beam of a house) incident because the hill range from Laimaton to Thangching peaks looks like the long sloppy beam from a distance. They said that early emigrant who settled at the *Loiching* foothill subsequently became known as *Loi-ching mee* (referring to the Lois or the Poireiton group). This *Loiyang* story seems to have occurred much before the event of *Pidonnu: The Chothe lady and Chingkhei the Moirang king*, the great tragic love story commonly performed as plays by the Meitei.

27. *Tao*: These subordinate names probably refer to Thao clan of Chothe who settled near *Loiching* or western hill or Laimaton hill ranges. They are probably the village leaders or lay villagers who provide company to the Bodo-Cacharis or Mayang (Bengalis) the immigrant asylum seekers to the state.

28. *Khwairamband bazaar*: Shangkham said that the only world's Women's Bazaar "Khwairamband Ima Bazaar" is derived from this inter-feud fight at the fish auction market between Chothe and Kharam where a Chothe man was killed (2006: 2, 44-45; also see Parratt, 2005:148). This incident occurred among few Chothe who settled near Polo ground around Kangla (Imphal) and the Kharam on the north-west near Sagolband. Subsequently, the market came to be pronounced as 'Khwairamband bazaar' after the event, deriving the name from the word 'Kharam pan/ban' (lit. the blocking/fencing of Kharam people) where a fence was put up against the Kharam from further attacks since the king was in favour of Chothe people.

CHAPTER - 3

Chothe Institutions

Introduction

Sociologists, in order to understand the nature, behaviour, function and structure of a particular society primarily focuses on institutions like: kinship and marriage, political, economic and religion. Such institutions serve as the backbone in the sustenance and development of a society. They are the products of collective activities of folkways, mores and norms that regulate the social system for the advancement of a society. These regulations or the standard customary norms or laws are guided by their own intrinsic principles. Institutions are abstract in nature, significantly represented by rules, signs and symbols often seen in formal organisations. Social institutions are universal, as they exist in all types of societies. Many sociologists like Durkheim viewed that religion is the first formal institution, followed by the political and economic institutions, while family and marriage systems are the informal institutions of a simple society. As society expand and grows from simple homogeneity into complex heterogeneity, its social, economic and political institutions also evolve to cater the needs and demands of the people and to facilitate inter-relationship networks. According to K. Praveen Parboteeah and John B. Cullen, social institutions regulate societal activities through a freedom or constraint duality of prescribed behaviours that results through incentives, coercive and normative constraints shaped not only organisational forms but also at the individual-level, especially values regarding work (2003: 138, 145). For example, Monica Heller (1995) points out that, the proper use of language by certain organisations and groups can be exercised to wield power or resist certain major decisions. This is made possible because of the guided norms of the organisation or the social institution established by these groups to strengthen their unit and maintain the system.

Definition: Many scholars have defined institution but so far no consensus on one common definition has been achieved. Oliver E. Williamson asserts that, we are still very ignorant about institutions, despite the enormous progress witnessed in the study of institution in the past quarter of twentieth century. He opines that since institutions are very complex and the chief cause being our ignorance, a unified theory of pluralism should be accepted. There being many instructive lenses for studying complex institutions, pluralism is what holds promise for overcoming our ignorance (2000: 595).

MacIver and Page defines institution as, "Established forms or conditions of procedure characteristic of group activity", while H.E. Barnes defines institution as "The social structure and the machinery through which human society organised, directs, and execute the multifarious activities required to satisfy human needs" (see Rao, 1998: 106). Similarly, *Dictionary of Sociology* defines that, social institutions consist of all the structural components of a society through which the main concerns and activities are organised, and social needs (such as those of order, belief, and reproduction) are met. According to Gordon Marshall, the above definitions are of the views postulated by Herbert Spencer and Talcott Parsons, for both it was central to the notion of society as an organism or functioning system (2006: 317-318). These definitions and concepts point to the formal or informal structural organisations which arise naturally out of human needs and necessities. These definitions are supported by Scott (1995) and Turner (1997) who also views, social institutions are structures that evolve in societies to organise human interactions for positive causes. They provide individual actors with sense making and taken-for-granted heuristics to know what is legitimate, reasonable and appropriate to them.

Types of Institution: Institutions are categorised into primary and secondary. The primary institutions comprise of family, marriage, religion, political, economy (property), while the secondary institutions are the education systems, laws, parliamentary legislatures, and any other constitutional organisations. But according to Olsen and Turner, the core institution system include the economic, kinship, religion, political, legal, educational, and stratification systems (1991, 1997: 8). We find kinship institutions comprise of: family and marriage; the political institutions: parliamentary legislature and legal matter; the educational institutions: various academic and training centres; the economic institutions: banking, corporation enterprises; and religious institutions: denominations and various church organisations.

Torsten Persso (2002) affirms that political institutions used the tools of modern economics both in theory and practice for constructing the equilibrium theory of macro-economic policy. According to him, the macro-economic policies are shaped by political institutions; empirically, the electoral rules, the choice of fiscal policy instruments and the incidence of corruption or rent sought by politicians (2002: 884).

Later sociologists like Max Weber, Ralf Dahrendorf, Talcott Parsons, N.J. Smelser, S.N. Eisenstadt, etc. primarily focus their attention on institutional study like religion, economy and political institutions in order to explain the conflicting nature within the system.

But Alpha C. Chiang says that among non-economic factors, religion stands out as an important, if elusive, force in shaping economic behaviour. In spite of his appreciation to Max Weber for linking religion with economy, he expresses his unhappiness towards western scholars for their disinterest in the Oriental religious beliefs and practices (1961: 254). S.N. Eisenstadt also describes the interrelationship between social and economic institutions. He says the Israel's economic values, social orientation and ideologies are shaped by following both traditional and modern social values. That is to say the Yishuv economy was a combination of a continuously expanding colonisation – both agricultural and industrial, and the driving force or motivation in the expansion of their economy is a largely non-economic factor because the set of institutions and its values are exclusive (1956: 146-47). Similarly, N.J. Smelser (1965) elucidates the relations between the economic and non-economic aspects of social life – how these aspects overlap and how they influence one another. But it is W.W. Rostow (1959) in '*The Stages of Economic Growth*' who gave the best paradigm in generalizing economic history in the form of five stages of economic growth, designated as (1) The Traditional Society, (2) The Pre-conditions for Take-off, (3) The Take-off, (4) The Drive to Maturity, and (5) The Age of High Mass Consumption. He opines the problem lies after crossing the last stage that is already developing in few societies. The first, second and third stages of Rostow paradigm fits into Daniel Learner's '*The Passing of the Traditional Society*' that described the gradual change of Ankara society of Turkey from the traditional to modern outlook by discarding the old and accepting the new ideas in the developmental process. This transitional behavioural trend seems to be similar with the Chothe society.

Kinship: Marriage and Family

The name Chothe (including the Purum of T.C. Das) took centre stage in social anthropology during the period 1950-1970, because of the prescriptive marriage alliance system or the preferential matrilateral cross-cousin marriage system which is practiced by the Chothe. This particular system was first highlighted by Claude Levi-Strauss' in his theoretical paradigm of, '*Les Structures Elementares de la Parente*' (1949). This work was criticised by

George C. Homans and David M. Schneider (1955) from a different perspective. Rodney Needham (1959-1960's) an ardent scholar, received this criticism seriously and argued in support of Claude Levi-Strauss' 'alliance theory' and propagated his own synonymous theory called 'matrilineal connubium' or 'marriage in cycle', which are all based on the empirical data provided by Tarak Chandra Das' book, *The Purums* (1945). Subsequently, numerous renowned anthropologists like, Frank B. Livingstone (1959), Floyd G. Lounsbury (1962), Charles Ackerman (1964), William H. Geoghegan and Kay Paul (1964), George L. Cowgill (1964) and William Wilder (1964), etc. argued and debated against one another on the subject, which continues even today amongst various eminent sociologists and anthropologists. Robin Fox and others have referred Chothe marriage under 'asymmetrical and symmetrical' of complex marriage system in their studies (1967: 210). In fact, Nitul Kumar Gogoi made a critical study on the above debate and rightly stated that "...though majority of the Purums have been converted to Christianity they continue to follow the prescriptive law for their marriage" (1989: 51).

The Chothe practice patrilineal descent system. They also practice exogamous prescriptive matrimonial alliance system, in which matrilateral cross-cousin (MCC) marriage, or marriage with mother's brother's daughter (MBD) is most preferred. There are seven eponym clans and seventeen sub-clans, a total of twenty-four, according to B.K. Das Gupta (1985: 74), (see Table 11). The significance of Chothe marriage system is that there is a clear concept about their marriage rules. There is no direct exchange of wives between the lineages or sub-clans or clans. They marry girls only from the prescribed lineages or clans set by their marriage rules, and taking girls from un-prescribed lineages or clans is strictly considered as a breach which is against their marriage-social norms.

Nitul Goigoi (1989) affirms that the Chothe practice a prescriptive marriage system. Marriage with father's sister's daughter (FZD) is prohibited because they believed it is cognate. Therefore, their girls are exchanged indirectly among specific lineages or clans that operate in cycle which may complete the rotation in the third or fourth generations or it may not at all. This indirect exchange of girls is possible because of the triadic structure they maintain among: (i) wife-giving, (ii) wife-taking and (iii) unrelated or distant relatives or neutral groups. Das and Needham also points out as: (i) a boy's or rather his father's sib, (ii) his mother's group of sibs, or rather the group from which his wife is recruited, and (iii) his sister's husband's group of sibs, i.e. the group of sibs in which his sisters are married - this is sometimes his mother's mother's or his mother's mother's mother's sib (Das, 1945: 123, 125; Needham, 1958: 80, 81). Therefore, marriage functions in cyclical manner, where one clan accepts a girl from another clan or sub-clan, and gives its girls yet to another clan or sub-clan. So, no particular clan or sub-clan is superior or inferior in the Chothe society (Yuhlung, 2007: 61). By descent, the male head of the family or lineage or clan line is called as *shapa* or *pipa*, while the daughter's line is refer as *sheinu* or *sarrnu* (*ni-ngol* in Meitei). By this descent rule, many scholars viewed Chothe society to be a dyadic or moiety in structure. But in the case of marriage system their society is broadly divided into three groupings, as indicated above.

(i) Forms of Chothe Marriage

The Chothe practices three types of traditional marriage, viz.: (i) *Nu-ngak loh* (Arranged marriage), (ii) *Mou-sem/ Mourui* (Love marriage) and, (iii) *Tlang-chom neilah* (Elopement/ Force marriage).

The first type of marriage *Nu-ngak loh,* literally means 'wooing or courting a girl by visiting/ staying' in the girl's house. It means 'Engaged/ Arranged marriage'. This is like a pre-nuptial engagement, commonly practice in early days by common people who do not have enough wealth to pay the bride price immediately, and agreed to serve the three years marriage labour service by staying/visiting in the girl's house. When a boy attains a marriageable age, he himself or his paternal relatives (not parents) seeks a suitable girl (often MBD) for him. If positive signal is noticed, alone with his paternal grandfather/ uncle goes to his desired girl's house with a wine pot (*zuchom leizu*) and a rooster, and officially negotiate and proposes the girl. If the girl's parents accept the marriage proposal, they dine and drank together as part of the agreement. Thereafter, an auspicious day is fixed for a boy to begin his visit/ stay in the girls' house. On completion of the three years marriage labour service, *Inlamtinni* (Home coming) ceremony is performed during *Innampei rhin* festival. After that the two lovers are married in a simple ceremony called *mourui* (bringing the bride) by paying symbolic some basic bride price, where the bride is escorted by friends to the boy's house (Hiyang, 1985: 20-21). In the past, this is the most common and preferred form of marriage among the Chothe for its idealness, stability and adaptability.

The second type of Chothe marriage is known as '*mousem*' (make/ seek a bride) or '*mourui*' or '*ruihong*' (bringing the bride), which is a kind of both 'love and arrange marriage'. It is a marriage mutually solemnised when a boy finds a girl of his choice or his soul mate from within the prescribed clan or outside the community. Often, the boy comes from royal family or higher status or was rich. In other words, it is a 'Royal marriage' (of kings and princes). It is solemnise when the boy and the girl, as well as when both parent's agreed to the marriage proposal by paying the bride price immediately without serving the traditional three years marriage labour service. Only the

Table 13: Chothe Clans and Sub-clans According to Various Ethnographers

J. Shakespeare 1912/ Clans	J.K. Bose 1933	R.C. Roy 1936	T.C. Das 1945	B.K. Das Gupta 1985	C. Charles Yuhlung 2007/ Sub-clans
Kiang	Hiyang	Hiyang	Kheyang	Khiyang /Hiyang	Aihung, Impi, [Ingte], Rungkung, (Hulpu)
Marem	Marim	Marim	Marrim	Marim/Mareem	Rimphumchong, Rimkung, Rimkelek, Pilling (Piring), (Musom)
Makhan	Mekhong	Makhang	Makan	Makan	Kankung, Makan-te, (Laisik)
Thao	Thao	Thao	Thao	Thao	Thao-kung, Thao-run
Irung	Jurung	Jurung		Yuhlung	Tangkim
Piring	Piring	Piring	Parpa	Parpa	No sub-clans
			Rungkung/ Rangshai	[Teyu]*	

Note: See also Needham 1960a: 238. Piring or Pilling is now accepted as sub-clan of Marim. * It is found that a family of Teyu a sub-clan Rangshai still exist in Tampakhu village.

prescribed and select paternal kins of the bride are allowed to eat the meat and drink the wine brought by the boy's family; other members are restricted to partake. This *mousem* marriage is also known by some as *maan-loh,* meaning 'demanding the bride price', and now it is the most common form of marriage.

The third type of Chothe marriage is known as '*tlaan-chom neilah*' (marriage by elopement or force marriage). This can be further sub-divided into two categories: (i) consent of two lovers to elope against the wishes of their parents, and (ii) the force elopement against the wish of a girl (force marriage). The first category usually occur when a boy falls in love with a girl outside his prescribe clan/ village/ community, which is common among the youth. The second category occurs often with superior class people when they so desire a girl outside their community or as part of revenged due to past enmity or hatred.

(ii) Marriage Obligations for the Breach

If a boy forcefully marries a Chothe girl, he is obligated to perform certain marriage ceremonies to legalise the marriage. That means, if a Chothe girl marries outside her prescribed clan or village or non-Chothe boy by breach, especially under the third type of marriage (Elopement- *Tlaan-chom neilah*), the boy has to fulfil certain obligations one after another to make the marriage legalise and validate officially in society, without which the marriage is consider invalid.

These ceremonial obligation has deep underlining meanings for Chothe. In the past, Chothe girls are considered as very dear and highly invaluable assets of the family. In view of this, a girl is given to only the most loyal and trustworthy person or friend, who can risk his life and fulfilled the wish of a dying man in certain cases. Therefore, material gifts or money are considered secondary, rather loyalty and trust is treated as vital in establishing the marriage alliance. Hence, bride-price are symbolic gift accepted by the girl's parent, so that it becomes accountable in future to the boy, in case he failed to keep his promise or betrayed one's trust. So, to legalised the marriage and accept the boy as the 'amakpa' (son-in-law) or as the compatriot, first he has to prove his loyalty to the father-in-law. Thereafter, only he may forego those marriage ceremonial obligations to legalise their love marriage. The marriage ceremonial obligations to legalise the love/breach marriage are: (i) *Phung-tlaanglam,* (*ii*) *Loukhatpa* and (*iii*) *Maanshipa.*

(i) ***Phung-tlaanglam****:* If a boy and a girl elopes, immediately on the next day, the boy's family or relative has to inform to the girl's parent about the elopement. Then, based on the (positive) outcome of the decision of the girl's parent, the boy has to pay a penalty fee/fine called *Phung-tlaanglam* meaning 'Fine imposed for marrying outside the prescribed clan or village or by non-Chothe boy'. This penalty fee is paid to the village council on behalf of the girl's family, where pieces of the meat is shared to important villagers and the left portion is cooked and eaten by villager committee. The penalty pig signifies that one of their daughter's has been eloped/ married. The fine is a pig (size of five *wei* or *wai* i.e. the pig's neck should be about 2.5 feet in diameter) and a bottle of wine. The girl's family members are prohibited to eat this meat and drinks brought. In case, this *Phung-tlaanglam* is not given on time, the girl's family with the support of the village authority has the legal right to avenge as war against the boy's family or village or community on the pretext of stealing their precious girl/ daughter. Only after paying this penalty fee, the marriage negotiation and other marriage obligatory ceremonies like *Loukhatpa* and *Maanshipa* can take place and make the marriage legal and valid. Otherwise, the marriage is consider invalid and the girl is not permitted to visit nor enter her parent's home even at the time of her parents' death. Perhaps, if the girl's parent initially refused to accept the penalty fee, it means that they refuse to give their girl to the concern boy. In such cases, a marriage conflict occurs between the boy and girl's family/ villagers.

(ii) **Loukhatpa:** Literally 'Loukhatpa' means 'Uplift/ acceptance' from being denied. This is perform any time after *phung-tlanglam* (penalty fee) is paid. The latent function is that since the boy and the girl are considered outcast because breach of marriage, they first has to seek apology of forgiveness to the girl's parent in order to legalise their marriage in society. This is possible only after the girl's parents forgive and accepts to bless them as their daughter and son-in-law (*Amakpa*). This particular act of reconciliation initiated by the boy with the girl's parent in order to legalise their marriage in society is known as *Loukhatpa*. Only after this act the couple are permitted to perform the bride-price giving ceremony and receive the blessing from the parents-in-laws. Those who followed the right approach of wooing a girl in accordance to their traditional custom are exempted of this act.

(iii) **Numei Maanshipa:** In Chothe, '*Numei maanshipa*' literally means 'giving bride-price', whereas the Meitei term it as '*Potshemba*' (gift preparation). This bride-price giving ceremony is perform only after undergoing all the above mentioned obligated customs. This is the last and important marriage ceremony, in which if the girl's parents accept this bride-price without any disagreement, the marriage is consider officially legal and valid, whereby the couple receives the blessing from the girl's parents and kins. Thereafter, the son-in-law becomes *Amakpa* or *Maksa,* lit. the Compatriot or Alliance partner. They said in the past, depending on the nature of family's relationship and position the *loukhatpa* and *maanshipa* are performed much later after the elopement. Normally, when the couple's relationships are stable and the boy after proving his loyalty and responsibility to his wife, children and his father-in-law, or after the family's conflict is resolved.

(iii) Bride Price

Except for the common traditional '*Numei loh*' or 'Arranged/ Engaged marriage', all other forms of marriage (love or force marriage) have to pay the bride-price (*Numei maan*) as a symbolic token of the boy's 'loyalty and a trustee' alliance partner. The significant is that the bride price/ gift are tokens that would be accountable to the boy in future, in case of any eventful situations like death, heir to the throne, conflict or estrangement. In other words, among the Chothe like any other old tribal societies, it is the loyalty, sincerity and honesty that matter most in relationship in the past as part of group solidarity. In this way, each bride price or gift has its distinctive marks recognised by the family and kin group accountable to him by the objects. So, the value of bride price/ gift becomes a symbolic affair or secondary among Chothe, instead the obligated loyalty of the boy to his wife and his wife's lineage is considered more important than any material or gifts money.

Traditionally, the Chothe bride-price (*Numei maan*) of a boy demanded comprises of: a gong (*shum*), a pig or a basket of boiled meat (cow or mithun), along with three traditional shawls [(*awa ampi*, one each for her paternal grandfather (*A-pu*), paternal uncle (*ateerpa* or *pipa* or lineage head) and maternal uncle (*ma-pute*)], a very good spear and knife (with tip curved downward), two hoes or small spades, a bottle of wine (*Zu*), a pot of rice beer (wine signifies for father-in-law and rice beer for mother-in-law), and an amount of Rs 500 (five hundred in one-rupee coins only). This tradition of giving bride price/ gift is known as '*Numei maansipa*'. Gong (*shum*) was considered a highly valuable gift off all the gifts.

Here, only the prescribed and close paternal kins of the bride are allowed to eat the meat and drink the wine brought by the boy's family. Other village members are restricted to partake but normally another separate pig or cow may be killed as part of the marriage feast where all expenditures are borne by the boy. So, this marriage is also known as '*maan-loh*', meaning 'demand of the bride price', which applies to allies groups of people.

In case the *ateerpa/ ateirpa* (Paternal eldest uncle) expired the shawl is given to her father or eldest brother (Yuhlung, 2002: 4). The girl in return receives blessing from her parents and some (movable) material gifts. For the Lamlanghupi villagers until and unless those ceremonies are performed by the boy, she is not permitted to visit nor entitled to receive any material gifts from her parents. But according to *Chothe Lim Abom Manipur* (CLAM) the Chothe Apex Body's resolution passed on 11th October 1985, if a girl marries outside her community the boy has to pay rupees five thousand (5000) per year in lieu of the marriage labour service, which amounts to Rs 15,000 for the three years besides other penalties of a pig and a pot of wine.

(iv) Polygamy and Divorce

Polyandry is not practiced at all by Chothe. Polygamy and divorce do exist but it is not encouraged. Widow, widower and divorcee if they so desire can re-marry only after fulfilling certain customary obligation. In case, if a man wishes to legally divorce his wife, he has to pay a fine, equal to bride-price to his ex-wife's family to signify that their marriage has been dissolved and they are not related by marriage anymore, then only he can remarry any girl. Similarly, if a girl seeks for a divorce from her husband, she has to pay return the bride-price to her ex-husband, then only she is legally free to remarry. This marriage law applies to even young widows who desire to remarry a man from another/ different clan/ outsider.

(v) Inheritance

Among the Chothe it is the youngest son or ultimogeniture of the family who inherits the family's movable and immovable property like estate/ land. Although *Pipa* the eldest male or the primogeniture is the legal head of the family or lineage or clan, he does not inherit the family's property, but he is the successor of his father or as the lineage head. Such system is also prevalent among the Ao, Zeliang, Kom, Hmar and other tribes of North-east.

(vi) Teknonymy

The Chothe kinship terminology and teknonymy is varied and complicated. A man or woman may be addressed, referred, identified and introduced in different ways by a person, depending on the criteria of his/ her descent and marital relationship. For example, one specific and unique marital term is *Amak-pa (Maksa),* which literally means 'Alliance or compatriot' which specifically refers to only "son-in-laws" by the wife's parent/ lineage/ clan members only. He (*Amak-pa*) is also address as *u-pa* or *ebye* (brother-in-laws) by his wife's brothers, or as *arrang* (aunty's husband) by his wife's niece and nephews, or as *apu* (grandfather) by his wife's great grandchildren. On the other hand, in term of his descent relationships, he (*Amakpa*) is also addressed as *a-pu* (grandfather), *a-pa* (father), *a-teerpa* (elder paternal uncle), *a-tun/ a-pate* (younger paternal uncle), *u-pa/ aya/ ata* (brother) depending on his lineage relationship with the ego. And *Uu/ U-nu* refers to elder lineage sister, *A-uu* to elder sister-in-law. Such similar and different terminology also applies to any girl or woman depending on her marital and descent relationship with the ego (Das, 1945:125-6, see Table 5, Yuhlung, 2007: 58-61).

Table 14: Kinship Terminology

Chothe	English	Chothe	English
Apa	Father	*Ateerpa*	Elder paternal uncle
Anu/ Amma	Mother	*Ateernu*	Elder paternal aunt
Apu (any aged person)	Grandfather	*Atun/ Apate*	Younger paternal uncle
Api	Grandmother (any aged person)	*Apute*	Maternal uncle (Younger)
Upa/ Aya or Ata	Brother	*Atu*	Grandchild/ children
Auu/ Aya	Sister	*Ate*	Great grandchild/ children
Ibai/ Eby	Brother-in-law	*Arang*	Aunty's husband
Uu	Sister-in-law	*Ani*	Aunty
Maksa	Son-in-law/		

grandson-in-law.

Besides, the Chothe use a prefix of the eldest child's name while referring or addressing a man/ woman by peer groups or elders as a sign of respect and courtesy, instead of calling directly by their actual birth names. Such teknonymy does not allow the younger Chothe to address their elders by their names; if one does they considered disrespect and also confuses the lineage groups. Such refined courteous behaviour and descent attitude in their tradition shows the Chothe tribe to be in advanced.

Till today, the Chothe adheres to their prescriptive marriage system, where MBD or a girl of mother's clan is the most preferred choice. Although the trend has substantially declined in the recent years due to certain factors as provided by Cheithou Charles Yuhlung, like increased marriage rates with other tribes, exposure and advent of Christianity, despite still showing stability in their prescriptive marriage rules (see Table 3 in, 2007: 51-52). Anyone violating their traditional prescriptive marriage rules are severely penalised by the Village Council with huge fines and sometimes they are expelled from the village.

(i) Political Organisation: Structure and Function

The Chothe political or administrative system is gerontocratic, hierarchical, non-hereditary and democratic in nature. They have no written records or constitution of their own. They function based on the custom and tradition handed down by their forefathers. They have no hereditary chief, unlike other similar tribes of New-Kuki. The chief takes the decision depending upon the consensus or mutual understanding of *Hu-bungkung* i.e. Village Council, comprising three houses or units viz.: (1) *Urinta bungkung* (Council of Elders), (2) *Tang-ngarinta bungkung* (Council of matured adults) and, (3) *Nu-ngak Luthei* or *Luther bungkung* (Council of girls and boys/ youths) respectively.[1] On the criteria of the house or unit, the *Urinta* are the decision-maker and the *Tang-ngarinta* the executor of law and orders. The Chothe Village Council like any political system of the world have its own distinctive structures and functions, where each house/ unit is also arranged hierarchically, with specific roles assigned according to the structural position they occupy in the society. Their traditional unit's resting spots are symbolically represented by stones at their deity's site (see Pic. 6).

The *Urinta bungkung* and *Tang-ngarinta bungkung* form the main Village Council or the decision-making bodies because only *Tangsha* the senior most leader of *Nungak-Luthei bungkung* represents his unit in any village meeting. The Chothe look upon the *Hulak* and *Luplak* as husband and wife in the political affairs. They believe that the political stability depends upon the two in their mutual faith, trust, cooperation and transparency which keep the political system effective, efficient, reliable and stable. Perhaps, if any person wishes to make a request or appeal his grievances to the *Hu-bungkung,* the minimum traditional court fee is just a bottle of wine (*Leizu*) set as a norm. But sometimes a rooster or a pig might be required if the case is major. John Shakespeare has described the nature of the Chothe political system as, "All the Old Kuki clans are organised far more democratically than the Lushai or Thadou. Lieut Stewart in his *Notes on the Northern Cachar* says there is no regular system of government among the Old-Kukis and they have no hereditary chiefs as among the new ones. A headman called the '*ghalim*' is appointed by themselves in every village, but he is much more a priest than a potentate, and his temporal power is much limited. Internal administration among them always takes a provisional form. When any party consider himself aggrieved he makes an appeal to the elders or the most powerful householder in the village by inviting them to dinner and plying them with victuals and wine" (1912: 148-49).

Monarchy: The Chothe believed they had a monarchical form of government in olden days. But after the declined it gave way to feudalistic and eventually becomes a gerontocratic system. The *Moirang Ningthourol Lambuba* (*MNL*) like *Cheitharol Kumpaba* (*ChK*) manuscript described that 'the Chothe King Natoi Nachaoba' was defeated by the Moirang king in the *Lungsukbung* (*Nungsuk*) battle (Singh, 1982: 93). Their oral history also speaks about the existence of many Chothe villages once ruled by a monarch (see MNL) in the region behind Thangching peak around Henglep called

Lungsukbung region. They claimed their predecessor were great kings (*A-reng*) who fought and died in many big battles. Even today, according to their custom and tradition, the head chief is symbolically regarded as their Monarchical king, where other villages' chiefs are considered federate kings/ chiefs of the tribe in the council who occupy positions both in the *Urinta* and *Tang-ngarinta bunkung* groups. For example, the formal courtesy addressed to their king/ chief in their Thanks-giving (*Thoukeipa*) ceremony by *Tang-ngarinta* and *Nungak-Luthei bungkung* members shows the structural and functional aspect of monarchism (see Pic. 27). This may be seen at micro level.

"Ka-reng-ngo, ka-thou-o, thanglei luthei, tui luthei, thanghung luthei, thingchu naruipa keichu nazu nabu bakka luiya na-sikan lonna nowe inn tin ne-ang no meshou-we".

Literally it means: "My King, my Lord, we; the youth in-charge of food and drinks, youth in-charge of water and youth in-charge of drums is very thankful to you because we have drank so much of your wine and ate enough of your food you offered. So, we are afraid that we may not be able to perform our duties (*Sikan*) and even return to our homes". (This thanksgiving ceremony is addressed to their king by the specific three youth leaders). The words used and action performed in this traditional ceremony implicates that the Chothe had a monarchical and feudalistic system that enjoyed the political hegemony over others in the past like the Chinese or Japanese. Later it became democratised and gave way to the gerontocratic form of government. The significant is that even today this ancient courteous behaviour of formal tradition is still observed during their annual festivals and important rituals, besides preserving other distinctive socio-political, economic and religious life.

1. *Nu-ngak Luthei (Luther) Bunkung*: The bachelor or youth's organisation is known as *Nu-ngak Luthei bungkung* (lit. girls and boys house/ unit). And their regular meeting place is called as *Ruishang/ Loishang* (lit. friends/ youth's house) which is a boys' dormitory. Sometimes it is called as *Sikan-Inn* (lit. beat house) since corporal punishments were carried out for the noncompliant youth. The Nagas called such dormitory as *Morung* generally, since each tribe have its own term. In the modern context, such youth dormitory in a village may be identified with education institution, boarding school, hostel or the youth club as it served the centre place of learning and training for the youths. The Lamlanghupi Village Council allows their youth to function and organised their activities from one of the member of Council of Elders' house since, such dormitory house is no longer built. Tomalsing Yuhlung a respondent said that, "In earlier days, all the village youth gathered in the dormitory and they were trained artisan, warfare, disciplined and imparted with moral values and education under the able-leadership and command of *Pakhang-lakpa* of *Tangnga-ringta*". This *Pakhang-lakpa* is assisted by the youth leaders appointed on the basis of their seniority and leadership qualities from each lineage or clan, although preferences are given to the eldest son of a family or lineage. The youngest youth recruited is term as *Leibak* (lit. bought with fine). Later, they are elevated batch after batch based on seniority and experiences to the highest hierarchy position. The hierarchical positions of *Nu-ngak Luthei bungkung* are:

(i) *Tangsha* - one each first from Hiyang and Yuhlung clans,

(ii) *Hancha* - one each from Hiyang, Yuhlung and Marim clans,

(iii) *Hithang* - one each from any three clans and,

(iv) *Leibak* - comprises all the boys above 14/15 years, who have been inducted into the youth congregation after performing the initiation (*leibak manpa*) ceremony. In case of a girl initiation it is called as *Nu-ngak manpa* (capturing of a girl). It has the structure of a military.

Whenever a Village Council meeting is called for, only the *Tangsha* represents on behalf of all the youth (Hiyang, 1985: 22). The *Tangsha, Hancha* and *Hithang* are dynamic bachelor leaders acting like platoon leaders in their units who have their own followers of *Leibaks* to assist them and carry out the orders from the higher authorities of *Urinta* and *Tang-ngarinta* members. These youth leaders are also responsible in the recruitment process of the younger boys into their unit. The girls too have their own dormitory, usually hosted at one of their seniormost girls' residence. All the girls gathered at her home, especially during the annual festivals. She oversees the junior girls and accordingly programms them. But it is *Pakhanglakpa* who decides and gives the final decision to all the youth irrespective of boys or girls, since he is the overall in-charge of the department of youth affairs.

2. *Tang-ngarinta Bungkung*: This house is also known as *Laihu ruishang* (*loishang*), meaning 'caretaker of the deity' because they are practically responsible for the maintenance and safety of their deity, sacred religious items and all other socio-political and economic activities. These members are all married men, who occupy the political hierarchical positions, status and powers next to the Council of Elders (*Urinta bungkung*) by their life experiences. So, they are known as *Tang-ngarinta,* meaning 'matured adults'. These leaders carry out their own roles and responsibilities according to their assigned position they occupied in the political hierarchy. They represents the seven junior *pipa* or lineage/ clan's heads or as executive leaders. Their hierarchical and functional roles assigned are:

(i) *Pakhang-lakpa* (Chief -In-charge of the Youth/ Superintendent),

(ii) *Zupai* (Wine Manager),

   (iii) *Lomjui-ulin* (Senior Team Leader),

   (iv) *Lomjui-jaima* (Middle Team Leader),

   (v) *Lomjui-noupong* (Junior Team Leader),

   (vi) *Zujong-ulin* (Senior Wine In-charge) and,

   (vii) *Zujong-noupong* (Junior Wine In-charge).

According to the Chothe, *Tang-ngarinta* members besides, assisting in almost all the ritualistic activities, do carries out the socio-political affairs and participates in the Village Council (*Hu-bungkung*) decision making. They handle any emergency cases and acts like the modern bureaucrats and executives, who took charges of the youth battalion and executes the social norms as laid by the Village Council. They also supervised the people in case of law and order problem. They trained and disciplined the youth from time to time at the bachelor's house (*Ruishang/ Loishang*), sometimes punishing the disobedient youth with a special stick called "Sikan-chei".[2] Their position, status, role and responsibilities are well designated and assigned accordingly who are accountable to the Elders. But in case of any vacant position arising due to death or surrendering of one's position under certain circumstances it is filled at the earliest by the person who occupies the immediate junior position. Similarly, the rest of the official members ceremonially succeeds the hierarchical position one after another.

3. *Urinta Bungkung*: The highest political decision-making body of the Chothe Village Council (*Hu-bungkung*) is known as *Urinta bungkung* (lit. Council of Elders). This Council of Elders has seven cabinet positions which is hierarchically arranged according to customary law. The members are usually represented by each *Pipa* the eldest male/ head of the lineage's (*inku*) or clan (*phung*). The chief (*Hulak*) occupies the highest cabinet position. He is the ultimate decision maker. There is no room for any arbitrary acts for the chief and assistant-chief (*Hulak* and *Luplak*), since the council exercise authority based on the consensus of the house on mutual understanding like the British Constitution. They are mostly aged persons, who are highly respected, honoured and trusted by the society for their vast knowledge, experiences and their expertise in diverse fields. In case a cabinet dies, the subordinate person in line occupies his position. But here, in case a member of *rui* dies, the position is replaced by the seniormost person from the same clan/ lineage, sometimes taking from lower house.

Besides, the seven cabinet post, the rest of the members in the Council of Elders are called *Rui* (lit. Comrade or fellowship). Although, they occupy higher elite status and position as members of the elders they do not enjoy absolute power and authority like the cabinets. So, all these political leaders functions their own roles and responsibilities according to the designation of

Table 15: The Socio-political Structure of the Village Council (Hu-bungkung) of the Chothe (See also CLAM, record book p. 5)

Category	A. The Village Council or Hu-bungkung of Lamlanghupi the Western group			B. Hu-bungkung of the Eastern and Central cluster groups	
Type of houses	1. Urinta bungkung	2. Tangnga-rinta bungkung	3. Nungak-luthei (Ruther) bungkung	1. Phamnei-ngei or Hloukal (Ruling party)	2. Loumi (Opposition party)
1	Hulak (H. Thambaijou)	Pakhanglakpa (M. Marachou)	Tangsha (H. Yaima)	Hulak	Hancha
2	Luplak (Y. Tomal Singh)	Zupai (UO)	Hancha ulin (H. Ibochou)	Luplak	Hithang
3	Zupai (UO)	Lomjui ulin (UO)	Hancha noupong (Y. Sanjoy)	Hancha (Pakhanglakpa)	Loumi-Hancha
4	Keirung ulin (H. Bokul Singh)	Lomjui jaima (UO)	Hithang ulin	Zupaipa	Loumi- Zupaipa
5	Keirung noupong (Selung), (UO)	Lomjui noupong (UO)	Hithang jaima (UO)	Keirungpa	Loumi- Keirungpa
6	Hachari ulin or Changrui (Th. Jatra Singh)	Zujong ulin (H. Gulap Singh)	Hithang noupong (UO)	Selungpa	Tlongthichaoi ulin
7	Hachari noupong or Changrui (M. Kundo)	Zujong noupong (P. Nandi)	Leibak (youths)	Changrui or Rui or Hachari	Tlongthicha oi noupong

Note: The names of present western village authorities are also given, where (UO) stands for 'Un-occupied' or 'vacant post'. Marim Marachou holds the post of Pakhanglakpa from August 2007 onwards after Th. Nabadip died.

the department assigned to them (See also T.C. Das, 1945:179-182). The *Urinta* members are like feudalistic nobles or ministers of modern democracy. The seven clan's heads or cabinet positions of *Urinta bungkung* and their equivalent functional roles are:

(i) *Hulak* (Chief, decision maker),

(ii) *Luplak* (Assistant Chief or Deputy Prime Minister),

(iii) *Zupai* (Wine Manager or Assistant Deputy Prime Minister),

(iv) *Keirung-ulin* (Senior Treasurer of rice-barn or Home Minister),

(v) *Keirung-noupong* or *Selungpa* (Junior Treasurer or Finance Minister),

(vi) *Hachari-ulin* (Senior Supervisor or Minister of Transport and Communication) and,

(vii) *Hachari-noupong/ Changrui/ Rui* (Junior Supervisor/ Minister of Information and Broadcasting, Other promoted member of elders are placed in this rank).

The Differences: The difference in the Chothe socio-political structure and village administration between the Western group and with that of the Eastern and Central-cluster develops after the two latter groups left the main Western parent group without their chief many centuries ago (see Table 13). It is said that the Eastern group was led by *Luplak* while the Central-cluster was led by *Hancha* and *Hithang*. Therefore, since the quorum for the Village Council was insufficient they were compelled to rearrange the three-tier original houses of *bungkungs* into two-tier as; (i) *Hloukal* or *Phamnei-ngei* (Ruling house) and (ii) *Loumi* (Farmers or Opposition party), (Rimkung, 2003: 12.b). The Western Chothe, however still adopts the gerontocratic three-tier political system in its entirety till date. But gradually the Eastern and Central-cluster Chothe have changed to an elective system where the village chief and its council of members are elected for five years period. After they were converted to Christianity the new five years tenureship system is believed to have strengthened since they could not adapt to their age-old rigid socio-religious and political systems.

Every society has its own sets of moral codes of conduct and behaviour. So, it becomes the duty of each unit's leaders to safeguard and preserved their Chothe cultural identity by conforming to their socio-political and cultural norms. For example, any youth committing a serious criminal act like killing a person or had breaches against the social, religious or marriage norms not only degrades his/ her reputation but also his/ her whole family and clan. Further, it directly affects the status and position of an honourable person who is in authority representing his/ her clan. Thus, the village elders' time to time reinforces their social-moral values to the youth from being defamed.

Even today, we see in their daily interactions their behaviours are filled with courtesies observable in the way they eat, drink, food and drinks/ tea served, folkways of greeting elders, dressing code for boys and girls, etc.

Interestingly, this study shows that many of the respondents who are above fifty years of age, especially the village elders and matured adult irrespective of Christian or non-Christian like Yuhlung Jate of Ajouhu wish to retain their age-old socio-political system i.e. they preferred to continue their indigenous gerontocratic, hierarchical, democratic and non-hereditary political system, provided the chief are educated and learned. They cherished their age-old traditional form of government, considering it is ruled by people who distinguished themselves with varied experiences and high reputation unlike the young leaders. The elders find the young leaders selfish, impatient, corrupt, and self-centred and acting on their human impulse rather than being meticulous with the pros and cons of the issues, often resulting into political chaos and instability. For example, Rengngir of Leininghu says that, "Some of our village chiefs (*Hulak* and *Luplak*) of Central cluster from the villages of Tampakhu, Ajouhu, Chumbang, Leininghu, Old-Wangparal, New-Wangparal and Chothe Khunou had been impeached by the Village Council because they are found involved in many mismanagements and scandals of corruption resulting in political turmoil and instability of the village". But respondents, who prefer the new political system opines that the gerontocratic chiefs and elders in authority are mostly illiterate, lack diplomacy and cannot conform to the modern governance system as they are rigid in their outlooks and slow in making decision.

(ii) Promotion and Coronation Ceremonies

The traditional Chothe socio-political system is gerontocratic, non-hereditary and hierarchical in structure. The members are ceremonially promoted and coroneted, succeeding one after another on the criteria of seniority and availability of the vacant position in each political house. In case, their chief or any political members dies, the vacant position is filled at the earliest ceremonially by the immediate person occupying in the hierarchy. According to Chothe elders, three main coronation ceremonies are to be performed by any Cabinet Council of Elders (*Urinta*) to become chief in the future viz.: (i) *Ruihong* or *Phamkeipa,* (ii) *Tolaihong* or *Phambakpa* and (iii) *Phamtakpa.*

But after performing the first ceremony *Ruihong*, the person is yet to perform another three very important minor meritorious promotional ceremonies in order to occupy the main cabinet position in the Council of Elders, without which, he cannot perform the other two coronation ceremonies to succeed as village chief. They are: (i) *Kui git* (ii) *Thong git* and (iii) *Petai.*

Other lower political members perform a rather simple ceremony while succeeding.

Traditionally, the king (*A-reng*) or chief (*Hulak*) occupies the highest position in Chothe society or village. As long as he lives, he decides and heads the society. It is not hereditary, unlike other similar tribes where chieftainship is hereditary. If a Chothe chief dies, his position is immediately succeeded by Assistant-chief (*Luplak*) only after he performed the other two coronation ceremonies of *Tolaihong/ Phambakpa* and *Phamtakpa*.[3] Similarly, on the basis of their traditional political norm, the rest of the members also succeed one after another the vacant cabinet positions in the Council of Elders (*Urinta bungkung*) house of the Chothe Village Council (*Hu-bungkung*).

Likewise, any member from the *Tang-ngarinta bungkung* (Council of matured adult) including *Pakhanglakpa* on the availability of the vacant position may join the Council of Elders as *Rui* (lit. friend/ follower) only after performing the *ruihong* and *phamkeipa* i.e. promotion or coronation ceremony. Perhaps, if *Pakhanglakpa's* position is found vacant in the *Tang-ngarinta bungkung*, his position is ceremonially succeeded by *Zupai* or *Lomjui Ulin* as priority is given to senior most citizen in the line of hierarchy. So, on the basis of this hierarchical succession, any lower vacant position in the *Tang-ngarinta bungkung* is succeeded by the seniormost leaders from the *Nu-ngak luthei/r bungkung* like by *Tangsha, Hancha or Hithang* with simple promotion ceremony unlike the cabinet or elder members. Likewise, the senior *leibak* (boys) in the *Nu-ngak luthei bungkung* accordingly succeed the above vacant positions i.e. *Tangsha, Hancha* and *Hithang*. Thus, among the Chothe we see that as one move up higher to their socio-political hierarchy from house to house/ unit their promotion and coronation ceremonial fees do increases, so also, the ceremony becomes from simple to complex because of the status value, power and authority they command.

As described above, the first coronation or initiation ceremony of the Chothe Council of Elders (*Urinta bungkung*) is called *Ruihong* (*Rui* = comrade/ bring; *hong* = enter). *Phamkeipa* means 'promotion/ coronation' feast. Initially the person offers a rooster and a pot of liquor (*leizu*) to the council in any of the major festivals and seeks the permission to enter their house. If the village council agree on his request, he organised a promotion feast (*phamkeipa*) to show his gratitude since he has achieve the status of *Rui* in the Council of Elders. The rooster is killed and cut according to their socio-religious custom of *saram-ngaram* (cutting the meat and fish in accordance to the norm). The meat is cook and distributed accordingly to the seven cabinet members in the Council of Elders.

However, another very important aspect is that for any *Rui* member in the Council of Elders who wishes to succeed as cabinet members and even desires to become chief of the village in the future, he has to perform the three important promotional ceremonies viz.: (i) *Kuigit* (ii) *Thong-git* and (iii) *Petai*. The first important promotion ceremony is called "*Kui-git*", meaning 'piercing the ear'. It is done on any auspicious day of the year by offering a pig and a pot of liquor (approx. 20 litres) to the Village Council. After a simple invocation rite the concern person's ear is pierced with a needle and he wears a metal ear-ring, signifying he truly now belongs to the aged group. The second promotion ceremony is called "Thong-git", meaning 'piercing of the spinal cord'. The significance of this is to test his patience and virility to be considered as a wise old aged man. Then, the third promotion ceremony is called "*Petai*", meaning 'helper/ assistant to wrap'. On completion of this third promotion ceremony he is designated and occupies the position as "*Hachari/ Changrui*". This means that only after a person performed all these three promotional ceremonies he occupies the lowest cabinet position of *Hachari/ Changrui* in the house of Council of Elders of the Chothe Village Council (*Hu-bungkung*).

In the month of April 2008, Gulapsing Hiyang (65/M) of Lamlanghupi was inducted to *Urinta bungkung* who earlier hold the post of *Zujong-Ulin* in the *Tang-ngarinta bungkung*. He performed the promotion ceremony of *Rui* to be a member in the Council of Elders. But the council agreed to double promote him to the *Petai* or *Hachari* post because the position was vacant and there are few *Urinta bungkung* members only.

The second major coronation ceremony is *Phambakpa* (Coronation) or *Tolaihongpa* (litter or palanquin) is performed especially by the three highest position holders among the Council of Elders i.e. *Keirung, Luplak* and *Hulak* respectively while succeeding one another, usually after the dead of their old chief/ king. According to them, only the appointed deserving chief/ king uses the litter or palanquin (*tolai-hong*) symbolising power and authority, whereas the others are forbidden to sit in the palanquin.

The third coronation ceremony of the Chothe Village Council is called "*Phamtakpa*" (directing the position). Performed only after the *phambakpa* or *Tolaihong* ceremony, where all the members of the Village Council (*Hu-bungkung*) gathers to officiate and indicate the chief's throne/ seat/ position arranged in their socio-political hierarchy. The most important aspect of this ceremony is the "thing-bompa" or "thing-tumpa" (called *cheithapa* in Meitei) i.e. counting of sceptre sticks or scrolls of each cabinet members contain inside a small bamboo basket (basket is like a filtering bamboo mug called *sack* or *poi*).[4] In such ceremony all the members equally contributes their fee except *Keirung-noupong* who offered only two liquor pots while *Luplak* offered a rooster and a pot of liquor respectively. In this way, the Village Council of Elders are promoted ceremonially by offering a grand feast and paying the customary fees and succeeded one another, if there is any vacant position in their socio-political hierarchical system (See Table 12).

The *Tolaihongpa* is a simple offertory ceremony, part of the *phambakpa* where the new in-coming chief is honoured with a litter or palanquin by the villagers as deserved to be called as chief/ king. These two terms are used synonymously implying coronation of a chief/ king. Khedon Khiyang (90/ M) said that, "In olden days the *Tang-ngarinta* members on any auspicious day before a week or a month would take the king's litter or palanquin to the new chief/ king's house and request him to accept the litter brought. If he agreed, the youth carries him to the deity's place *laman* (*laimang* in Meitei) followed by the villagers to officially and ceremonially honour him as their new-crown chief/ king. At the deity's site a short simple ritual is performed by the village priest (*thiempu*) by offering prayer, seeking blessing and also consulting divination for him".

The rightful chief/ king, on his coronation day is officially honoured the chieftainship of the village or society with their traditional king's headgear and a shawl by the *Keirung* and *Zupai* after a simple rite of *tongkaipa* and *zurum*.[5] To commemorate his chieftainship, as the new crown chief or king he offers a big community feast to the entire villagers. He also invites relatives, friends, socio-political leaders, dignitaries and other village chiefs. His near and dear ones, friends and relatives honoured him with shawls and other items as gift. Such coronation feast and celebration is said to last the whole night and even continued till the next day with singing, dancing and drinking. However, all the *maksas* (brother/son in-laws) and *sarrnus* (sisters/ daughters) of the concerned chief supervise the whole celebration like receiving the guests, cooking, killing of animals (fowls, pigs or bison (mithun) and also serving the food and drinks to the invitees. But the tradition of carrying the chief/ king in the litter or palanquin (*tolai*) is no longer practiced by any Chothe villages now.

**Table 16: Fix Amount of Customary Fees for
Coronation Feast (see T.C. Das, 1945:176)**

Rank of the officer	Equivalent term in English	No. of pigs to be offered	No. of wine pots (zu) required
Khullakpa (Hulak)	Village Chief	3	20
Luplakpa (Luplak)	Assistant-chief	3	20
Khunjahanba	Village/ Lineage leader	2	10
Zupanpa	Wine secretary	2	10
Keirungpa	Rice-barn secy.	2	10
Selungpa	Finance secy.	2	10
Hachari (Changlai/ Rui)	Matured adult followers	1	07

Village Court: So far, the system of exquisite coronation ceremony and seating arrangement of the traditional Chothe Village Council's Court i.e. *Hu-bungkung* is still maintained and practiced by the Lamlanghupi villagers. It is a great opportunity to see such distinctive ancient court and the seating arrangement still preserved till date, although it is symbolically represented by plain wooden seats instead of elegant throne or chairs. One can notice, the seating position of their political hierarchy arranged on the veranda of the chief's house, instead at *Laman* or sacred-grove especially on *Lamleh-thoipa* (*Panthong iratpa*) and other criminal court cases day (see Pic. 2). The remnants of such village court at *Laman* are found in the old settlements of Old and New-Wangparal villages.

Another particular democratic political custom of the Chothe noticed is the consensus decision taken based on mutual understanding by the members of the village council. For example, if a person within the group is supposed to move up in the socio-political hierarchy by offering the promotion feast but he cannot effort to do so because of financial or personal problems. Then this opportunity is given to his immediate junior with a green signal to move up the hierarchy, which occur when the post remain vacant beyond a certain period of time. The senior member gives way to his immediate junior with a proposal. But, if the immediate junior is reluctant on moral ground, then the council reconsider the senior member's problem, thereby making concession to the customary fees, and who let him performed a simple symbolic feast. But in most cases, his lineage and clan members rescued him with contributions and boring certain expenditures required for the grand feast in uplifting him to occupy the coveted high position and status in the society.

Although some differences between the Western group (Lamlan-ghupi) and with that of the Eastern and Central-cluster groups are seen in the position's name, stages and also in the nature of coronation. But the functional aspects of the designated positions are the same. The fixed customary amount or fees in early days for promotion and coronation ceremonies given by T.C. Das have not changed much (see Table 12). But, if one is wealthy and rich he has the liberty to host and offer the feast with more grandeur menus and attain more fame, respect and social prestige in the society.

Customary Land Law: In the issue of village land dispute and family property, the village chief is the absolute decision-maker based on the consensus opinion of the village council members. If any person or group or tribe encroached their village territory for jhum cultivation or cuts down trees from their reserved forest without prior consultation, then the offender will be avenged with war or with heavy penalty of a pig (of 6 *wais* size) and a bottle of wine, thereby asking him to return what belongs to them. This law of disputes applies to all irrespective of villager or non-villager. The fine depends on the degree and nature of the crime committed.

Any marriage breaches like elopement and dispute is settled by the chief based on the council of members' views with heavy penalty of a pig (six *wais* size) and a bottle of wine. Any thief, man or woman found guilty is penalised by complete saving of his/ her hair and applying lime and turmeric paste all around the person's body, and to parade naked the whole village by shouting himself he is the thief (*kei inn lupa mee-ye*), and imposing a penalty fee of a pig and bottle of wine.

(iii) Some Important Persons in the Society

Besides the political members, there are certain specific persons who play important roles in the Chothe society. They are: (*i*) *Thiempu* (priest), (*ii*) *Assain or Ashei* (assistant priest who assists in any ceremony), (*iii*) *Thao-lum* (oil manufacturer) and, (*iv*) *Rengchang* (in-charge of musical instruments), (*v*) *Sapu* (in-charge of meat/ cowherd), (*vi*) *Athem* (propitiating deities) and, (*vii*) *Thirsu* (blacksmith), (see Gupta, 2000: 17).

Thiempu, the village priest is sometimes identified as local medicine man. He occupies a high status in the society because he is highly regarded, respected and given due reverence for his social responsibilities though he does not have any political power like any of the village council members. The female priestess is called *theimpi*. She also performs certain minor rites and rituals. But she plays an important role during child-birth and in the child's naming ceremony. There are two types of *thiempu*, one is the officially assigned village priest who belongs to *Thao, Marim, Parpa* or *Rangshai* clans and he is the deity's keeper, while the other *thiempu* is a professional priest or medicine man an expert in the art of magic, witchcraft, charms and spells, and has vast knowledge on herbal treatments for various illnesses. He performs rites and ritual for different kinds of sick patients but he cannot perform important community or village rituals. In case, the actual head priest was unavailability for certain important rituals, the task is carried out by the assigned assistant priest called *assain-pu* or *ashei* who usually belongs to either of the clans mentioned above. It is a religious taboo for people from other clans to perform village rituals. Another important person is the subordinate priest (*athem*) who arranges items for any important ritualistic ceremonies. The *Thao-lum* is the linseed manufacturer. *Rengchang* is in-charge of the king's musical instruments like drums (*hung*), gongs (*shum*), bagpiper (*ruicham*), mithun horns (*siki*), mouth instrument (*changchou*). The *Sapu* (Cowherd) is responsible to supervise and distribute any ceremonial or festival meat according to the traditional norm and also oversee the social decorum. The blacksmith (*Thirsu*), though does not have any political position, is an important person in the society for his distinctive profession. The socio-political and economic lives of Chothe people are well described in the book of T.C. Das (1945).

Chothe Economy

The Chothe economy may be classified as an indigenous tribal economy because the majority depends on the natural resources that surround them. Agriculture is the main stable economy of the people, who practice both wet and jhum (slash and burn or shifting) cultivation. Except agriculture, there is no other specific common economy carried out by the entire Chothe community. Their secondary income varies from region to region, since they are all located in different geographical settings. Those settled near the valley do practice wet cultivation while the villages which inhabits on the top or slope of the mountains like, Khongkhang, New-Wangparal, Old-Wangparal and Lunghu still engages in jhuming. Except Lamlanghupi, all other Chothe villages depends their livelihood on forest produces like firewood, timber, bamboo, vegetables, fruits, bamboo handicrafts, etc. But nowadays this indigenous economy is shifting towards the modern mode of economy as large number of them is found interested in the secondary and tertiary service sectors (see Table 14 and 15).

The Chothe society as a whole is undergoing a complete transformation as compared to some sixty years ago or more, from the underdeveloped socio-economic stage to modernised advance stage of development. Each village is now electrified. Almost every family owns a colour television (even with Tata-Sky TV network connection), Video Compact Disc (VCD) players, radio, tape player, telephone and mobile phones, etc. Roads and sanitation are improving, automobile owners are increasing, thatched roofs have been replaced with tin, *kacha* types of houses have become a semi-*pucca* and *pucca* houses. Attitudes, lifestyles and food habits are also changing. The people have become more materialistic, adapting to modern and western cultures influenced by movies, songs, social interactions, exposure, western education besides others critical factors, that is why, the Chothe rich indigenous culture and heritage is seen gradually dilapidating.

Most Chothe elders claimed that there was a kind of economic division of labour in olden days on the basis of gender. They said like farming, hunting, fishing, collecting fire wood, construction of houses, guarding the village, etc., and other heavy major works were done by men, while the women cooked food, looked after the babies, brewed rice beer and wine, collected vegetables and fruit from the jhum fields and occasionally helped in plantation as well as in the harvest. Men involves in village political administration while women were excluding from participation. The unmarried daughters helped their mothers in cooking, pounding rice, plucking cotton, yarning, weaving and with other domestic chores. T.C. Das with regards to the Chothe indigenous industries stated that, "Spinning and weaving are the two most important industries of the Purum (Chothe). Cotton is grown in individual *jhums*. Almost every household produces sufficient quantity of this stuff to meet his annual necessity" (1945: 100). They claimed in the past some of their colourful clothes made from their own cotton and loom were exchanged with salt, earthen pots and other metallic objects with their neighbouring valley people. Today, the Chothe does not grow cotton anymore, they depend the yarn from markets. The value in traditional division of labour is also declining.

(i) Eastern Chothe Group

As observed, the Khongkhang villagers are the hardest working people among all the Chothe community, despite their geographical setting located on the sloppy mountain peak. The village is blessed with rich natural resources that still enjoy the fruit of abundance.

Jhuming: The Khongkhang villagers still practices their traditional slash and burn or Jhuming cultivation. Clearing and burning of their forest area begins usually in the months of March-April, where each individual or family carved out its own plot from the main village forest areas. The plantation began within one-two weeks before the expected monsoon rain. The whole forest area belongs to the community, so no individual without prior permission of the village chief/authority may use any part of the forest land for his own benefit. If anyone desires to use the land for himself, he may notify to the village authority in its meeting. The jhum fields are usually very large, approximately 20-30 hectares. But while clearing it about 30-40 per cent of the forest trees is wasted and about 40-50 per cent is sold to the valley people in Kilo-ton (KB-5x5 sq. ft.). The rest is used by them. The price of the firewood and charcoal depends on the quality and size of the logs and the current local market rates.

Joined Labour or Group Working (*Lomrui or Lomjui*): The Khongkhang people still maintains a remarkable old feature of indigenous joined labour or group working system characterised by a strong community feeling in their socio-economic activities, like the 'Self Help Group' (SHG). There are two type of join labour. Firstly, for example a person may invite relatives/ friends/ neighbours to help him on his plantation/ harvest/ threshing, etc., by assuring them to provide food, drinks and other refreshment items for that day only. This type of 'join labour' is known as "*Lomrui*", meaning 'working with friends'. Similarly, another join labour or group working when organised among 10-20 or more individuals who voluntarily agreed to work in each member's field on rotation basis as per the mutual agreement of the scheduled fixed, is known as "*Lomjui*", meaning 'following the working scheduled'. The term also implies as 'following the team leader'. The synonymous word for *lomjui* is "*jaitha*", literally it means 'plantation of talisman', which is understood as 'sound sleep', but the latent meaning is that one owes one's labour. Traditionally, such group is formed voluntarily among relatives, friends or immediate neighbours. But now the groups are often formed within an organisation like the church, youth organisation or women's society, etc. This kind of joint labour or group working is organised when the work requires a large number of individuals like in wet and jhum cultivation for ploughing, plantation, harvest, threshing, house construction and social functions. In case, a member is unable to join the group on the scheduled day the concerned person sends a substitute, his/ her family member. But if he is absent without prior information, he has to pay a fine, agreed by the group.

Bamboo Shoot (*Antui*): The Khongkhang Chothe is famous for its fermented bamboo shoots called "Antui" (in Meitei *soibum*) that serves as a delicacy for any types of pork, chicken, fish and chutney dishes in the state. It is one of their main incomes. The village is rich in natural forest resources like timber, charcoal, wild-animals, fruits and vegetables. It is also favourable for the growth of variety of bamboo species like *Bambusa tulda*, *Dendrocalamus giganteus* and *Melocans bambusoides* too (Laiba, 1992: 116). After the plantation season, the villagers early in the morning by 4-5 am during August-October they usually ventures deep into the forest about 1-3 kms to collect this specific bamboo shoots and return by 9-10 am. Soon after their lunch, they peel and sliced the bamboo shoots into small pieces either at their home or at a relative or friend's house where they chit-chatted, gossiped and cracked jokes and spent their day doing the work. The simple folk living style needs to be admired for a strong sense of community feelings and harmony. The sliced bamboo shoots are washed and deposited in a big bamboo basket (about 500-1500 litres capacity). The basket is then, wrapped air-tight with the wild-yam leaves (*Baira abu*) or plastic sheets and is left to ferment for a minimum period of three months (see Pic. 86). The longer it ferments, it taste better.

This fermented bamboo shoot (*antui/ soibum*) has high demand in the neighbouring markets of Moreh, Pallel and Kakching. They sold it in bulk. The current price ranges from rupees forty to one hundred per kilogram. Ironically, this very special Khongkang Chothe '*antui*' is popularly known by many as *Kakching soibum* because it is mainly available in Kakching market. Another reason is that the Chothe does not have the knowledge to patent their special product. M.T. Laiba described that the fermented bamboo shoot is rich in protein, free amino acids, soluble sugars, ascorbic acid and thiamine. This bamboo shoot contains the chemical composition of lactic acid, titrable acids (mainly, formic acetic and lactic acids) and volatile acids (formic and acetic acids), (1992: 116).

Hunting and Fishing: Since T.C. Das' last visit to the Chothe Central-cluster group, the environment and many economic aspects have considerably changed. The thick forest once with many wild animals and varieties of vegetables had depleted. Hunting is no longer a part of their old tradition for most of the Chothe villagers, except for the Khongkhang people and few neighbouring villages of Maring, Lamkang and Thadou-Kuki living around the area. Khongkhang still carry on recreational activities of hunting and fishing because they have thick forests, gorges and streams. There are about ten persons in Khongkhang who own licensed guns for hunting wild-animals like deer, wild-boars, jackals, leopards, jungle fowls, monkeys, etc. They also use different types of indigenous animal traps (*Chaang*) and fish traps (*ruu*). Hunting is often carried out individually or in group. But fishing is usually done in group. The Khongkhang villagers fishes in the Lokchou stream and other nearby streams during January-April. They used different traditional methods like fishing nets (*Inn*), net-baskets (*anga-ru*), bleaching powder, dynamos, local made grenades and varieties of indigenous leaves, barks or roots of many poisonous shrubs called '*Uo*' that are pounded before use. They usually fished in deep waterfalls, cleavages and shallow streams.

Khetrichou said in olden days, "the Chothe sometimes fished at Leimatak River and Loktak Lake and other big streams". But now the Chothe of Lamlanghupi and Central-cluster group fished in the nearby catchments, watershed areas, small streams or water clogging areas while some families rear different types of fishes in their own pond for domestic consumption. The Chothe hardly sells their fishes and domestic animals in the market.

Fruits: Variety of fruits (*thei*), especially citrus and other indigenous vegetables are found abundantly in Khongkhang than in other Chothe villages or other adjoining villages. Fruits like mandarin oranges (*theithum*), *theirupok* (a kind of fruit like an apple that is extremely sour), lemon (*theithui*), mango (*theinou*), jack-fruit (*theipong*), fig (*theichang*), goose-berry (*theichura or suru*), pineapples (*kehom*), banana (*amot*), tezpatta (*Cinnamomum tamala*), etc. is grown in this area. There is a good scope for commercialisation of these fruits.

(ii) Economy of the Chothe Central-Cluster Group

Agriculture is the main economy of these people. In earlier days, rice, banana, yam, cucumber, pumpkin, melon, water-melon, chillies, soya-beans and variety of beans were cultivated in their jhum fields. After they moved down at the foothills near the valley and taken to wet-cultivation, most of them had given up to jhum cultivation, planting indigenous fruits and vegetables. Their production has been substantially reduced to mere kitchen garden. They now entirely depend on almost every valley produce like rice, potatoes, cabbage, mustard, dhal, peas, salt, sugar, tea, milk, fish, meat and others, except for firewood. The villages of Ajouhu, Tampakhu, Phantu, Leirungtabi, New-Wangparal sells forest produce like firewood and timber to the neighbouring valley people. Sometimes they leased the forest area for a certain period and the money becomes the corpus-fund of the community.

The secondary source of income of Central-cluster is mostly derived by selling firewood and different handicraft products to the valley people. They have specific names for each type of basket depending on its shape, size and design. T. C. Das has categorised the baskets into four types based on design and usage: (i) Carrying basket (*Laan*), (ii) Storing basket (*Tai*), (iii) Haversack basket (*Laan-wang*) and, (iv) Tray basket (*Barei*) respectively (1945: 95). Different types of carrying baskets are known as *Nunghai laan* (swinging carrier basket), *Laander* (semi-hole basket) and the rest of carrier baskets are identified depending on the shape and size by using a suffix of *asinte* (small) and *alokpa* (big). There are broadly four standard measuring storage baskets [see Table 16(ii)]. The other varieties of baskets are known as *Tai-don* (plinth basket), *Tai-wang* (basket with small holes), etc. The haversack is known as *Pai,* and a suffix of *asinte* (small) or *alokpa* (big) is used for its size. The fourth type of basket, shaped like tray or flat in design is call as *Buhu, Balei, Lungnik* and *Wai-wang. Buhu* is the largest tray basket generally having a diameter of 5-6 ft., while *Balei* the most common winnow has a diameter of 2-2 ½ ft. in circumferences. The former two types are tightly knitted but the *Lungnik* and *Wai-wang* are loosely knitted like nets. The *Lungnik* has smaller holes compared to *Wai-wang* that has larger holes measuring about one sq.cm.

The Chothe also competes with other tribes like Maring, Moyon, Monsang, Anal, Lamkang in their craftsmanship of carpentry and handicraft works. The valley people entirely depend on hill tribes for variety of handicraft products like bamboo and cane baskets, winnows and other craftsmanship. The price differs in the quality and size of the products. For example, a simple *Taidon* costs rupees twenty to fifty; while a good quality *Shangphai* the standard measuring basket cost about Rs 300-500 (see Pic. 92). Most of these handicraft products are sold at Pallel and Kakching markets.

In spite of earnings on an average of about Rs 100-200 per day, the majority of Chothe villagers did not save or invest their income (which could be more now). The society that was once self-sufficient is now economically poor and dependent unlike their neighbouring communities Anal, Lamkang, Moyon, Kom, etc., whose socio-economic condition has improved in the past few decades. The sad fact is that, many Chothe of Central-cluster have lost over their land ownership rights to the neighbouring Meitei, since they sold it directly or indirectly by leasing out to meet their financial crisis. Besides, many of their indigenous plants and vegetables also have disappeared as they no longer practiced jhum cultivation.

(iii) Western Chothe Group

The Western Chothe, unlike the Eastern and Central-cluster groups primarily depends on agriculture i.e. wet-cultivation and grows variety of paddies (rice). But their secondary source of income is derived from selling their distilled liquor or alcohol (*leizu*) especially to the neighbouring Meitei communities (see Pic.70). People who brew and distil liquor do rear piggery that greatly supplement to their income because pigs are highly valued and has high demand even in the market. Almost every family has small kitchen garden to meet the shortage of vegetable supplies. The Western Chothe men-folks are generally enterprising and self-employed in various professions like house construction, carpentry, drivers, etc. Group hunting and river fishing has become a myth since they no longer practised it anymore after they settled at the foothills, surrounded by paddy fields. Often meat and fishes are purchased from Bishnupur and Ningthoukhong towns. Families owning pond rear variety of fishes meant for only family's consumption. Hongpa said that "in the earlier days, they extensively reared or domesticated a number of animals like horses, goats, sheep, bison (Mithun), cows, buffaloes, pigs, dogs, ducks, chickens, swans, cats, etc. but today only few household rear such animals due to the lack of pasture ground besides other socio-economic reasons".

The Western Chothe like their Central-cluster group critically suffers from land ownership rights. They claimed their country covered the entire area of North Churachanpur (Henglep Constituency) extending up to the present Bishnupur town. But now their area has been considerably reduced to just a few acres since many communities had encroached. They said that in olden days the land value was very cheap and their great forefathers would simply exchange with some rare metallic objects or sold it directly for just a few rupees a big plot of their land especially to the immigrant valley people (Meitei/ Cachari) and other surrounding tribes after they befriended their forefathers with a bottle of wine or a rooster. For example, Hongpa Yuhlung (72/M) said, "My grandfather exchanged the whole mound cultivable area of a hill to a fellow immigrant Meitei for just a rooster and few rupees. Now I own a very small portion of cultivation land that is to be distributed among my six sons. But later nothing will be left for my grandchildren anymore". Cheidon Hiyang (38/M) similarly stated that, "My grandfather sold away our huge arable land about 20-30 hectares for just a sum of rupees two hundred to a neighbouring immigrant Meitei who settled near the Loktak Lake. So, I am poor now because what was left is very small to be shared among my five brothers". These are few examples, how the Chothe lost their rights over land ownership to the surrounding communities. It is also seen that during 1980's till 2000 many Chothe sold and leased their cultivable land either to bribe or buy government jobs for their educated children or for pursuing training or further studies outside the State. All these indicate that the Western Chothe is striving with difficulties especially in their socio-economic spheres. Their problem seems to lie in their economic backwardness, narrow attitudes, idealistic views, sense of minority, love for sedentary life, lack of exposure and connection with outsiders.

Occupation and Employment

The most stable job sought among unemployed Chothe youth is government jobs. The motivation for entrepreneurship or self-employ is lacking although some began their inclination. The Table 14 shows out of 2675 population, only 184 (6.84 per cent) individuals are government employees. Out of 184 government employees there are only seven gazetteer officers, viz.; (i) Thao Hopson of Tampakhu, the Sub-Deputy Commissioner (SDC), (ii) Hiyang Sichong Ibohal of Lamlanghupi, Executive Engineer (EE), (iii) Yuhlung Standhope of Laininghhu, the Election Commissioner, Under Secy. (EC), (iv) Maigai John of Lamlanghupi, a Veterinary Doctor, and three Lecturers, (v) Hiyang Romo of Lamlanghupi Assistant Professor in Department of Mathematics, Delhi University, (vi) Thao Paingam of Ajouhu and (vii) Makan Davan of Chumbang are Lecturers in United College, Chandel.

The villages of Tampakhu, Lamlanghupi, Phantu and Chumbang showed more employees in the category of Govt. Civil Employees. In the category of Active-Services: (polices and armies) Chumbang, Tampakhu, Chandolpokpi consecutively ranks first, second and third respectively (see Table 14). Overall Chumbang, Tampak-hu, Lamlanghupi and Phuntu ranks first, second, third and fourth in the total number of government employees. Many Chothe viewed that the state is very partial in offering jobs to the tribal. Some believed that the corrupt socio-political system of the state and their poor socio-economic condition are responsible for many graduates working in different underpaid private institutions as they do not have enough money or political backing to bribe Ministers and high Officials. In the bribery culture of Manipur bidding the highest amount for any government job is very intense. Keidi said "It is an open-secret; even a Peon's post is worth rupees fifty to eighty thousand. So, if the position is bigger one the bribe's price is more in term of few Lakhs".

Despite the government's effort to educate and develop the villagers through various rural developmental projects and schemes like *NRIGES,*

Table 17: Distribution of Occupations Government employees (Personal data 2004-05)

Govt. employees	Ajouhu (Purum khullen)	Bethel Happy land*	Chandonpokpi	Chothe Khunou	Chumbang (Purum)	Khongkhang	Lainingbu	Lamlanghupi	Lamlangion*	Leiruingtabi*	Lungbu*	Lungleh*	New-Wangparal	Old-Wangparal	Phatu (Chandrapoto)	Salemhar*	Tumpakhu (Purum)	Ziontiang	Total	Percentage
No. of households	38	4	19	14	72	49	35	53	13	5	6	10	25	21	54	10	72	31	531	-
Total Population	164	13	91	67	336	291	204	296	42	27	39	50	138	111	260	42	332	186	2689	-
Person in civil services of various dept's.	-	-	3	-	17	10	8	21	6	-	1	2	-	-	20	2	24	-	114	4.23
Person in active services (Police & Army)	3	-	6	4	22	4	2	5	-	-	-	2	3	4	5	-	8	2	70	2.60
Total	**3**	**-**	**9**	**4**	**39**	**14**	**10**	**26**	**6**	**-**	**1**	**4**	**3**	**4**	**25**	**2**	**32**	**2**	**184**	**6.84**

Note: Asterisk (*) denotes new settlements not recognised yet by the Census of India.

conducting workshops and seminars on numerous socio-economic and political issues, schemes on tree re-plantations, construction of roads, maintenance or repair of roads, construction of sanitary, drinking water reservoirs, low cost latrines, emphasis on the use of Bio-mass gases, etc. it is disheartening to say that much is done despite these numerous projects and schemes offered. Due to diversion of funds in many ways, majority of the actual rural benefiters are seen neglected or they did not get the expected benefits from such programmes. However, the Chothe in general is rapidly changing from traditional to modernisation and westernisation like any societies or the 'Coorgs of Mysore' where the Lower-class groups Sanskritised themselves to be like the Brahmins or the Upper-Class groups as studied by Srinivas', and also like the Ankara town of Turkey where their age old-traditional values were replaced soon by modernisation and westernisation values as described by Daniel Lerner (1972).

Table 15 shows the exclusive Chothe population engaged in agriculture and other allied economic activities. The total number of individuals engaged in agriculture and other Non-Government services is about 887. But out of which 521 (i.e. 19.37 per cent) are prominent farmers, and 366 [(887-521), (i.e. 13.61 per cent)] are individuals engaged in Non-Government organisations and other private institutions as self-employees. Specific self-employed women comprises 181 (i.e. 6.73 per cent), the vocational weavers comprises of 81 (3 per cent), private school teachers 32 (1.2 per cent), private vehicle drivers 8 (0.29 per cent), Catholic Nuns 3 (0.11 per cent) and Evangelists, reverends and pastors comprises 44 (1.63 per cent) respectively. The total number of self-employees (both men and women) is almost double the total number of government employees.

The number of person engaged in the secondary and tertiary service sectors including government and non-government sectors is about 550 (366 + 184) i.e. 20.45 per cent which is slightly higher than the total number of farmers 521 (i.e. 19.37 per cent), (see Table 14 and 15). This indicates a movement in labour force from primary to secondary and tertiary job sectors.

Measurements: Length and Volume

The most common Chothe indigenous standard measurement unit of length is called "wei/ wai/ vai", meaning the left length of a man's fist with pointed thumb. This unit is used in measuring the length, height and breadth (size) of a pig, door, window, basket, etc. The unit of a short distance is measured in term of "Lam" or "Lam-chei", meaning 'standard yard stick' which is the outstretched arm length of a mature man. Thirdly, unit of volume is measured by a storage basket. The standard storage basket is *Shangphai* (*Shangbai* in Meitei) often used for measuring the amount of paddy.[6]

Table 18: Distribution of Chothe Occupation: Non-Govt. Employees (Personal data 2004-05)

Occupations	Ajouhu (Purum khullen)	Bethel Happy land *	Chandonpokpi	Chothe Khunou	Chumbang (Purum)	Khongkhang	Laininghu	Lamlangkhupi	Lamlangon*	Leirungtabi*	Lungnu *	Lungleh *	New-Wangparal	Old-Wangparal	Phaini (Chandrapoto)	Salemihar*	Tampakhu (Purum)	Ziontlang	Total	Percentage
NFarmers	73	5	22	7	19	33	26	23	8	2	15	9	41	17	59	6	45	111	521	19.37
Women self employees	-	4	3	11	11	55	23	26	6	7	-	-	-	4	-	-	31	-	181	6.73
Weavers	5	1	-	1	6	3	17	13	2	-	2	-	3	13	-	6	6	6	81	3
Private school teachers	-	-	-	3	9	1	-	12	1	1	-	-	1	1	-	2	1	-	32	1.2
Drivers	-	-	-	-	-	1	1	2	1	-	-	-	-	-	-	-	2	3	8	0.29
Nuns (Sisters)	-	-	-	1	-	-	-	-	-	-	-	1	-	-	-	-	-	-	3	0.11
Evangelist and Pastors	2	-	3	2	8	4	2	3	-	-	-	1	6	3	-	-	-	10	44	1.63
Total	81	10	28	25	59	96	71	82	17	10	17	10	50	38	61	15	87	130	887	100

(Please note that under the women self-employed category I have clubbed enterprising professions together who comprise of small shop owners, bamboo shoot and fire-wood sellers, artisans, liquor distillers, etc.)

Sometimes, *Lam* or *Lam-chei* is also used for measuring the amount of paddy after threshing. The paddy is piled up like a pyramid after threshing and winnowing, and is measured by *Lam-chei*; firstly, the based or circumference of the paddy gathered and then the height from the base to the tip portion.

The amount of paddy is calculated in term of *shang-pot,* on the basis of their indigenous arithmetic method [see Table 16(i) and Table 16(ii)]. These traditional measuring units are still used by the Lamlanghupi. But the Eastern and Central-cluster Chothe have discarded the method of *lam-chei* and *shangphai* and have replaced it with kilogram and "tin" (a twenty litres mustard oil can, influenced by the neighbouring valley people).

Table 19(i): Chothe Standard Measurement of Volume in Indigenous Units

Sl. No.	Units in Chothe	Literal meaning	Equivalent volume of each unit
1.	Khut-kot	Plunge of a hand	The bowl of a single hand. This is the smallest unit of volume.
2.	Khut-chop	Bowl of hands	The bowl of two hands of an adult (appx. A quarter or 200-250 ml or kg)
3.	Meeruk	Share basket	It is the smallest standard measuring basket for small quantities. Used for measuring uncooked rice. About 2½ khut-chops.
4.	Masung tai	Sharing inside, (*tai* means any storage basket)	This is the smallest measuring basket for volume for larger quantities. Equivalent to ten-fifteenth *khut-chops*. The diameter of the circumference is about 1 sqft. and appx. ½ ft high (appx. 1-1½ kg or lit.)
5.	Laitaang tai	Matured basket	This is a quarter basket, equivalent to two baskets of *masung tai* (appr. 10-12 kg or lit.)
6.	Leekhai or Lee tai	Half-basket or half-shares	This storage basket is equivalent to two *laitaang* or four baskets of *masung* basket.
7.	Shangphai	Paddy collected in basket by surfacing plain/ paddy basket	This is the largest standard storage basket. Equivalent to four *laitaang* or two *leekhai* baskets (Circumference = 2.3 ft, High = 1 ½ ft. app.)
8.	Shangpot `akha	One full load of paddy/ a bag full.	This is the amount of two *shangphai* or four *leekhai tai* of paddy. Almost equivalent to 100 kgs of rice bag.

Table 19(ii): Chothe Standard Measurement of Length in Indigenous Units/Methods

Sl. No.	Terms in Chothe	Literal meaning	Equivalent length of each unit
1.	Wa-ei or Wai, Vai	Left fist or wide or throw or grip.	This unit of length is measured from the base of one's closed left fist to the tip of pointed thumb of a matured man's hand (appx. 5 inches or ½ ft.)
2.	Khut-kap	The length of a hand/fingers	This unit of length is measured from the tip of a thumb to the tip of a middle finger (appx. 6 inches).

(Contd...)

3.	*Khut-taang* (*Cubit*)	The length of	This unit of length is measured from the base of an elbow a man's elbow to the tip of his middle finger. (appx. 1½ ft.)
4.	*Lam-chei* (*Fathom*)	The length of a man's arms or	This is a standard yard stick. Equivalent to the length of fully stretched arms of a standard yard stick mature man. It is measured from the tip of his right middle finger to the tip of his left middle finger. The length is approx. 6 ft. (approx. 24-25 *wa-ei*).

Indigenous Rice of Chothe

The Chothe seems to have varieties of indigenous paddies/ rice. Some of them are: (i) *Shang-maichamnu* (wrinkle face paddy), (ii) *Shang-jaire* (good health paddy) (iii) *Shang-koinu* (curve paddy), (iv) *Shang-likte* (tiny paddy), (v) *Shang-ningshiton* (oily paddy), (vi) *Chithou-ahang* (black sticky paddy), (vii) *Chithou-angou* (white sticky paddy), (viii) *Chithou-asan* (red sticky paddy), etc. These paddies are taken as feminine and derived the name from the nature and shaped of it. There is also a myth that says a rat helped them bring back the paddy of an old woman that was carried away by the strong river current while fleeing from a war. According to them, in olden days the seedling of paddies are preserved in big dried bamboo tubes fitted with a tight lid, while some wrapped them tightly with a cloth or store them in earthen pots. Nowadays they preserved in big bamboo baskets and gunny bags. Many Chothe indigenous paddies are believed to have extinct, since the majority of them have taken to wet-cultivation and used only High Yielding varieties of seeds (rice) provided by the Indian Council of Agriculture Research (ICAR) Imphal, Manipur considering to be more productive. But it is found that only few Chothe families of the Eastern and Central-cluster still uses their old indigenous paddies as it is more suitable for their jhum cultivation. The villages located close to the valley favour wet-cultivation and used local paddies known as *Phourel, Moirang-phou, KD, Hui-kap, Angan-phou* and *RI,* etc.

Chothe Beverage and Wine (*Zu*)

Since time immemorial the Chothe have been brewing different types of beverages like rice-beers, wine or liquor that form as an important part of their food item. According to their nature of rites and rituals certain types of rice-beers and wine are used. The Chothe call any types of alcoholic beverages; rice-beers and wine (liquor) as "Yu/ Zu". There are four distinctive types of wines (*Zu*); but three are rice-beers named according to the method of brewing viz.: (i) *Zu-ngou* (white rice-beer), (ii) *Zu-ting* (fermented cooked rice-beer) and (iii) *Shawai-zu* (fermented husk rice-beer); and (iv) The last one is the distilled liquor known as *Lei-zu* (lit. sold wine), (see Pic. 69 and 70). The most important substance required in brewing rice-beers and liquor is yeast called *A-choi,* meaning 'the touch'. It is prepared by powdering the *ngoupok* (dried germinating seeds of the paddy) and little piece of *jangzu* (dried bark of a kind of climber plant found in the deep forest). The two flours are mixed well with water and made into small round cakes. Then it is placed above six inches high husk bed specially prepared in a safe corner and is covered with some straw and old blankets and made it dry for about two weeks. The quality of rice-beers and liquor depends very much on the quality of such yeast. Different methods of brewing rice-beers and the liquor are also found mentioned in T.C. Das work (1945: 87-90) sub-titled as, *'Drinks and their Preparation'.* Rice-beer is brewed even today for self-consumption and for festivals. Commercial distillation of liquor is practiced in Lamlanghupi by both the Christian and non-Christian families as their secondary economy. Customers are mostly the neighbouring Meitei and other tribes. At present a bottle (750 ml) cost Rs 20 and contains between 20 to 40 per cent v/v of alcohol.[7] The quality of alcohol varies from season to season, and also from family to family.

According to some Chothe elders, *Api Shang-nginluh Shang-ningthum* the first daughter in their genealogical myth was the first woman to brew wine. But Roushi said the old widow in their legend *'Api Shorkim Yuhlung'* was the first woman to brew rice-beer (*Zu*). According to him, one sunny day *Api Shorkim Yuhlung* after working the whole day returned home hungry exhausted and tired from her jhum field and was desperately looking for something to eat. She found nothing except her old rice package wrapped in the wild-yam leaves meant to throw away. When she opened it she got a sweet smell that tempted her to taste it. Later she found the taste was good and happened to eat more. But after awhile tired and intoxicated, she feels sleepy and slept away. The next morning she realised that she had a sound sleep. Thereafter, she began to experiment secretly and enjoy herself the fermented rice in different forms as rice-beer. One day some village youth went to invite her for a wedding feast and one of them asked her for some water to drink, instead she (*Api Shorkim*) offered her rice-beer to them, on the pretext that she did not have fresh water. The youth after drinking later realised that it was refreshing and boosting their strength. Thereafter, the news of the rice-beer spread in their village and those interested began to visit her house. Some youth who enjoyed her drink requested her to stop working in the field and rather insisted her to brew rice-beer for them who willing to pay the price for it. Thus, *Api Shorkim* became the first Chothe woman to prepare *Zu/ Yu* (wine) the rice-beer that becomes a very important food habit/ menu of the Chothe, so also in their socio-magico-religious activities too.

In olden days, the practice of using wine in a child's naming ceremony and other ritualistic activities is also described in the sacred text of *Chothe*

Thangmei Pakhangpa (*CTP*). The elders of Lamlanghupi have given an important account of Chothe wine connected with the early Poirei (Meitei) king. It is said that one day the Chothe king invited the Poirei king for dinner and offered him his best wine (*Sawai-zu* the fermented husk rice beer). The Poirei king compliment the Chothe king that his Chothe wine was the best in the entire country that he had never tasted which was so refreshing after his long journey. Then, the Poirei king enquired the Chothe king in which customary ceremony their wine was most sacredly used. The Chothe king replied that the Chothe used such special wine mostly sacredly first on their child's naming ceremony and other significant magico-religious ceremonies too. The Poirei king on learning assured the Chothe king that he too would follow the Chothe custom to keep up their friendship. Thereafter, it is believed that the Poirei (Meitei) king declared a decree in his kingdom that Chothe wine shall be used in any child's naming ceremony, and is believed to have initiated by himself this custom among the Meitei. Until recent times, it is believed that this custom had been practicing by the succeeding Manipuri kings and other royal families when they bore a child who sent men from the palace to get Chothe wine for the ceremony. The Chothe as part of their courtesy and friendship to the king provided the palace men a shawl if the child was a male and a sarong (*Mekla*) for a girl, besides giving their special wine. Later, when the demand for Chothe wine/ liquor increases among the valley people, this particular local wine/ liquor came to be known as *"leizu"*, meaning 'wine that is bought' by others. The Chothe claimed that this tradition was in practice till the time of Maharaj Chandrakriti of Manipur (1850-86), who was also known as Naochinglen Nongdren Khomba a close ally of Chothe (Hudson, 1908: 114).

Types of House

According to Y. Jatrasing, Y. Maipak and Miss H. Atonpi (65) there are three types of Chothe houses (Inn/ een). They are: (i) Pongshang, (ii) Shangkai inn and (iii) Shangte.

The pongshang is an elongated house built above the ground with open courtyard or veranda. The front part is decorated in "X" style craved with wood and is little higher than the back part. The hearth is kept in the centre of the house. For example, the bachelor's house (ruishang/ loishang) design is a type of pongshang constructed in the village.

The Shangkai inn/ een means the elongated hut/ house. It is rectangular in design with equal high in the front and back unlike the pongshang house. It has a veranda and the inner part is divided into three section. Most Shangkai house is built on plinth where the front door is normally faced towards the east and with a back door towards the north-west. It is built with wooden/

bamboo pillars, straight beams and the roof was covered with thatch. The first section of the room on the south is the master bed room where father sleeps. The second section or the middle is the mother's bed and the third section on the extreme southwest is the daughter's bed. While boys sleeps on the first and second section opposite to their father's and mother's bed, or in the bachelor's house if adult.

Shangte means 'small hut/ house'. It often refers to jhum hut or any extended room or separate small house with single room built around the main house like for storage room.

Notes

1. *Bungkung:* The word "Bungkung" literally means 'rhizosphere of the banyan tree'. But it means 'around the base of a banyan tree' (*Bung* - banyan tree, *Kung* – rhizosphere/ base of a plant). In olden days, the three political houses/ unit of the Chothe village council i.e. *Ulinta, Tangnga-rinta and Nungak-luthei bungkung* are symbolically identified with three separate monolithic stones erected at some corner around the banyan tree or sacred grove. So, whenever a village council meeting is called for or festivals are held, people gathered around their own respective monolithic stones, thus, it derives its name. The remnants of such places still exist around the sacred grove of Lamlanghupi, New-Wangparal and abundant Old-Wangparal (see Pic. 60, 61).

2. *Sikan-chei:* It means *thrashing/ wiping stick of an animal*. It refers to a special cane-stick used by *Pakhanglakpa* the *Tangnga-rinta* leader to discipline any village youth for their misbehaviour, thief or disobeying the socio-religious norms especially on the last day of the festival. The functional application of this cane-stick is like the policeman stick.

3. *Tolaihong* or *Phambakpa:* Literally *tolaihongpa,* means 'bringing or carrying the palanquin', while *Phambakpa,* means 'feast of merit or feast of social position/ status'. Both terms are synonymous. The Palanquin symbolises power and authority, and only the deserving person can be seated. The former is ancient term associated with palanquin/ litter while the latter is considered a laymen term for grand merit feast.

4. *Thing-bompa, thing-tick pot* and *sackpoi*: These terms implies a different literal meaning that significantly refers to a very important political ceremony practiced by the Chothe in olden days. It refers to the distribution of political portfolios and functions, where the members can exercise their veto power and authority sanctioned through that secret scroll sticks. These secret scrolls or sceptres are now symbolically represented by simple bamboo sticks. It is traditionally kept secretly on the left side of the veranda of a *Luplak's* house in a 'small basket' called "*sackpoi thing*", meaning 'secret scrolls container'. Traditionally, these sticks are taken down from the hiding place on the first and last day of the *Innnampei Rhin* festival only. The procedure of '*Thing-bompa*' is that if there is any vacant position lying in the village political hierarchy (especially in *Urinta* and *Tangnga-ta*) the post is/ are filled on such festive occasion, while others who still occupy the positions are reminded their positions, or in case of any

change, it is re-shuffled. This ceremony is carried out by the *Zupai* who placed the sticks (scrolls) on the ground, numbered and re-assigns them. The position unoccupied or scroll not received is removed symbolically from the main group position in row. The Meitei called this annual practice of distribution and counting (re-assigning) of such political portfolio by a stick as 'Cheithapa/ Cheitharol Kumpapa', (see S.N. Parratt, 2005). It probably owes it origin to the early Pong/ Shan/ Kachin people, whom the Chothe and other old tribes of Manipur continued this tradition as part of their ancestral connection.

5. *Tongkaipa* and *Zurum:* The term *Tong-kaipa,* literally means 'pronouncing or stretching or spelling the words' which actually means 'prayer'. So, when any kind of drinks or meals are being served to a person, a person offered a prayer with the wine and meat on the ground thanking Gods, seeking blessing and also protection from any kind of evils.

   The *zurum* means 'the custom of passing the wine glasses'. Soon after offering a prayer or *tongkaipa* the *zurum* act follows where the wine is being served by a *rui* to all the members present in the house/ occasion on the basis of their seniority or hierarchical position - *Hulak* to *Ruis* and lay members. While offering this drink/ wine they strictly follow their courtesy custom, where the server by his right hand holds the glass at the bottom and his left hand supports his right hand at the base of the wrist, and by slightly bending his body.

6. *Shangphai:* This is the largest Chothe standard measuring basket, approximately about 2 ft. in diameter and 1½ ft. High (see Pic. 92). The paddy is always measured in basket by levelling with a bamboo pipe call *Utong.* Rimlil Marim (56/M) of Lunghu said the term *Shangphai* is originally a Chothe word, although now every Meitei uses. According to him, 'Paddy' in Chothe means "Shang", but Meitei call it is as "Phou"; while 'the Valley/ Plain' in Chothe means "*Phai*" (flat land/ valley), but in Meitei it is call as "Tampak". So, he said in the early days the Meitei have acculturated many Chothe and other indigenous tribal languages in their social discourses but now the reverse is happening because the valley people have become dominant cultural group.

7. The alcohol percentage (20 to 40 per cent v/v) of Chothe liquor brought from Miss Donnu Yuhlung of Lamlanghupi was measured by Dr R.K. Singh, Department of Biochemistry, NEHU, Shillong.

CHAPTER - 4

Chothe Mythology:
The Basic Foundation of their
Belief and Practices

Introduction: Myth and Legend

The *Concise Oxford Dictionary* defined myth as 'a traditional narrative usually involving supernatural or imaginary persons and embodying popular ideas on natural or social phenomena, etc. It is a traditional story accepted as history; which serves to explain the world view of a people usually connected with religion'. Therefore, the story of a person or people related with an event after many years become a history; later the history becomes a legend; and thereafter, the legend becomes a myth. In Greek *muthos,* it means 'just a tale or mythos something one utters, in a wide range of senses: a statement, a story, the plot of a play'. But for Plato, the first known user of the term, *muthologia* meant no more than the telling of the stories, like the Greek tales of Perseus and Medusa, Odysseus and the Cyclops, Oedipus and Iocaste or Hermes and the cattle of Appolo (Kirk, 1998: 8).

But Stith Thompson (1955) argued that myth is somewhat different from an ordinary folktale. Accordingly, he defined myth as something that "has to do with the gods and their actions, with creation, and with the general nature of the universe and of the earth" (1955:484). This distinction between myth and folktale is seen very narrow, since it is often found confusing with one another because the folktales of some primitive societies are also connected with gods and demigods. The folklorists consider all myths as religious (sacred) stories but not all religious stories are myths; religious stories that involve the creation of the world (like the story in Genesis) are myths. However, religious stories that do not explain how things came to be in their present form (i.e. the legendary stories like hagiographies of famous saints, heroic persons) are not myths. It is stated that it was the early Christian theologians of the Greco-Roman, who first started to use the term "myth"

(Greek *muthos*) to mean "fable, fiction and lie" (Eliade, 1968:162). So, any mythical story is viewed by the Christian as a lie or a false story that negates their views or cannot be proved.

Malinowski and Mircea Eliade opine that one important function of myth is to provide an explanation for rituals. Eliade notes that, "In many societies rituals are considered important precisely because they were established by the mythical gods or heroes" (1968:7). But Robert M. Wallace (1987) says that Blumenberg suggest we shall discover myth, in its own way, also seek to produce a mastering of reality without which human life would be impossible.[1] This is why, every community or society or country has its own story, history, legend and myth in different forms that resulted out of historical eventful incidents comprising things like the first man and woman, a great warrior, a great religious reformer or a political leader, a famous hunter, a skilful magician that can be distinguished from others. All these stories may not necessarily have a connection with gods and goddesses or nature-myth or myth-ritual but are accepted as great tales because of the intervention and connection with gods in their experience and overcoming the hurdles. In short, myth can be understood as a complex story of a person and its surrounding compressed into a simple mythical story related with gods and goddesses or creation of the world, while the others may be considered as folktales or history.

Levi-Strauss (1972) in *The Structural Study of Myth* asserted that 'Myth of one culture is astoundingly very similar to the myth of a different culture', this he believes and proposed that there must be some universal law which guides basic human thought. This 'universal law of basic human thought' is seen in the mythical concepts of cosmology, animism and totemism like Oedipus, Zuni and Hopi origin myths. According to Levi-Strauss, each myth may seem unique, but it is this similar principle of 'universal law of human thought' that shows seemingly similar elements with one another, which he said is based on the criteria that "mythical thought always progressed from the awareness of oppositions toward their mediation" (1972: 299). In other words, myths consist of (1) elements that oppose or contradict each other, and (2) other elements that "mediate" or "resolve" those oppositions (*ibid.*). This 'similarity principle' of universal law of human thought does not necessarily mean that all myths of different culture of the world are exactly identical and have same structure and function, rather he means that most myths that oppose or contradict, mediate or resolve follow a similar trend in the construction of their beliefs and ritualistic practices (*ibid.:* 300). This assertion is criticised by Malinowski and G.S. Kirk that despite the similarity, many elements contradict itself. Therefore, William A. Lessa and Evon Z. Vogt stated that the term "myth", should be used advisedly as a convenient general label for an enormous diversity of narrative styles, contents, forms, and functions (1972: 249).

In a sense, it is believed that a large part of mythology is based upon a belief in 'soul or spirit' that is 'animist' or 'animism'. Myths that portrayed plants, inanimate objects, and non-human animals as personal beings are examples of animism in its more restrictive sense. But large amount of mythology focuses largely on corporeal beings rather than spiritual ones, the latter may be entirely absent in some cases. For example, the mythology of the Australian Aborigines largely focuses on corporeal, non-spiritual beings. The later mythology began to include numerous complex ideas about future life and purely spiritual being, as a result the overlap between mythology and animism widens. So, it is believed that a rich mythology do not necessarily depend on belief in many spiritual beings but on the criteria of possessing certain religious elements of supernatural characteristics. Thus, the idea of spirituality emerged only at the later period. Such features are observed in the context of the Chothe mythologies too.

Chothe Indigenous Religion

The Chothe though believed in one Supreme God (monotheistic), yet practices polytheism. They worship a host of cosmological gods, nature gods, village gods, house/ family gods, forest/ land gods and river/ water gods, etc. They called their god's according to the nature, characteristic and power endowed like *Thangvan-Rengpa* (Heavenly King) or *Chungthieng* (Almighty God), *Tui-laihu* (Water God), *Pu Lungchungpa* or *Pakhangpa* (Rain God), *Sanamahi* (God of Wealth), *Leimaren* (God of Fertility), *Shanglung* (God of paddy), *Shunglung* (*Bumbu*) means deities of four directions/ village gates), besides many other minor gods and goddesses. Similarly, various British Political Administrators like McCulloch, Hudson, J. Shakespeare, William Shaw, and national scholars like T.C. Das, Ansari, M. Kirti Singh, T.C. Tensuba and Bareh remarks in their anthologies, ethnographies and books that the Chothe worship the gods of *Pu Lungchungpa, Pakhangpa, Pu Soraren, Sanamahi* and *Leimaren*. They also believed in totems, superstitions, dreams and magic too.

Like many cultural myths of the world, the Chothe mythology also has its own distinctive genealogical myth which mediates or resolves their mythical belief of "*Pu Lungchungpa*" in the person of "Chothe Thangwai/ Thangmei Pakhangpa" the legendary king of Manipur. Therefore, the most important fundamental principle of Chothe indigenous religion lies in this doctrine of avatar or reincarnation or re-birth of *Pu Lungchungpa* their Supreme Guardian God of earth as 'Pakhangpa', which formed the bases of their animistic or ancestor-worshiper that is practiced till today.

Pu Lungchungpa: According to Chothe genealogical myth, they believed that from time immemorial they are the descendants of the 'Dragon-Python god' called as *Pu Lungchungpa,* literally "'One who sits above the rock' or 'the One above'", derived from its sitting behaviour, symbolising Emperor/ King/ Authority. By some, the Dragon-Python god since belong to the serpent family is also called as *Ruipi Santai Rengpa* lit. 'The red horned Serpent king'. The Chothe like other people symbolically identifies the Dragon-Python with the "God of Rain/ Sea". His majestic life is represented by "Rainbow". Therefore, the Chothe's headgear and their flag is designed in the rainbow pattern. *Pu Lungchungpa* the Dragon-Python god is believed to have the power to transform himself into anything like stone, tiger, human, etc. So, when he incarnates into human form, he is known as "Chothe Thangwai/ Thangmei Pakhangpa". Thus, the Dragon-Python God in ancient Chothe term is known as *Pu Lungchungpa* the assumed Principal Heavenly Guardian God of the Chothe, whom they believed to have saved and protected them from the clutches of the lower gods and also from the ferocious Tiger King (*Kamkeirang-rengpa*). This genealogical myth is built around the mystical personality of the Dragon-Python (Water/ Rain god) entrusted by the divine Heavenly God (*Thangvan Rengpa*) to be the protector and benefactor of the Chothe people.

The Chothe mythical story centres around three characters i.e. (i) the Celestial/ Heavenly/ Abode gods, (ii) the Lower gods and, (iii) the Mankind; a triangular entity represented by the Dragon, the Tiger and the Human Beings; symbolising the Good, the Evil and the Ignorant man. This triangular or the trinity concept is also seen among other religious group of the world like Catholic. Subsequently, after many centuries *Pu Lungchungpa* fulfilled his promise by interceding in human form and resolved himself as the avatar or Divine-incarnate in the mystical person of "*Chothe Thangwai/ Thangmei Pakhangpa*". His childhood name in Chothe is known as *Mei-ngai* (lit. a child with a protruding tail).

Pakhangpa's mysticism re-instils the religious zeal of the Chothe because of his manifestation to the promised he made long ago that he will come someday and dwell among his people when settled a prosperous life. According to their folktale, when Pakhangpa transformed and appeared to his people as a young stranger they failed to acknowledge him as the Divine-incarnate. Later, he fell in love with *Daishin* the eldest daughter of *Surou* (also known as *Tarang*) a chief of a Chothe village and impregnated her. When his identity was sought for his anonymity he mysteriously disappeared. Later Daishin bore a son 'Mei-ngai' (who came to be later known as Pakhangpa). Since, the people are unaware of His divinity as the avatar they denounced him as an 'illegitimate child', and ignorantly banished him and his mother from their country. Pakhangpa and mother lived at Langthabal, Imphal for few years and later moved down south (around Moirang) during the inter-tribal war. Subsequently, he grew up to be the most audacious youth and earned as the most trustworthy person from the Moirang king, who later succeeded the king after his death (being a foster son). But not forgetting his root and origin, he asked his Chothe people to perform certain rite and ritual to absolve themselves from their past sins. Some rituals like *tuihumpa* (rite for the water), *lamleh thoipa* (village gate rite), *pumningpa* (baptism), *ta-sanpa* (divination) and taboos (*ashei-asi*) practiced even today are said to be somehow connected to the legend.

Some similarities between *Chothe Genealogical Myth* with other tribes of Manipur are also seen, particularly with the cognatic indigenous tribes like; Kharam, Tarao, Koireng, Anal, Maring, Lamkang, Chiru, Kom, Aimol, besides others from different sources. For example, J. Shakespeare mentioned that the Lamkang originated from a place "on the *Kangmang* hill, away to the south, there is a cave, out of this came a man and woman, and were eaten up by a tiger that was watching. A god who had two horns, seeing this horrible sight, came out and drove away the tiger, and so the next couple to emerge escaped and became the ancestors of the Lamkang" (1912:150). Accordingly Mrs Y. Tharaklei (96/F) on the basis of the folktale says that, "The Maring came out of a cave only after a bull that belonged to a Chothe widow pushed out the rock that covered their cave for which they had paid thirty pieces of silver coins to that Chothe widow". Whatever, it signifies that all these tribes are related in one way or the other as belonging to common (old) cognatic group.

A close affinity also exists between the Chothe and Meitei base on religion, where the Chothe indigenous religion and the Meitei Sanamahi religion both emphases on "Pakhangpa". The Chothe and other cognates knows Pakhangpa as "*Chothe Thangwai/ Thangmei Pakhangpa*", and to the Meitei popularly known as "*Nongda Leiren Pakhangpa*" as their avatar, both referring to the same person i.e. the first historical king of Manipur. The former associates him with his childhood and as a great conqueror in the south, while the latter as a mythical divine king for this greatness in the northern valley of Manipur.

The concept of spirituality among the Chothe exists from the early stage and this spiritualism is re-strengthened through Pakhangpa, as the avatar of their God *Lungchungpa*. Tensubu remarked that "The God Pakhangpa is believed to be a Dragon-Python" (1993: 46). Further N. Sanajaoba also pointed out that "Pakhangpa has a supernatural power to transform himself into anything like a stone, a tiger, a dog or a human being, and can even take human birth at any time and place" because he is endowed with divine supernatural powers (1991: 104). From this perspective, the Chothe socio-religious historical myth can be divided into two categories on the basis of the historical period as; "Chothe Genealogical Myth" and the "Legend of Chothe Thangwai Pakhangpa", since the elements of opposition and contradiction of this myth fits into Levi-Strauss' paradigm in the legend of resolving concept.

This Chapter particular focuses on the oral history of *Chothe Genealogical Myth* and the legend of *Chothe Thangwai/ Thangmei Pakhangpa* which is the foundation of the Chothe religious belief and practices, as provided by different Chothe village elders like H. Thambaljao, Y. Maipak, Y. Tomalsingh, H. Gulapsing, Pr. Roushi, Mk. Neilut, Pr. Wailum, Pr. Herachou, K. Hamunchao and Pr. Vincent (Babu), besides many other elders and leaders. The *Chothe Genealogical Myth* contains almost all elements of a religious myth which is evolutionary in character (nature-myth) that resolves or mediates in the legend of *Chothe Thangwai Pakhangpa*. The genealogical myth is based on oral narratives plus the recorded work of Khiyang Manjou (1982) of Khongkhang titled as, '*Chothe Athouna*' (Chothe's Origin) written in the Chothe language. Similarly, the legend of '*Chothe Thangwai Pakhangpa*' is based on their oral history as well as the sacred manuscripts tilted as, '*Chothe Thangwai/ Thangmei Pakhangpa*' (*CTP*) that have been preserved and kept as sacred for many centuries. There are also other very important manuscripts like *Moirang Ningthourol Lambuba* (*MNL*), *Cheitharol Kumpaba* (*ChK*) and few select literatures of Manipur that has sound referring to the existence of the *Chothe Thangwai Pakhangpa*.

Chothe Genealogical Myth

The *Chothe Genealogical Myth* is deliberately elaborated here because no literature, exclusively studies the Chothe indigenous religion apart from their socio-cultural aspects. Another important reason is to provide readers sufficient data to analyse the evolutionary development of the Chothe socio-religion and ethno-history, and understand the culture from the light of their indigenous religious beliefs and practices. The deliberate elaboration is also credited to Clyde Kluckhohn, who critically remarked that the writings of J. Frazer, E.B. Tylor, E. Durkheim and others provided insufficient primary data or description in their classic books to substantiate in their arguments, with a view that they analysed it from the peripheral points where the readers are made to believe with their hypotheses (1972: 98). All these facets insist me for a descriptive study, and it is hoped will help readers to analyse the subject from different perspectives and speculate what is religion and culture on the basis of his/ her interest. This Chothe myth basically focuses to the time when gods and mankind had direct interrelationships.

The Genesis of Mankind (*Mameeshi*): According to *Chothe Genealogical Myth,* "In the beginning, between the abode of (Gods) Heavenly and Earthly kingdoms there was no human beings at all excepts the gods only" (*Amating-nga Thangvan-Shimlei anih kai hinna 'mameeshi' tapa hi amphuino-e, leihu mani chakka amphui-a*), (Khiyang, 1982). But one day, all the Higher and the Lower gods assembled at 'the Centre of the Universe where the Light and the Darkness (Sun and Moon rises) originates' (-*Koikung suhlam shimni sukna munna*) in order to find out the most suitable creature to serve them and would lighten the burden of the lower gods who have being complaining about their heavy workload (*Ibid.*). So, the lower gods first brought a water creature called '*Ngavok*' a Dogfish (*Sp.Channa punctatus*). But the higher gods after examining it were not satisfied, so they sent it back into the water. Then, they brought '*Uitok*' a frog, still the Gods were unsatisfied. Next, they brought '*Ajongpa*' a monkey. But the higher gods were still unhappy; dejected with the ugly physical appearance of its tail and body hair, was sent back to the forest leaving on a banyan tree. The lower gods were unhappy too, since they were unable to please the higher gods. Ultimately, they decided to create a new living being in the image or shadow of God, and thus created a man (*A-pa*) and a woman (*Nu-mei*). In Chothe, these human beings are called as "Mameeshi/Mamalsi", meaning the 'Mankind', literally "His Left Shadow" or the "Images of the Creator" (*Ma* = His; *Mee* = shadow; *Shi* = left). The higher gods seeing these beautiful perfect humans (*Mameeshi*) gladly accepts, and therefore gave breath of life. Thus, *Mameeshi* or mankind came into existence on earth created in the 'image of God's left shadow', and were kept at *Koikung* the centre of the universe i.e. the earth.

The Division of Mankind: Since, the lower gods were responsible for the welfare of mankind they began to use the human beings according to their own wish and will. Subsequently, it is said many of the lower gods began to fear that human beings might assault them sooner or later since they became populated, powerful and unruly. Therefore, the lower gods decided to destroy mankind before subjugating themselves. The Heavenly King (*Thangvan Rengpa*) and the Mother of the Earth (*Shimleinu*) decided to have their own child, in case the lower gods determined to do away with the human beings. Later these two powerful gods (Heaven and Earth) bore a lovely son. On the other side of the world, it is said that the other powerful gods i.e. the Moon (*Tha-pa*) and the Sun (*Ni-nu*) also bore a beautiful daughter whose face shines like gold. Since, the Heaven and Earth's child (son) was cute and lovely they became apprehensive that some of the wicked lower gods might steal and claim as their own child. So, these powerful gods secretly hide him inside a rock. The child grew up eating every morning the dew (*Sumphai adon* lit. cloud shoot) that grows above the big rock (*Lungpi*). With the passage of time, the human population substantially increased and became chaotic, unruly and powerful. So, the lower gods ultimately decided to divide the human beings into clans (*phung*) instead of destroying them. Thus, mankind was divided into different clans, sub-clans and scattered to different directions of the world.

Disappearance of the Child: The Heavenly and Earthly (Cosmic) gods too decided to give their beloved son in the care of lower gods, with a thought they would give him a name and a clan among human beings. But when the Cosmic gods went to get the boy he was nowhere to be found, since he had disappeared from the hidden place, this upsets them. Meanwhile, the Dragon-Python King (*Pu Lungchungpa*) and the Tiger King (*Kamkeirang rengpa*) were also on their way to the Abode Council's House to demand their shares of human beings since both did not get it as both were absent on the distribution day. When the Dragon King with his assumed son the Bottle-Gourd (*A-Uum*) were on their way to the house of council they suddenly heard a child's cry at a brook side. When the bottle-gourd out of sympathy persuaded the Dragon to take the child along with them, the Dragon saw the Tiger from afar wagging its tail and approaching them. The Dragon reluctant to disclose about his discovery of the child to the Tiger, he quickly wrap and hid the child inside the cave.

The First Agreement between the Dragon and the Tiger: As soon as the Dragon met the Tiger, he enquired the Tiger's destination. The Tiger told him that he was on his way to the abode council's house to claim his human share, so as to bring up some human beings as his descendants. Further, the Tiger soberly expressed his humiliation and resentment that the lower gods have begun to ignore his greatness, since they took the decision of human distribution without informing him. Hearing this, the Dragon also expressed his sentiment to the Tiger that he too did not get his human share nor was he informed about it. So, he has decided to destroy all mankind with landslides. The Tiger instantly interrupted and said he too was thinking to kill and suck all the lower gods' blood. But the Dragon asked him to calm down that the lower gods could overheard their plans, and he (Tiger) being a carnivorous animal will not be able to kill all the lower gods unlike him. So, the Dragon requested the Tiger to do him a favour. The Tiger proudly reacted to the Dragon, whether he had denied any of his requests before. But the Dragon did not fully trust the Tiger, with a belief that 'carnivorous animals are forgetful'. So, he insist the Tiger to swear "If any of us break our promises, all our thirty-two teeth shall fall" (*E-hongnga aluita shaita ngak-nenopa meeha aha somthum-ani tickhap su-o ta, washak thakke*), (Khiyang, 1982). When both swore, the Dragon brought out the hidden child and hands over to the dumbfounding Tiger, asking him to take care of the child until he returns instead of going to the council's house. In case, if he did not get their shares, he will bless, protect and multiply the child to be their descendants.

The Gods Submit before the Dragon King: When the Dragon reached the abode council's house he saw all the lower gods in chaos, afraid of the Heavenly King (*Thangvan rengpa*) and the Earthly Queen (*Shimlei-nu*). Because they believed they will be punished to death if they did not find their secret child at the earliest, since he had disappeared from the hidden place. It is said that in the midst of the commotion a decree was also announced that to whosoever informed them where about the child or admits to taking the child will be forgiven. Learning the information, the Dragon took advantage of the situation and appeared before the scene, and threaten all the lower gods assembled there that he had conspired with his other six powerful Cosmo Gods/ Kings to punish the culprit for stealing and hiding the child near a brook, if no one admits it. Further, he also told them that his friend the Tiger King has decided to kill all of them for ignoring his social status. With these awesome words, all the lower gods suddenly bows down before the Dragon-Python King requesting him to have mercy at least by sparing their lives. Taking advantage of this critical situation, the Dragon asked them to surrender all their wealth and power including human beings or else he will join the powerful Gods and the Tiger, and destroy the whole earth with landslides separating the gods and the human beings forever. The lower gods trembled in fear and ceded to the Dragon's wish, by seeking apology and acknowledging him as one of the powerful Gods who could do anything and everything like any other great powerful Cosmic Gods.

The Second Agreement between the Dragon and the Tiger: Accordingly, it is said that when the Dragon returned from the heavenly council's meeting, he told the Tiger not to worry anymore because all the lower gods had submitted themselves before him and so all the human beings including the child belongs to them. But the Dragon said to the Tiger that since both of them cannot bring up the child together as they lived in different places, he will bring up the child under his protection and blessing. However, the Dragon felt doubtful and insisted the Tiger and the child also should swear, with a belief that in the near future they might misunderstood and kill one another. So, the Dragon persuaded the Tiger to swear before him that he will not harm the child. The Tiger agreed and swore, "My human grandson, if I, your grandfather happen to kill you mistakenly let your gods who created you kill me. But even if I die let your gods re-incarnate me from my bones in the next re-birth"

(*Katu mameeshi unga-o napu keina ihongnga nangta thet-man a-lechu, katu navon choih ngeina napu keita that shuh-o, chutihleiko napu keichu voiha thileko voiha saruh ha navon choih ngeina ringthou pishi suh-o*), (Khiyang, 1982). As per the deal the boy also swore to the Tiger, after which both courteously bow to each other and bid farewell.

The Dragon become the Principal Guardian God for the Heavenly Child: The Dragon, then took the child to the Heavenly Abode where the Seven Powerful Celestial Gods live, and requested the Heavenly King and the Earthly Queen to discharge the other peer gods like the Sun, the Moon, the Storm (Wind/ Air) and the Fire from being on halt/ inactive, since he has found their beloved child at a Brookside, if not he feel all the lower gods and human beings would die of suffocation. The Heavenly King and the Earthly Queen on hearing the good news granted the Dragon's wish and the world was restored to normalcy. Thus, on the basis of the decree, the Dragon became the Principal Guardian God and the first mythical ancestor of the Chothe people (the descendants of Ka-chokte/ Ka-choite and Thanidam).

The Dragon Named the Heavenly Child *Kachokte* (*Kachoite*): The Dragon king took the child to his cave and gave him a name saying "My dear grandson, since I, your grandfather have brought you this far from the brook side by holding you and stirring the lower gods, you will need a name to identify your settlement in future by your descendants. So, I named you as "Ka-chokte/ Ka-choite", meaning "the child that I hold or stirred with",

> (*Katupa nangchu apuna kuiput kuilei yaiya kachokka kaluih phaosouchu, katu naramingangchu anungtinga natu-nate ngei pha-nungtinga dangnata apuna naraming "Ka-chokte or Ka-choite" ta bohshingnge*), (Khiyang, 1982). Henceforth, the descendants of *Ka-chokte/ Ka-choite* became known as *Chokte = Choite = Shote = Zote = Chawte = Chote* and *Chothe* tribe.[2]

Kachokte **Marries** *Thanidam*: After many years *Kachokte/ Kachoite* grew up as a strong, young handsome man. The Dragon King seeing him always alone felt sympathy and decided to find a suitable girl for him. After searching for a long time, he finally found a girl the secret daughter of the Moon and the Sun gods. The Dragon approaches his friends the Moon and the Sun gods, and sought the hand of their beautiful daughter for *Kachokte* with an assurance of equal blessing and protection to both as the guardian god. The Moon and the Sun gods became subservient to the proposal. So, the Dragon brought the girl along with her helpers across the big river on his back and introduced her to *Kachokte* (*Kachoite*). On that day itself, the Dragon gave her a name as, "Tha-Ni-dam" (*Thanidam*), literally 'the Moon and Sun are alright'. The Dragon explained her that when he initially approach her parents (Moon and Sun gods) they were very apprehensive and worried. But now that they are happy, so he has named her taking both her parent's names. Thus, she got her name as *Thanidam*. Subsequently, *Kachokte* married *Thanidam,* and became his beloved wife.

Beginning of Veneration, Divination and Ritual: One day, the Dragon-Python King (also known as *Ruipi Santai/ Lungchungpa/ Pakhangpa*) called upon the two grandchildren and instructed them the basic socio-religious and cultural norms they should follow in the future. Accordingly, he first asked them to invoke to the rock before they gather any food (cloud's shoot/ dew drops) growing 'above the rock' (*Lung-chung*) by venerating their parents' names i.e. *Thangvan Rengpa-Shimlei Rengnu* and *Thapa-Ninu* to allow them to gather foods every morning. Secondly, the Dragon brought a rooster and a hen, and explained that if the rooster crows it tells them that it is dawn. The hen will lay about 15-20 eggs that would help them in many ways. Thirdly, the Dragon asked them, if they need anything in future they should always offer a roster/ chicken by cutting into 'seven meat shares' (*Salam sari*), only then he will be pleased and oblige their request. But if they wanted to know the sign whether their request is approved or disapproved, they can find out from the chicken-leg's divination (*Aike-jan*). In such cases, if the right leg of the fowl overlaps the left leg it indicates a positive sign, but if it's in reverse form a negative sign. The degree of approval or disapproval seems to depend on the degree of overlapping. In this way, the Dragon instructed other customary norms, the passing of the seasons, months and years, and also taught them when and how to harvest and store foods for future uses.

Descendants/ Progenitors of Chothe (*Kachokte* and *Thanidam*): As years passed by, *Kachokte* (*Kachoite*) and *Thanidam* became prosperous and bore seven siblings i.e. five sons and two daughters. But another version claims, it is nine progenitors i.e. seven sons and two daughters. They are (1) Khiyang (Khiang/ Hiyang), (2) Yuhlung/ Zulung, (3) Makan, (4) Mareem/ Marim, (5) Athao/ Thao, (6) Parpa and, (7) Rangshai, while the two daughters are (8) Singinluh Singinthum and (9) Chonginglu Chongingchong. The Dragon King examines after each of their birth carefully and accordingly named and blessed them, who thus, became the first progenitors/ clans of the Chothe.

Mythically, it is said that the Dragon King named the first son as *Aihung* (lit. rooster's crow) because he was born at dawn when the rooster crowed. So, the Dragon told his parents that he shall also be known as *Keyang* (*Khiyang/ Khiang/ Hiyang*), lit. Relief after parturition. Since, his mother relieves herself after giving birth to him and his name shall also bear as his clan's title (*phung*). Thus, the first son came to be known as *Aihung Khiyang/ Khiang/ Hiyang*. Similarly, the Dragon named the second son *Zulung /Yulung / Yuhlung* (lit. intoxicated with wine) because he was born when his parents were brewing wine (*Zu/ Yu*) and were drunk. But the Dragon assured his parents that he will grow up to be intelligent, a capable leader and a good administrator because of his calmness. The third son was named *Makan* (lit. who stop the fight) since he was born when his father was stopping the fight between his two elder brothers i.e. *Aihung Keyang* and *Zulung*. The Dragon noted that the child will be a great craftsman since his hands constantly moves. When the fourth son was born they were happy and merry, so the Dragon named the child as *Mareem/ Marim* (lit. merry or happy) and assured that the child would become a great priest or magician (*Thiempu*) where all gods and human beings would fear him, because he found the child sound asleep when his parents brought to him. The fifth son was named as *Athao/ Thao* (lit. fatty or oily) because he was born during the spring festival when his mother was preparing a special dish with linseed oil (*Saningtha sathao tha kamma soiya amleiya*) to offer to gods as part of the custom. So, the Dragon assured them that he will grow up to be a great warrior.

Later, two sons were born. The sixth child was named as *Parpa* (blooming) because he was born when the flowers were blooming. So, the Dragon assured the parents that he will be wild and free, without much worry. The seventh child was named as *Rangshai/ Riangsai,* (lit. furious person). Ssome said it means erection of a stone, since he was born during man-animal conflict. The Dragon assured that he will grow up to be in the forefront in times of wars and battles to defend his people.

The eighth (or sixth) child being a daughter; the Dragon named her as *Sheinu Shingingluh Shingingthum* (long sweet-scented linseed) by assuring her parents that whatever food items she prepared with her hands will always taste good, since she is quiet and composed with folded hands, even inside her mother's womb. The last ninth (or seventh) child was named as *Chongnginluh Chongnginchong* (lit. wealthy and prosperous) by the Dragon since she was born when all were happy and content with their lives. As indicated by her palm, the Dragon assured her parents that she will grow up to be a very beautiful girl like an emerald. She will also be creative and an excellent weaver. These are some of the basic mythical personal attributes and traits endowed and blessed by the Dragon King to the first progenitors of the Chothe people.

Dragon Arrange Marriages: With the passage of time, the sons and daughters of *Kachokte* and *Thanidam* grew up; accordingly the Dragon King arranged marriages for all. They said that *Aihung Khiyang* the eldest son married *Shinrung; Yuhlung/ Zulung* married *Paihudam; Makan* married *Theishinni; Mareem* married *Tuanshinni: Athao* married *Neiamni; Parpa Theishu* married *Neirung,* and *Rangshai Mera* married *Reinem* (These are based on myth).

The Dragon's Blessing: It is said when the Dragon finished providing each of them with a wife, he called one by one and formally blessed each of them according to their own inborn personal attributes, character and traits. The Chothe believes that such distinctive features are still visible amongst certain members of their clans. The eldest son *Aihungpa Khiyang* is blessed to be Dragon's right man who will shoulder every responsibility by overseeing the welfare of the people and decide internal issues as the head of the lineage/ tribe on his behalf.

The Dragon, then blessed *Yuhlung/ Zulung* saying that he will become a potential leader and chief, since he has diplomatic skill, and also assist his elder brother in making decision. However, the Dragon cautioned that since he is clever and intelligent he will have some jealous enemies to obstruct his path but he will outwit them by his wisdom. In case of any serious trouble he will personally come to assist him. Further, the Dragon instructed him to give the chicken's liver and heart to his elder brother in any sacrificial offerings.

Similarly, the Dragon blessed *Makan* that he should take the magnificent strength of his grandfather the Tiger (*Kamkeirangpa*) and provide all the necessary weapons like swords and spears to all his kins, so that they can defend their country like the Tiger. The Dragon also asked Makan to make sacrificial offering to the Tiger at the beginning of each year so that his weapons remain strong like the jaw and claws of the Tiger, and bring back his people from any battles. The Dragon suggested that if he maintains a close relationship with the Tiger by offering annual gifts the Tiger could reveal his secret techniques of warfare and improve his craftsmanship. His heavy heart and depressed mind will also unfold and live a prosperous life with many descendants. But the Dragon cautioned him that the lower gods and neighbouring tribes may wage war together against him out of envy, and if he wants to defeat his enemies he should perform the annual rites to the Tiger because the magnanimous strength of his weapon lies with the Tiger.

The Dragon, then called upon the fourth son *Mareem* and told him that he should be the priest of his people because he has been blessed from birth with the power to dispel and cast away the evil spirits. His magical charms will be very powerful and even the gods will be scared of him. The Dragon reminded him to perform all the necessary rites and rituals according to the divination instructed.

Likewise, the Dragon blessed the fifth son *Athao* that since he is strong and brave he will be a great warrior. Therefore, he should defend and protect his village in the absence of his brothers, so that, no savages and barbaric people can enter their village. Moreover, the Dragon said his descendants will enjoy fame and popularity by outstanding acts and his daughters will be well known for their beauties.

The Dragon blessed *Parpa* saying that he will prosper and his descendants will be spread to places far and wide, while *Rangshai* will be a brave warrior helping his brothers and will be in the forefront of any war and battles.

Like the sons, the daughters of *Kachoite* and *Thanidam* were blessed. The Dragon assured *Shinginluh Shingingthum* that she will be like the grandmother of a house. Whatever food or drinks she prepared will always taste good and pleasant. No one will be able to compete the quality and taste of her food.

Lastly, the Dragon blessed *Chongnginluh Chongnginchong* that she will be creative and will weave beautiful clothes for her brothers and kins. The first cloth would have to be named as "Amtin-amwai" or "Awa-ampi", meaning 'pure and bright motif' or 'mother of all bright motifs' and the rest she could be named according to the motif.

The First Ancestors of the Chothe: Thereafter, the first great progenitors of Chothe had many children. Accordingly, the eldest son of *Aihung Khiyang* is believed to be known as *Shangthun* (lit. the rice carrier). *Yuhlung's* eldest son is *Tangkim,* assumed to be the first leader and chief/ *Hulak* of Chothe. *Makan's* eldest son is *Kanshu Kanrung* who became the best craftsman. *Mareem's* eldest son is called as *Kengjang/ Lukung* the first priest/ magician (*Thiempu*), while the fifth son *Athao* is believed to have three sons viz.: *Thierang, Mushin* and *Tubei.* The *Parpa's* eldest son is *Shumhel,* and *Rangshai's* eldest son is called *Thiershu.*

Preparation inside the Cave: After many years, the people in the cave became overpopulated and congested. So, the Dragon King asked the giant monkey to remove the slab of rock that covered the opening of the cave so that they all could come out and live freely on the surface of the earth. As commanded by God, the monkey opened the cave and the Chothe people come out. But, soon the Tiger (*Kamkeirangpa*) who was waiting outside the opening began to kill and ate them one by one, since he could not recognised his descendants. So, all the surviving Chothe returned to the cave and the monkey immediately closed the opening of the cave. Henceforth, they lived for another seven years inside the cave. During those days the Dragon explained his plans how to overcome the ferocious Tiger and how they should live in future. So, the Dragon-Python King asked *Chongnginluh Chongnginchong* the youngest daughter to weave clothes copying his striped pattern, in order to dupe the Tiger by wearing it, since both have similar patterns. The Dragon then asked *Shingnginluh Shinginthum* to brew wine (*Zu*) for him and the Tiger. He also asked *Kanshu Kanrung* son of *Makan* to make swords and spears.[3] Finally, the Dragon assured his people that someday he will come and live with them when they lead a prosperous settled life.

The Mythical Cave (*Huipithoranga*): Thus, after seven years, the Dragon once again commanded the giant monkey the guardian of the cave to open. When the cave was opened, *Kanshu Kanrung* son of *Makan* as instructed wrapped himself with *ava-ampi* the traditional shawl and sneaked out to face the Tiger holding the sword in his right hand and offered the wine (*Zu*) to the Tiger with his left hand. He told the Tiger that the wine was a gift from the Dragon-Python King his old friend. Then, *Kanshu* told the Tiger that his headgear and body pattern (motif of his *ava-ampi* shawl) is similar with his (Tiger) pattern, which is also similar with the Dragon stripes. Thereby, asking the Tiger that he has more black spots than him and challenges him to count if he dares believed. The Tiger was baffled, bewildered, drunk and confused, *Kanshu* promptly told the Tiger that they all belonged to the same clan. *Kanshu* insisted the Tiger, why he wanted to kill him and his people when their body patterns proved to be close relatives. When the Tiger became convinced of their brotherhood, *Kanshu* persuaded the Tiger to swear that 'if any of them happens to kill the other and his descendants in the near future the doer's thirty-two teeth will fall'. Coming to terms both *Kanshu* and the Tiger swore. In the process of *Kanshu's* distraction and conversation with the Tiger, all the Chothe men and women escaped from the cave and live on the surface of the earth. Henceforth, the mythical cave is known as "Huipi-thoranga/ Hurpi-thoranga", lit. 'The cave where the five brothers sprang out', refers to five clans.[4]

The First King *Tangkim Yuhlung*: It is said that as soon as they began to settle on the surface of the earth there arises a leadership conflict among all the eldest sons of the first progenitors. *Lakung Mareem* claimed leadership on the ground that he had cast away the forest evil spirits from the chosen settlement by his magical power. *Kanshu Kanrung Makan* claimed leadership for outwitting the Tiger; *Theirang Thao* for killing the Tiger; and *Tangkim* (*Tangkip*) *Yuhlung* because of the assurance given by the Dragon King. Since, they cannot come to a consensus to the issue, they thus, agreed to a bet that whosoever sees the Sun first on the following morning whether the eldest or younger one will be acknowledged as their first chief or king. Accordingly, when the rooster crow at the dawn all the brothers went in different directions in the darkness to see the first dazzling Sunlight. It is said *Lukung/ Kengjang Mareem* went towards north; *Kanshu Kanrung Makan* towards west; *Theirang Thao* on the south. However, *Tangkim Yuhlung* went east and climbed up on the top of a banyan tree, and saw the first morning's sunrise. Therefore, based on the agreement *Tangkim Yuhlung* became the first King (*A-reng*) of the Chothe people. Accordingly, as instructed by the Dragon, *Lukung Mareem* the priest performed the sacrificial offering to the Seven Celestial/ Cosmic Great Gods and also seeks the chicken-leg divination on *Tangkim's* coronation day.

From Myth to Legend: According to the Chothe village elders, a popular folktale called '*Shangtum shang*' describes an event that occurred during their migration. They said the Dragon King gave a bundle of paddy (rice) to

Shangtum the eldest son of *Aihung Khiyang*. A rat stole it and got lost during their journey. Since, they are in trouble situation, they reprimanded the forest god, and through his advice they smoked out the rat with chillies and got back their paddy. Similarly, at another stage of their migration, another bundle of their paddy is believed to have carried away to the other side of a big river while crossing it. Being helpless, they called the rat for help, who brought it back for them. They said it took seven years to complete the full plantation of their paddy by all. When the paddy plants began to fill its ears, *Lungkung Mareem/ Marim* offered the "Shanghong lethoi" (lit. thanksgiving rite for the paddy) in honour of their Powerful Cosmic Gods. Not forgetting the rat's help, the Chothe also offers a small quantity of their paddy for the rats after each harvest. If this is not done, they believed that the rats attack their rice-barn. This belief and rites was institutionalised and is still practiced by few indigenous believers of Lamlanghupi village.

Many similarities are seen between the Chothe and some Northeast tribes with that of Southeast Asian groups like the Chinese, Japanese, Taiwan, Korean, Tibetans, Bhutanese and Thais, etc. with regards to their myths, legends and stories, as indicated by their en route migration. Since, they have no any written records nor any serious work were done before, it is very difficult to distil the Chothe pre-history and distinguished between myths, legends and histories. But based on migration, the Chothe socio-cultural and religious history may be broadly divided into two categories as: Pre-history (myth) and History (legend). Their pre-history begins from *Huipithoranga* (the mythical cave) till *Lungleh-Waishu* (Lungleh district of Mizoram) settlement.[5] Their transitional history continued till *Lungsukbung* (*Nungsuk ching*) settlement in the south-western region of Manipur, and thereafter, their legend and history entered into landmark with the story of *'Chothe Thangwai Pakhangpa'*.

Brief Analysis of the Chothe Genealogical Myth

There are several elements in this genealogical myth that reflects religious significance apart from various other valuable socio-cultural and historical accounts. Some of the salient features that have religious significance under this study are:

1. The *Chothe Genealogical Myth* elucidates how the world originates. How living organisms and creatures including mankind came into existence, after a series of evolutionary stages. It explains that, in the beginning the world was completely empty and void filled with spirits (energy) only. But with the combination of the 'Seven' basic Cosmic Elements 'the first form of life began in water'. The first creation is claimed to be a water creature called '*Ngavok*' means a

'dogfish' (*Spe. Channa punctatus*). The second is said to be a land creature called '*Ajong*' (a monkey or an Ape). The third and final creation is known as '*Mameeshi*' means 'Mankind' (lit. the left shadow of God).

2. This myth describes their genealogical origin. The Chothe mythically believes that *Kachokte* and *Thanidam* are their first progenitors/ ancestors (i.e. son of Heavenly King (*Thanvan rengpa*) and the Earthly Queen (*Shimleinu*), and *Thanidam* the daughter of the Sun (*Ninu*) and the Moon (*Thapa*) gods. The Dragon-Python king accordingly becomes the Principal Guardian God as the protector and benefactor of the Chothe on this earth due to his transfiguration capacity. The tribe thus, derived its name from *Ka-Chokte/ Ka-Choite* as "Choite- Chokte- Shote- Zote- Chawte- Chote- Chothe". The myth describes the primitive stages of lives at the *Huipi-thoranga/ Hurpi/ Chinglung/ Shinlung* cave.

3. The Dragon-Python King is recognised as the intercessor between two Worlds i.e. Heavenly Gods and Earthly creatures (Mankind) because of his transfiguration potential or metamorphosis personality since other Cosmic Gods are invisible and intangible for the human beings to see and touch. Of all the Cosmic Gods, the Chothe believes the Heavenly (Sky) God *Thangvan Rengpa* as the most powerful God of all. The ancient Meitei even called the Heavenly God as *Pu Soraren* the controller of human destiny.

G. Elliot Smith (1919) in his book *Evolution of the Dragon* says that in China the Dragon is considered as the earliest mythological beast symbolising fertility of the earth and power of the emperor. According to the Chinese myth, there are fifteen meaningful gods in order of personal involvement. One of it is the *Lung-Wang* or the Dragon King, the Ruling God of the sea because he controls the weather especially the rain. He appears in the human form but can transform into a Dragon, especially when he makes rain and thunder. There are many folktales about his colourful life reflecting like a rainbow and an elaborate golden palace beneath the sea, and his symbol is one of the most popular symbols found in almost all ancient Chinese temples (Channa, 1998:143-144, 156).

As indicated above, many similarities are noticed between the Chothe and Sino-Tibetan Dragon myths. The Chothe address the 'Rain God/ Sea God' as 'Lung-chung-pa' meaning 'one who sits above the rock', symbolising the powerful dragon king. In ancient Chothe the term *Lungchungpa* or 'Lung-chwang-pa' means 'the rain God above the head', (*Lu* = head, or *Ru/* Luì = rain; *Chung/*

Chwang/ Vang = up/ high above; Pa = stands for masculine gender). From the analysis, the Chothe since early days like any Asian communities worships and revere the Dragon king as their Supreme Guardian god of the earth. The deep-pink or light reddish colour of the Chothe traditional shawl "Awa-ampi" motif is assumed to be the pattern and colour copied from the Dragon's body. The Chothe emblem, flag and headgear (*pun-rang*) has "Rainbow" pattern symbolising the radiance and life of the Dragon-Python King.

4. Like any other religion of the world, the Chothe religion also believes that certain numbers are very significant, sacred and profane. The number "Seven" (7) plays a very important role for the Chothe, especially in their ritualistic activities because they believe in the Seven Celestial Elements or Cosmic Natural Gods. They are: (1) The Heaven, (2) The Earth, (3) The Sun, (4) The Moon, (5) The Fire, (6) The Air or Storm, and (7) The Water or Rain, in which the survival of all life forms depend upon them. The religious philosophy is that all these Seven Celestial/ Natural Elementary Gods together created human beings from the 'left side of God's shadow/ image' and breathe forth life. The Chothe believes that their seven clans (*phungs*), seven bright Stars and also the seven big landmasses symbolically represent the seven celestial elements. The Khasi of Meghalaya too consider number seven as very important in their religious affairs since they claimed to be the descendants of the 'original seven household units'- "Ka khun Ki Ksiew U Hynniewtrep" (Nongkynrih, 2002:131). The belief in numbers as sacred or profane is found in almost all walks of life. For example, the Christian believe that triple six (666) is the number of the Beast or Satan. For the Hindu astrologers all numbers have their own significance depending on the individual personality (*rashi*). Likewise, for some cultural groups 'Odd Numbers' like one, three, five, seven, and nine are considered good and sacred, while 'Even Numbers' like two, four, six, eight are bad/ profane, or the vice-versa. For Chothe any ritualistic activities, day and items should always be in odd numbers like one, three, five, seven or nine reflecting the family of Cosmic-Elements.

5. In this genealogical myth, the Dragon and the Tiger portrays the nature of conflict in human lives. The conflict and mistrust that exists between the two animals is believed to have passed on to human beings that continue to exist in different forms. The Chothe believes that if two good friends have opposite characters like the Dragon and the Tiger they will always be in conflict but at the same time complement each other as bi-polar entity. M. Khundo and

H. Ibochou of Lamlanghupi Chothe gave a mythical story about the sacred treaty between the two animals. They said that 'till some twenty five years ago especially, during March-April and November-December on or before the full-moon a tiger and some monkey used to visit their sacred grove at Khuman (Old settlement area). They claimed of sighting a Tiger's footprint on their village road side and paddy fields that came down from the Laimaton hills to pay a visit to *Lungchungpa* (*Chothe Thangwai Pakhangpa*) at the sacred-grove as part of the traditional homage. On such nights, the atmosphere seem unusually still, by midnight the village dogs barks and howl in the direction of their sacred-grove, perhaps sensing the Tiger'. They claimed that a hole inside the Chothe sacred-grove (temple) directly connects to the hole at Kangla Fort, Imphal. Any ritualistic offerings like a fowl made at this sacred grove intended for the Kangla god seems to mysteriously appear at the Kangla fort's pond alive, signifying the symbolic offering made here.

6. Many Chothe still believes the distinctive personal traits, character and charisma found among certain members of their clans are attributed to their ancestors and the Dragon-Python's blessing who bestowed upon them. For example, most of the *Makan* men are said to be a good craftsmen and artistic while their girls are outspoken, idealist and lazy. The *Thao* men are brave and courageous, and outstanding in games and sports while their girls are considered assertive, beautiful and seductive. For example, *Thaowon Samtharnu* (Nungthil Chaibi) wife of King Charairongpa of Manipur is said to be a very beautiful Chothe girl. *Yuhlung* (*Zulung*) men are generally considered gentle, humble and diplomatic, and often occupy a high position in a society, while their girls are considered good natured but often control their husbands. *Khiyang* (*Hiyang*) men often occupy higher status in the village (by virtue of being mythically the eldest son) and their girls are hospitable, hardworking but defensive. *Mareem* (*Marim*) men are credited as skilful in magician but their girls are said to be introvert, clever and dominant. *Parpa* men being born free during spring season loves leisure and leads easy lazy life, while their girls are said to be hardworking, bold and dominating. The *Rangshai* men are considered argumentative and ill-tempered but their girl's are gentle and understanding.

7. The most significant of the Chothe genealogical myth is the assurance of Dragon-Python king that he will come and dwell with them someday when they live a settled prosperous life. After many centuries this prophesy was fulfilled by impersonating himself as a young stranger and manifesting his greatness through

his son *Chothe Thangwai/ Thangmei Pakhangpa* (*Nongda Leiren Pakhangpa*) the legendary divine king of Manipur. Initially, when people did not recognise his son as their Divine-incarnate they ill-treated him during his childhood. Firstly, they were unaware because of the time and place he would appear before them. Secondly, his son was considered illegitimate child since the identity of his father (assumed mythical stranger) was unknown to the people. Another most important feature of *Chothe Genealogical Myth* is the case of avatar or re-incarnation which is similar with other mythical stories like the birth of Lord Jesus Christ, or Lord Krishna of the Hindu god. This 'law of similarity' is well explained by Claude Levi-Strauss (1972) in his study of myth as the 'universal law of human thought'.

The Legend of Chothe Thangwai Pakhangpa

The *Chothe Genealogical Myth* is based on the Dragon-Python god and Tiger myth like most of the Sino-Tibetan speaking groups of people. The Chothe firmly believes in the cosmology and ancestral-spirits. They believe to have migrated from *Huipithoranga* a mythical cave (in southern China) to *Lungleh-Waishu* (in Mizoram), and later moved up to the present southern region of Manipur. As the legend begins where the myth ends; the Chothe legend also starts with the legendary King "Chothe Thangwai/ Thangmei Pakhangpa" or "Nongda Leiren Pakhangpa" probably believed to have existed before 700 or 1100 A.D. The Chothe folklore well elucidates the genealogical history of *Pakhangpa* but not his later life story. This legendary King *Chothe Thangwai Pakhangpa* is considered as the avatar or Divine-incarnate of *Pu Lungchungpa* or the Dragon-Python god who is their Principal Heavenly Guardian God the protector and benefactor of Chothe people. This legend re-instils the Chothe mythical religious beliefs and practices. According to Chothe elders, *Pakhangpa* the Divine-incarnate or supreme guardian god is always with them and His earthly resting abode is identified with the sacred-grove or banyan tree. The present Chothe sacred-grove of *Chothe Thangwai/ Thangmei Pakhangpa* is at Khuman village, Bishnupur, an abandon settlement of Lamlanghupi, i.e. half a kilometre away from their present village.⁶

The *Chothe Genealogical Myth* although in its origin is similar with other indigenous communities of Manipur, especially the so-called "Old-Kuki" tribes like Kharam, Tarao, Koireng, Kom, Anal, Lamkang, Maring, Moyon, Monshang, Aimol and Chiru and others. However, unlike the Chothe, the belief that *Chothe Thangwai Pakhangpa* as their Divine-incarnate of the Dragon-Python god is not found among these tribes. The Chothe for his mystical personality, extra-ordinary power and feats believed Pakhangpa as the avatar. Therefore, they revered and worshipped him as their Ancestor God.

Pakhangpa is known to various Meitei clans by 'eighteen different cognomens of Pakhangba' and the most common one is *Nongda Leiren Pakhangba* (Singh, 1986:271-272). Like the Chothe, the early Meitei also revere and worship him as their mythical and first historical king of Imphal (Kangla) Kingdom, although he is believed to be originally known as '*Chothe Thangwai/ Thangmei Pakhangpa*'. It is important to note that many among the Meitei are ignorant, and are confused about his real identity, childhood and parentage because of too many cognomen versions and the available written records are the distorted versions done by the later scribes during the seventeenth century Hindunisation process in Manipur.

In connection to the above Chothe myth and legend, it is believed that the later Meitei scribes and scholars have tried to link the Chothe Pakhangpa myth as their Meitei mythology with "Atiya Guru Sidaba" or "Kuptreng and Sentreng" by borrowing the idea of Hindu mythology. But it proves futility, since they failed to establish the link with Pakhangpa's origin and his parentage story. The various contesting opinions about Pakhangpa and his cognomens from different sections of Meitei further denied any acceptable version about the genealogical identity of Pakhangpa even among themselves, since the constructed history of Pakhangpa's origin and parentage are incoherent with the folklores in many respects. The Meitei historians too speculated about Pakhangpa's origin and parentage by constructing various myths and legends around his mysterious personality but they still cannot unearth. It is believed that the idea to distort and develop a new myth of their own (Meitei) by few seems to be because they wanted to establish a separate political and cultural identity by dominating the indigenous hill peoples. Thus, Pakhangpa's identity remains unsolved and is shrouded in mystery till today in the context of the religious history of Manipur.

This prevailing speculation is well pointed out by Prof. Gangmumei Kabui a renowned Manipur historian that "Nongda Leiren Pakhangba was a prince of mysterious origin, opinions about his origin and parentage runs from he being an Aryan prince from upper Burma to an adventurer from the Brahmaputra valley or the Himalayas to Divine-incarnate to put an end to anarchy in the land or an illegitimate child of a clan chief, made a ruler by his foster father" (2003:75). Further Kabui said that "The chronology of Pakhangpa is one of the most controversial issues in the history of Manipur" (*ibid:*90). All these confusions are believed to be because of Pakhangpa enigmatic personality and also the various distorted versions derived later after his death among various associated valley people. However, for Chothe people, there seems no confusion and doubt at all. Since, Pakhangpa is revered and worshipped till today as their avatar or Divine-incarnate of the Dragon-Python god (*Lungchungpa*) born to a Chothe lady. Therefore, the Chothe adore, revere and worships Him as their Ancestor God the Supreme Principal Guardian God of earth as the protector and benefactor of the people.

(i) The Oral History of Chothe Thangwai Pakhangpa

Kabui asserts that "Nongda leiren Pakhangba was extraordinary ruler, but his background before he became a ruler was comparatively unknown" (2003:85). But let us see what the Chothe oral history and the CTP manuscript have to say.

The Chothe oral history on the legend of *Chothe Thangwai/ Thangmei Pakhangpa's* origin, parentage and his background is described by different Chothe village elders like H. Thambaljao, Y. Hongpa, Y. Maipak, Y. Tomalsingh, H. Jaikan, Pr. Roushi, Mk. Neilut, Kh. Khedon, M. Mouchung, Pr. Wailum, Pr. Herachou and Pr. Vincent, besides many other elders and leaders is lucidly explained below. This Chothe oral history is firmly supported by various historical texts like *CTP, ChK, MNL* manuscripts and other literatures in the subsequent analysis on the origin, parentage, coronation, mysticism, secrecy, and death of Pakhangpa. First let us have a look at the Chothe oral history as given by them:

"Chothe Thangwai/ Thangmei Pakhangpa was the son of Daishin the eldest daughter of Yuhlung Surou (also known as Tarang, Nungkarakpa and Sanarakpa) one of the great chiefs of Chothe. Surou had two beautiful daughters namely; Daishin and Joushin. As he was getting old, the Dragon-Python (Pu Lungchungpa) their Principal Guardian God felt sympathy on him because he was the only descendant left in his family line after all his kin members died fighting in different battles. Moreover, Surou was a good man, so, the Dragon-Python God decided to bless him. Therefore, the Dragon-Python God transformed into human form and disguised himself into a strange young handsome man and appeared before Daishin who was working in her parents' jhum field. This mysterious young handsome man, who introduced himself as stranger, started frequently visiting Daishin in the jhum field. Thereafter, she fell in love with him. Later, when her father Surou came to know that she was impregnated by this mysterious young man, and she could not specifically identify him, he got infuriated and restless. In order to find out whether he is a demigod or human being, her parents asked her to pierce the mixture package containing turmeric, garlic, ginger, snail, eel, etc. when the mysterious young man comes to visit her again in the jhum's hut. Daishin, on her parents' advice pierced the mixture package and when the liquid drops down on the mysterious young man, he could not bear the smell and burnt of the mixture. So, he rushed to the nearby brook and disappeared forever, testifying that he was not human, but a

divine being. Joushin the younger sister, who was also working in the same field saw from a distance the strange young man transformation into python (only the tail) when she suddenly happened to look out in response to her sister's cry. When they reached their home, Joushin informed her parents about the incident. On learning the news, Daishin was prohibited by her parents from going to the jhum field from that day onwards. Daishin spent the rest of her days weeping. It is also said that she escaped many times from her house and took refuge among the neighbouring villages expecting to find her strange lover. But he never showed up. However, her lover appeared in her dreams assuring his existence and protecting her and the unborn child by different signs, directing and instructing her about the do's and don'ts of food habits and other religious taboos, which she should observe during her pregnancy. After nine months Daishin gave birth to a son "Thangwai". But later because of his protruding tail he was nicknamed by others as 'Mei-ngai-te" (Child with a tail). Since, the mysterious young man did not appear anymore after the incident to claim Daishin as his wife, Thangwai was considered as an illegitimate child by the society. Therefore, great Surou in order to save his image and status, attempted to kill the child three times without knowing about the child's divinity and supernatural power endowed as the Dragon's son.

In the first attempt, Surou took Thangwai into a deep forest and left him alone to die. But his mystical father, the Dragon-Python disguised as an old man and rescued him with his old friend the Tiger King (Kamkeirang Rengpa) who helped carry back the child to the village. It is believed that when the Tiger approached, the child's cry worsens. But the moment he saw the waging tail of the Tiger, he immediately stops. So, the Tiger tricked the child who slowly followed the tiger's waging tail till the middle of the village road. As soon as the Tiger left, the child began to cry. Soon some villagers heard it and took him to his mother. As Thangwai grows up, he became more notorious and often creates problems to his friends because of his extraordinary strength and power, especially while playing. So, his friends were annoyed and often refused to play with him. So, his mother compelled him to stay at home and play with his grandfather Surou.

The second attempt was made when Surou and Thangwai went to a forest. It is said that when they were climbing a steep mountain Surou on the pretext of slipping his foot pushed down a big boulder with his leg to kill Thangwai. But the child escaped by deflecting the boulder with his hand, being guided by the Dragon's spirit.

Surou made his third attempt when the young innocent boy Thangwai Pakhangpa followed him into the deep forest to fell trees. It is said that when the tree which Surou was cutting is about to fall, he asked the young boy to stand in the way of the falling tree and catch hold of it. Accordingly the boy obeyed going in the direction of the falling tree. So, Surou returned home thinking that young Thangwai might have been crushed to death by the tree. Since, the boy did not return home till the evening, his worried mother asked her father about her son. But her father replied that the young boy had left ahead of him and he must be playing with his friends. The worried mother searched the whole village but could not find him. Surprisingly, late in the evening, young Thangwai returned home with a log of the tree and asked his grandfather where to put it down. As suggested, he dropped it at their front courtyard. That night, young Thangwai told his mother the strange dreams he had during the day while he was crushed to asleep by the falling tree. Hearing the story, his mother realised that it was the Dragon-Python's spirit. So, she asked him not to disclose to anyone and also be afraid of it.

As the pressure of the villagers were mounting on Surou the village chief to decide on the fate of his daughter and the illegitimate child (Thangwai), he requested his daughter Daishin and young grandson Thangwai Pakhangpa (Mei-ngai) to leave the village soon. So, on one auspicious day, he gave them a hen and a rooster, with an instruction to move north and perform an egg-divination (artui-shan) and settle at the place where the rooster crows. Accordingly, it is believed that Daishin and young Thangwai moved north and settled near Langthabal on a small hill-slope where the rooster crowed. It is also said that often his grandfather visited them carrying some ropes, clothes, bamboo baskets, and fats for lighting. But during the inter-tribal wars in the northern region, Thangwai and his mother is believed to have moved down south and took refuge among the Moirang people. In due course, by his feats and merits, he soon became a great military leader and ultimately succeeded King Kongding of Moirang. Legend says that, thereafter he consolidated all the small southern kingdoms into a confederate unit, he then marched north and defeated all his rivals like Khaba-nganba tribe, and thus established the Kangla (Imphal) Kingdom. Subsequently, he also subjugated the other neighbouring groups and thereby became the first sovereign ruler of entire Manipur valley as 'Pakhangpa' (lit. the virile youth, in Meitei)".

Some of the missing stories and gaps of Pakhangpa's later life in the Chothe oral history are found mentioned in *Moirang Ningthourol Lambuba* (MNL) and other important historical manuscripts of Manipur (i.e. after he and his mother left the Chothe village). The MNL elucidated that Pakhangpa was at Moirang and was described as a great warrior. Because of his courage and bravery he was commonly known as "Thangwai Atengba", which means "an aide to the King Thangwai Kongding" in Meitei. He succeeded Kongding after his death. Later, Pakhangpa became one of the greatest kings of Moirang after defeating the great Chothe King Natoi Nachoupa in the fierce battle of *Chothe Nungsuk ching* (*Lungsukbung region*) and he acquired the titled "Thingkri Nachoupa" (lit. the big ear king who wiped out, it carries the meaning of two dialects).[7] Thereafter, he conquered surrounding small southern kingdoms one by one and consolidated into one big Moirang principality. Later, he mobilised a huge number of soldiers from the south, then marched towards the north and defeated the *Khaba-nganba* (probably the Maring/ Falam/ Poi tribe) and brought them under his direct control.[8] Pakhangpa confederated the Moirang principality of the South-east tribes, the South-western kingdoms (Chothe, Kharam and Koireng, Kom), the North-west kingdoms of *Luwang* (Liangmei, Maram, Thangal tribes) and the North-east kingdom of *Angom* (probably refers to a Tangkhul leader named *Angam*) under one administration.[9] Pakangpa thus, established fully the "Kangla Kingdom", and became the first Sovereign-Ruler of the entire Manipur valley by conquest. Subsequently, he subjugated the other adjoining hill tribes too. In this regard, some Chothe elders claimed that even some close Pakhangpa's relatives and three elders assisted him on his coronation day as per the Chothe custom and tradition. If the sources are to be true, this could be one reason, why tribal participation is still a must in any Meitei king's coronation or some other important ritualistic ceremonies (Kabui, 2003: 84; also see Chothe chief's coronation ceremony in Chapter - 3).

(ii) Analysis on the Identity of Chothe Thangwai Pakhangpa

To analyse and reconstruct the socio-religious history of the Chothe in the mythical person of *Chothe Thangwai/ Thangmei Pakhangpa* (or their ancestor God or the avatar of *Pu Lungchungpa* or the Dragon-Python god) and with that of *Nongda Leiren Pakhangba* (the first historical king of Manipur) to be one and the same person, first we need to de-construct the socio-religious history of the Meitei mythology from the available literatures and compare the contrasting views with the Chothe oral history and the CTP manuscripts with respect to his identity i.e. origin, childhood background and genealogy/ parentage for its authenticity.

(iii) Literatures on Chothe Thangwai Pakhangpa

There are very few literatures available on 'Chothe Thangwai Pakhangpa' which gave the account of his origin, parentage and background. The available literature are the record materials of Manjou Khiyang (1982) *Chothe Athouna* (Chothe's origin), the ancient sacred manuscript like *Chothe Thangwai Pakhangpa* (*CTP*), *Moirang Ningthourol Lambuba* (*MNL*), *Cheitharol Kumpaba* (*ChK*) and some remarkable books written by various British administrators and scholars like; J. Shakespeare (1912), Hudson, William Shaw (1929), M. Kirti Singh (1988) and K. Mangpu (2002).

Except for Manjou Khiyang's (1982) manuscript the rest of the literatures are written by outsiders either in Meitei or English. The CTP sacred manuscript is written in ancient Meitei script in paragraph form on a folded scroll paper accord with 167 paragraphs without the author's name. On its reverse side is the transliteration into Bengali script. This CTP manuscript along with some sacred archaic materials is preserved successively by the deity's keeper (lit. *leihu jokpa* or *Pakhanglakpa*) of Lamlanghupi Chothe Village Council. There is also a translated copy of the original manuscript written in Bengali script, retained by the village chief successively along with two celebrated historical necklaces related to the folktale: *Shantheihoi and Yangngeir* or known as *Lungthun maythranu* (see Pic.18).

A closer looked into the Chothe oral history, the manuscripts of CTP, MNL and other available literature seems to unveil one of the most controversial socio-religious histories of Manipur; that is, the origin and identity of *Chothe Thangwai Pakhangpa* (*Meingai/ Meetingu*) or the so called *Nongda Leiren Pakhangba* whose childhood and parents' identity is shrouded in mystery.[10] The above available literatures serve as the bases in filling up the incomplete history of *Pakhangpa* or the first Sovereign Ruler of Manipur. It also highlights similar beliefs of the Chothe and Meitei in the realm of animism, ancestor-worship and socio-cultural relations since contacted. Based on the Chothe oral history and other secondary sources we shall analyse the elements of Chothe Thangwai Pakhangpa's origin, identity and background, and also examine the identity of his parentage, his wife Leima Sunurembi/ Laisana, and thereby re-construct the socio-religious history of the Chothe and also the Meitei.

(iv) Chothe Thangwai Pakhangpa: The Sacred Manuscript (His Origin)

The sacred manuscript *Chothe Thangwai/ Thangmei Pakhangpa* (*CTP*) is in ancient language written in *Meitei-Mayek* (script) by unknown author in 1870 A.D. The reverse side of the manuscript is the transcription of the same story in Bengali script. There is also an abridged text of the sacred manuscript CTP written in Bengali script under the same title.[11] Like any ancient manuscripts of the Meitei, the statements are in the ancient form of questions, interrogative phrases, idioms and remarks. Many common people will not be able to comprehend the semantic and syntax of the text, since it is very cryptic, poetical and often in rhyme with deep underlying meanings. It can be understood only by those who have slight idea about the story and nature of people of that period.

The original CTP sacred manuscript has 167 paragraphs. The manuscript begins with the introduction (Para: 1-2) stating as, '*Chothe Thangwai Pakhangpa*' is a sacred manuscript which records the origin and identity of the Chothe tribe. The story is a very old history that had been destroyed during the Vaishnavism (Hinduism/ Sanskritisation) movement and was hidden from public knowledge in the early part of the eighteenth century'. It indicates that the author had re-constructed it with much difficulty from few ancient texts obtained after an extensive searched. During his field research the author met an old man, the elder son of Khaibam Yaimou Sagei (probably a priest) near Khujuman road (a village in Bishnupur). That old man told him the story of Chothe Pakhangpa from '*Tej Kumari*' manuscript. But he found the story was incomplete. So, he made a deeper research and fortunately met another man from Nagamapal (Imphal), who provided him a very good ancient manuscript called '*Sahui Loirempa Moirang Kanglarol*' that features more information on the history of Chothe Pakhangpa's origin and identity'.

Hence, it is seen that the sacred original manuscript *Chothe Thangwai Pakhangpa* is one of the most important historical accounts of Pakhangpa who (anonymous author) compiled with much difficulty based on the oral history and other available archaic materials, after the burning of all Manipuri/ *puya* books by the Hindu followers (see Pic. 8 and 10). The CTP manuscript is preserved by the Lamlanghupi village council as a sacred document. It is shown to only few selective villagers on certain auspicious occasions, especially after the annual festivals by performing a very strict ritual. Therefore, no researcher or any outsider has had any full access this to sacred CTP manuscript till today except S.N. Khelchandra who had abridged it. The abridged manuscript '*Chothe Thangwai Pakhangpa*' of Khelchandra has ninety-three (93) paragraphs and the front page reads as (below is the free translation):

(*Aruba leirikne, Meitei ariba mayekna eirambadagi, Bangla mayekta ethokpane. Kristabda 1870, gi Thawan ahanba humni panba, thangja numitta eiba loijabane*),

"*This is an important book which was initially written in ancient Meitei-Mayek (script) and rewritten into Bengali script. The writing was completed on Saturday, the 3rd of the first month of (Thawan) July-August 1870 A.D.*" (see Pic. 9 and 11).

The period 1870 of the '*Chothe Thangwai Pakhangpa*' manuscript indicates that the anonymous author under sponsorship had probably compiled and re-written it during the reign of King Chandrakriti (1850-1886) after the original historical writings had been destroyed in fire during Hindunisation process by King Garib Niwaz/ Pamheiba (1709-1748).

The *Moirang Ningthourol Lambuba* (*MNL*) specifically also indicates that Pakhangpa was one of the greatest kings of Moirang in Chapter - 19 entitled as, '*Chothe Thangwai Pakhangpa: Thinkgri Nachaoba*'. Since, the book did not record the period of any of the kings or dates of the events, some scholars considered it as a collection of fables. But one cannot deny the large amount of invaluable information provided by this MNL manuscript that described holistically the early culture and history of Manipur. Some still argued that MNL manuscript is much older than the *Cheitharol Kumpaba* the court chronicle book.

The legendary King Chothe Thangwai Pakhangpa since considered divine and sacred; the CTP manuscript begins the introduction in ritualistic form like any opening Hindu prayer:

(*Hung! Hayahe, heiyao; Nahalnong Chothe Mareipung, Yangthou lammahanbu, mayum Chothe meinungthou Khunpu Tarang khullakpa, loibi hao reima loiya Lenghoinu gi palem pibuknunggi, chingpal khom-ol angalla. Huiyai liklu ahanbibu phuina rakle haidabara. Adunong-gibu mayum Chothe mareipungda, Chingngu nongthou Sorarel, awang pakhang yoirenba, korou thangba nong-ningthouki, chingngu mityeng panchumpana, chingngu manongta-mpu, khoiyum shingtum luroi paina, nongtamkhire haidabara. Mamon phuina monggibu, Unbi Makan lamda leiraklabada, Mamo madom shatpina, maning shumlei tallabagibu, mapal Chothe panphoilau, madu khalei pam ngapabu, Thaushiraklabada chingngu manongdamgibu, Maman marau launa heina. Namu pong-oi shaktam lep, tubi marou heina langwol phoraklabagibu*), (CTP - Para:1, p.1, of abridged text).

The above CTP excerpt reads: "*Hung! Hayehe;* once in the kingdom of Chothe, Khamlang-Taopi (Daishin) the eldest daughter of the village chief Tarang (Surou) and queen Lenghoinu of the hill people found their daughter mystically pregnant. The Dragon-Python God (*Pu Soraren* in Meitei) of the north-western hills while wandering around spotted Khamlang-Taopi in her parents' jhum (yam) field and her beauty captivated his eyes. Therefore, the Dragon God transformed like a young handsome Pong man and met her in the field (CTP- Para: 1, p.1). Thereafter, he developed intimacy and frequently visited her in the jhum field. They had physical relationship, and Khamlang-Taopi was impregnated. Tarang/ Surou was hurt by his daughter Khamlang-Taopi's pregnancy news, who thereby accused all the village youth for seducing and impregnating her before he could declare her marriageable publicly. After repeatedly reprimanded by her parents to disclose the identity of her lover (the father of the unborn child), Khamlang-Taopi revealed that he was neither a Chothe boy nor any neighbouring youth from the 'Keke Chaopapung' (a Moirang village)", (CTP- Para: 2).

On hearing Khamlang-Taopi's confession, her father became more furious, doubtful and apprehensive about the unknown identity of the young stranger (i.e., his name, clan and village). So, in order to find out whether the stranger was a divine being or human, the angry parents instructed their daughter to hang the package containing mixtures of white linseed, onion, fresh yam, garlic, ginger, turmeric, snail and eel wrapped in the wild-yam leaves in the inner roof of the jhum hut just above his usual sitting place, and should pierced it when he comes visiting her:

(*Chothe mareipung shanglou mathel lang ngambabu, thangpak mem man, thoiding ngouja, panphuk panphoi, shoikari mayangba, thilhou, chanam, lilwai khomwai, shingkha shingthum, yaimu yai-ngang, tharoi khoujao, ngaparum ngaril khangkabol* (CTP-Para: 3, p. 2).

When the young stranger visited her jhum hut and sat at his usual place, Khamlang-Taopi as instructed by her parents pierced the package secretly during their conversation and few drops of the liquid mixture fell on his body. Though he initially sensed and expressed the unusual smell, Khamlang-Taopi convinced him that the smell came from her lunch package. Being a Divine person or demigod endowed with supernatural powers he cannot bear the smell and burn of the mixture on his body, so he immediately rushed to the nearby brook and disappeared.[12]

According to the CTP sacred manuscript, Khamlang-Taopi was prescribed with many do's and don'ts of the food habits and other religious taboos in her dreams by the demigod (her lover) after she became pregnant. As a result, it is mentioned that she did not go out of her house during the last four months of her pregnancy until she gave birth (CTP-Para: 28-32, pp. 16-18). In the following chapter, certain 'religious norms and taboo' instructed in her dreams are thereby discussed.

The CTP manuscript also states that Khamlang-Taopi (Daishin) gave birth to a son, who was named as "Chothe 'Thangwai' Pakhangpa". According to N. Vijalakshimi Brara, Pakhangpa is said to have been born on Thursday, the 15th lunar day of the Inga month (15th June) and all the Mangang worshipped their ancestors on this day (1998:86). Further, the Para: 32 of the CTP manuscript states that *Chothe Thangwai Pakhangpa* was named on the fifth day as instructed by the Dragon-Python god. This child naming ceremony appears to be similar with the Chothe custom (see the *Chothe child naming ceremony*). The Para: 32 of CTP sacred manuscript also mentioned that Pakhangpa was referred as "Lairen Meitingu" (lit. Python's protruding tail) especially by the Nangngoi (Moirang) people. According to the Chothe oral history, "Meingai" or "Meitingte" means 'a child with a protruding tail', believed to be the mark of his divinity. This particular term is seen interpreted by the Meitei from a different perspective as 'Lord of the kings'.

S.N.A. Parratt without any prejudice clarifies such incoherent notion and the misconception that "The use of the term Meetingnu (lit. Lord of the Meeteis) for king indicates that the chronicle is essentially the repository of the Meetei writing of history. It reflects the Meetei viewpoint against that of the other *yeks* or clan groups, as well as of other peoples, probably pre-Meetei autochthones (like the Chakpa and the Loi), while others are today classified as 'tribal" (2005:3).

Closer to the Chothe oral version is the M. Kirti Singh remarks that "another title for the king is 'Lairel Meidingu' meaning 'Lord, straight tail'. Pakhangba, being the Lord of the snakes is better known as Meidingu" (1993:55).

But in Para: 25 of the abridged *CTP* text or Para: 2 of original CTP and also MNL, Pakhangpa is referred as one of the greatest kings of Moirang, known as the subjugator of 'Thingkri Nachaoba'. Prior to identifying him as defeater of Thingkri Nachaoba, he was known as "Chothe Thangwai Pakhangpa" whose great (foster) father was known as "Thangwai Kongding Ahanba" and his mother as *Thamoirempi* the princess/ queen of Chakhakhong Mareempa.[13] Below is the text.

(*Keke Moirang ningthou Thinkgri Nachaoba touna kau-ae. Thinkgri Nachaoba kaudringeidi Chothe Thangwai Pakhangba tauna kauye, Keke Moirang Chothe Thangwai Pakhangba mapanthou ningthou Keke Thangwai Kongding ahanba kau-aena, panlem mama Chakhakhong Mareempa chanu leima Thamoirembi tauna kau-aena*), (CTP-Para: 25, p.15).

In accordance with the Chothe oral history, the Para: 13 of the CTP manuscript also described the third attempt made by Tarang or Surou to kill the boy (Pakhangpa). According to the CTP manuscript, Tarang cursed his grandson who neither knew his father's identity nor clan to go and catch-hold of the huge falling tree, so that he might be crushed to death.

(*Tarang makhoi shaona, pacha khangda shalai toukhangdaba-o nangbu pamel Uru tuple tare U-ngakluro,* (CTP-Para: 13, p. 7).

According to CTP- Para:14-17; 'Tarang returned home without the boy, but the young boy miraculously survived from the incident and surprisingly brought home the big log of the tree on his shoulder and drops down in their courtyard. This astonished his grandfather Tarang. It is said that the boy narrated everything about the strange dreams he had to his mother when he was knocked off by the falling tree and fallen asleep. He told his mother that a man came in his dream and asked him to pick up some particular falling dry leaves grown around the area and to keep the leaves on his shoulder where he would carrying the log'. However, the manuscript does not specifically mention which particular type of plant leaves it was. The man is believed to be the disguised Dragon-Python god. Daishin, from her son's dream realised that it was her lover the Dragon-Python god that saved her son's life. The manuscript also mentioned that she had many strange dreams and visions time to time foretelling and warning her about certain future consequences. It also mentions that in her dream she was asked to perform a ritual with seven (7) eggs (*Khuiyum* in Meitei), in case she suffered from shock or frightened (CTP-Para: 20-22). This indicates the spiritual connection between Khamlang-Taopi (Daishin) and the Dragon-Python god as guardian angel although he made visible to others.

In continuation, the Chothe oral history says that young Thangwai Pakhangpa grew up to be extremely notorious and a trouble maker among his friends whenever they played. He often landed up hurting others. His extraordinary strength and power surprises and horrifies the villagers. Unable to bear the shame due to his notoriety and as illegitimate child, his grandfather Tarang/ Surou asked his daughter Daishin to leave the village along with her son and settle far in the north. He gave them a hen and a rooster, with an instruction to settle at a place where the rooster crowed, and there, to perform the egg divination (*artui-jan/shan*). As ordered by his grandfather, young Pakhangpa and his mother left the village and marched north. It is believed that they first settled at Langthabal (near Imphal) on a mound close to the lake, since the rooster crowed and accordingly performed the egg divination.[14]

(v) Pakhangpa's Childhood and Parentage (Analysis With Other Literatures)

Other literatures that described Pakhangpa's origin and parentage and that support the Chothe oral history and the CTP manuscript are found in William Shaw (1929), M. Kirti Singh (1993), K. Mangpu (2001) and G. Shangkham (2006) to name few. Kirti Singh remarks that "The myth of Pakhangba recalls the association of the Meitei with the Chothe of the Kuki groups of tribals" (1993:153-154). This very important statement of Kirti Singh on Pakhangpa's origin, identity, parentage and the origin of Meitei and its association with Chothe are evidently substantiated in William Shaw's writing as firsth and account:

"There was a girl by the name Lenghoi or Nungmaidenga who fell in love with a large snake, which resided near the village. She was of the 'Chothe' tribe of Old-Kuki. To others the snake appeared as a snake but to the girl it was a very handsome young man. Eventually she became pregnant by the snake and a male child was born to her. He grew up and all spoke of him as father-less at which he used to be ashamed. His mother told him not to mind that but to go and make friends with his father, the snake. The boy was not afraid and met the snake who he

caught by the neck and the snake told him many wonderful things that were to happen to the boy. The boy then went and told his mother of this and she gave eggs to perform the "Arhtuishan" when searching for a new site where he was to set up a new village. He tried Langthabal first but because of inauspicious omens he moved to the middle of the valley where, on performing the Arhtui-shan, he found the place suitable and he founded a village there. Thus the Manipuris were originated. At that time they live like Kukis and Nagas but later a Brahmin came from the south who so impressed them with his preaching that they took on their present religion" (Shaw, 1929:47-48).

William Shaw in a nutshell has given the most undoubted lucid history of Pakhangpa's origin, his parentage, and the Meitei's origin- as the descendant of the Chothe.[15] Similarly, Mangpu Kilong also remarks that, "Sometime in 700 AD a Python-god fell in love with a lady - Lenghoi by name, of Chothe, a member of Old-Kuki who was renown as Pakhangpa" (2002:42, 54). Gina Shangkham as informed by her informants of Kharam tribe said that the Meitei king (Pakhangpa) was, "The son, born of the Chothe lady" (2006:45).

In this regard, most of the descriptions provided by these scholars in their literatures, including William Shaw are seen to be authentic as far as the sources and their writings are concerned without much inference. They obtained these sources of information from different groups of local folks based on their oral historical account, and it shows direct coherence with the Chothe oral narration, unlike Meitei scribes that produced various mythical versions.

Some of the mysterious eventful life of young *Chothe Thangwai Pakhangpa* missing in most oral histories after he and his mother settled at Langthabal; his growing power in the north; his caused of movement to the south; his first war and defeat by the Khaba-nganba; and his alliance policy with the Moirang kings are found mentioned in brief in the Chothe oral history and also in some other literatures. For example, Pakhangpa's existence at Langthabal in the north, his defeat by the Khaba-nganba and taking refuge at Moirang, and his mysterious personality as king of Imphal (Kangla) is described by Gangmumei Kabui and W. Ibohal Singh based on archive historical materials like *Cheitharol Kumpaba* (*ChK*) *and Moirang Ningthourol Lambuba* (*MNL*). Pakhangpa life and battles, as a great warrior and conqueror in the south, and also as the greatest king of Moirang before he became the first sovereign king of Imphal valley Manipur are well described in *Moirang Ningthourol Lambuba* (*MNL*). His origin and parentage, passionate romantic relationship with Sunurembi (his beloved wife) is well elaborated in the sacred manuscript *Chothe Thangwai Pakhangpa* (*CTP*). But the Meitei historians wrote the accounts of Pakhangpa based mostly on MNL and Chk manuscript therefore, their history is never complete since the third most important sacred CTP manuscript is never consulted by them besides the Chothe oral history.

The cause of Pakhangpa's movement toward south, Kabui writes "According to *Chakpa Khunta Khunthok*, Nongda Leiren Pakhangba when he became of age, fought against the Khabas under the leadership of Khaba Nungchenba. In the struggle, Pakhangba was defeated by Khabas (*Khaba-nganba*) and Pakhangba was forced to take refuge in Moirang principality" (2003:83). This apparently suggest that Pakhangpa after being defeated by the Khaba-nganba the northern (*Koubru*) group fled south and became an aided or alliance partner with King Kongding Ahanba (the elder son of former Moirang King Tushemba). This suggests that his mother Khamlang-Taopi being a beautiful young lady probably married Kongding or became one of his concubines. The evident is that as part of the tradition Khamlang-Taopi changed her name and thus came to be known as "Thamoilempi" in the south. While Kongding was referred as the foster-father or guardian (*Mapan-panthou*) of Pakhangpa (CTP- Para:58, 61, p. 30).

The story how Pakhangpa perfectly engineered and became one of the most successful and the greatest king of Moirang, how he acquired the name "Thingkri Nachaoba", and his treaty of "Taibelou Pukphat Sapeilou" (The elongated inter-locking hunting field) in the south with Thokchao the eldest Angom (Angam) prince of Tangkhul is well elaborated in *Chothe Thangwai Pakhangpa* (CTP- Para: 90, p. 46) and in *Moirang Ningthourol Lambuba* (*MNL*). His treaty at *Taibelou Pukphat Sapeilou* proved to be a landmark event.[16]

Moirang Ningthourol Lambuba (*MNL*): Pakhangpa at Moirang

The manuscript *Moirang Ningthourol Lambuba* (*MNL*) is also considered as one of the most important historical texts of Manipur. The Chapter nineteenth titled as, '*Chothe Thangwai Pakhangpa: Thingkri Nachaoba*' exclusively deals with Pakhangpa describing him as one of the greatest kings of Moirang of the ancestor god (*Purek lai*).[17] The similar account is also found in the *Chothe Thangwai Pakhangpa* (*CTP*) manuscript. According to MNL and CTP, Pakhangpa was also commonly known as, "Purek lai Thangwai Atengba", meaning 'the aided ancestor god of Thangwai Khongding' because he helped subjugate the people living on the south and western areas of Moirang which King Khongding and his predecessors could not do so (Singh, 1982: 90, CTP-Para: 83, p. 43). Khongding was the eighth king of Moirang. MNL also provides detailed account of his conquests, successful expansion of his kingdom and the new titled he acquired in the south, often as great warrior.

Pakhangpa, after his victory over Koireng, Kharam and also Chothe by defeating the great Chothe King Natoi Nachaopa in the fierce battle of *Nungsuk-ching* or *Lungsuk* of the south-western kingdoms, began his campaign in the south and south-east region against the small kingdoms of *Sugunu Ewaita* and *Ashong Khunlen* who gained control over them after devastating battles.[18] According to MNL, Pakhangpa plundered and burnt the entire village of Ashong Khunlen a village beyond Sugunu Ewaita inhabited by Poirei.[19] He defeated the youngest son of queen Peyai the huge and brave warrior, and the brave King Salikpu (Singh, 1982: 95-96, CTP-Para: 88-89, pp. 45-46). Thus, Pakhangpa brought all the southern kingdoms directly under his control by breaking all their ancestral socio-political equations and ties.

Moirang Ningthourol Lambuba like the CTP manuscript states that Pakhangpa after unifying all the small southern kingdoms accepted a truce with Thokchao the eldest son of Kouburel Angom-ngagi of the northern kingdom and a treaty was made between them at *Taibelou Pukphat Sapeilou* near Khuijuman/ Bishnupur (Singh, 1982:97, CTP- Para: 90, p. 46).[20] This treaty of alliance between the two leaders may be considered as the turning point in the history of Manipur as it resulted in overthrowing the rival Khaba-nganba by the combined forces. Kabui said while staying in Moirang, Pakhangba organised support from Moirang Chaopa Mathipa and Sapon Sanoupa who whole heartedly helped him. The combined forces of Pakhangpa completely destroyed and defeated the Khaba. Some Khaba surrendered to Angom Puleiromba while others fled to hills and lived in the southern Tangkhul region (Kabui, 2003: 83, see also Kamei 2004: 46).

The hidden motive of Pakhangpa's was to take revenge of the northern Khaba-nganba since they ousted and humiliated him when he was young at Langthabal. Therefore, in the south-west as he grows up he slowly campaigned and consolidated the various small kingdoms around Moirang like Kumbi, Wangoo, Ethaiwas and Sugnu region. Later, considering insufficient army he turn his eyes towards the western kingdoms like Koireng, Kharam, Liangmei and also defeated the Chothe king in the battle of *Nungsuk laan*. As he gathers the army and prepares for his attack, he made Thokchao the eldest son of Kouburel Angom-ngagi who was also seeking an allied partner. Taking the advantage of the situation Pakhangpa made truce with him and jointly ousted the Khaba-nganba of the northern kingdom. Thus, Pakhangpa's champion has put the power of Khaba-nganba to an end in the north and established his historical Kangla Kingdom and as the sovereign king at Imphal.

Meitei Mythology of Pakhangpa

G. Kabui the renowned historian of Manipur states that "The origin of the Meitei is shrouded in mystery and the study on the subject is greatly influenced by the religious faiths and the political ideologies of the Meitei themselves, thus making the problem highly speculative and controversial" (2003:15, see notes on *Meitei* and *Poireiton*). Thus, some local scholars disagree with the Meitei mythologies relating to the origin and identity of Pakhangpa as described by the earlier scribes. So, these speculation and controversies may be further analysed by incorporating the oral history, the *CTP* and other manuscripts.

According to Meitei mythology, there are four Pakhangbas, viz.; (i) Loimanai Pakhangba, (ii) Leinung Lonja (*Ariba*) Pakhangba, (iii) Lolang Pakhangba, and (iv) Nongda Lairen Pakhangba. Of the four, Nongda Leiren Pakhangba is considered as the historical King according to *Cheithourol Kumpaba* record, while the rest are considered as mystical Pakhangbas, besides the other eighteen cognomens given below (Kabui, 2003: 75). One of the most popular mythical versions which tried to construct a connection between the myths of *Sanamahi, Pakhangpa* and the legendary King Pakhangpa is the *Sanamahism* religion.

According to this Meitei mythical version, *Atiya Guru Sidaba* the Supreme God and the creator of the Universe, and his wife *Leimaren Sidabi* had two sons. The elder brother is known as *Ashiba* or *Kuptreng* or *Sanamahi* and the younger known as *Konjin Tuthokpa* or *Sentreng* or *Pakhangpa*. One day their father, Atiya Guru Shidaba floated down the river in the form of a dead cow to test the faith and wisdom of his two sons. Sanamahi thought the cow was already dead and stinking, so did not bother. But Sentreng recognised his father and performed the funeral rites. Based on this view, he is known as 'Pakhangba', lit. 'One who knows the father' according to Meitei version. Again their father asked both of them to go round the universe and whosoever wins the competition will succeed as king. While Kuptreng was attempting to cover the entire universe, Pakhangpa, on the other hand went around his father's pedestal seven times, on the advice of his mother considering he was weak and young. Thus, on the criteria of the test prize, Pakhangpa became the royal king of the earth and Sanamahi was made the house/ family god (Kabui, 2003:57, Singh, 1986:396-7).

Many scholars like K.C. Tensuba attempted to clear the above mythical and historical uncertainties by affirming that "N.L. Paakhangba was not that Paakhangba, the younger brother of Sanna-mahi the son of Yaibirel Sidaba and Leimarel Sidabee, which was in fact, not historical but something like a religious story reflecting the concept of the creation of life of the earth" (1993:137). Similarly, Gangmumei Kabui asserted that, "The tradition of Pakhangpa as their divine King of the earth and Sanamahi as spiritual deity of the Meitei perhaps was a myth created by rulers of Ningthouja dynasty founded by Nongda Leiren Pakhangpa in the late historical time to give a garb of divinity to the king" (2003:57).

In this connection, W.I. Singh (1986) states that there are eighteen cognomens of Pakhangba as mysticism seen from different accounts by the Meitei (that began by 16th and 17th century A.D. in the pursuit of Tantric culture), in order to please the autocratic rulers of the kingdom. The eighteen cognomens are: (1). Nongta Tukuplik, (2) Nongtreng Apumba, (3) Leinung Lonja Ariba, (4) Laloyang Tanouba, (5) Nongpok Poklen, (6) Umtha Ningthou Yoirmba, (7) Chingwang Ningthou Atenba, (8) Laiyingthou apanba, (9) Ching-U Langba Apanba, (10) Leinung Longja Pakhangba, (11) Lai Pakhang Atengba, (12) Tangja Leela Pakhangba, (13) Lolang Pakhangpa, (14) Tubi Yoi Nongta, (15) Nongta Lairen Pakhangba, (16) Ningtem, (17) Sa, and (18) Javista (Singh, 1986: 271-272). Such was the variant names.

(i) Pakhangpa's Coronation at Kangla (Imphal)

According to G. Kabui, soon after the defeat of the Khabas and the Poireiton groups, Pakhangpa was crowned as the New Sovereign-King of Kangla (Imphal) by the three great leaders viz.; 'Puleiromba the Angom chief, Luwang Langmaiba (Luwang priest) and Ningthem Apanba of the Mangang (the ruling prince of Mangang) by pouring Nongjeng pond water on the body of the King Chothe Thangwai Pakhangpa and Queen Leima Sunurembi or Laisana' (2003:84-85). Kabui also said that many of his leaders and relatives attended his coronation ceremony, as it was performed in the indigenous manner. According to the *Chakparol* manuscript Kabui describes that 'Kansurol a leader of the Chakpas sent four persons namely Chakmaringba, Langmaringba, Mungmaringpa, Ngangan maringba to call Pakhangpa from Langthabal to Kangla for the coronation where they guarded Pakhangpa during the coronation, ... All the people were invited to the ceremony, Pakhangpa along with his Queen Laisana were formally coronated.[21] According to *'Shanglen Puba Puya'* manuscript, the coronation ceremony was performed on first Saturday of Kalen (June/ July) the Meitei lunar calendar' (*ibid:* 84-85).

G. Kabui further said that, on his coronation day the poets and singers gave Pakhangpa (Meingai) the regal title "Tubi Yoinungda Nongda Lairen Pakhangba" (literally in Meitei, a son bore of the Rain Python God through a lady by intercession).[22] This points how Pakhangpa acquired his divine name (in Meitei dialect) from his valley admirers. It is said to be a common (tribal) practice in the past to compose folksong honouring one's greatness. The song often expresses the nature of one's success, victory or achievement and deeds, thereby giving the person a new titled or identity for his greatness. As a result, he was given the title, "Meitingu or Meidingu" a phrase referred to as a 'demigod with a tail' (*ibid:* 84-85).

Thus, we see the metamorphosis of Pakhangpa's name changing from: *Thangwai* to *Meingai, Meitingte* to *Meetingu; Chothe Thangwai Pakhangpa* to *Thingkri Nachaoba; Thangwai Khongding* to *Nongda Leiren Pakhangba*, and so forth (the cognomens), known differently to different groups of people by his relationship. Some by his mystical life and others by his feats. Pakhangpa to distinguish himself among the equals with other Ningthoujas/ Royal clanships finally established his own identity as head of "Mangang" clanship, and was crowned as the first Sovereign King/ Emperor of Kangla (Imphal) Kingdom by combining two principalities of Moirang and Kangla.[23]

(ii) Death

The mysticism of Pakhangpa did not just end with his mysterious childhood activities and parentage, but continued even after his death. The Chothe elders said that Pakhangpa is believed to have conspired and killed by his enemies using magical charms. Some claimed he died after he revealed his secret strength to his beloved (persuasive) wife, though he was not supposed to reveal under any circumstances. In this way, the Chothe believes that a man should never disclose all his secrets or very confidential matter to his wife, no matter how much he loves her. If he does, it is believed that he will not live long.

According to Kabui, Pakhangpa and Laisna lived in constant fear of the Khaba with great risk since he defeated them. And that one Khaba rebel named Huitao Tington Khaba Tousuba ambushed and speared Pakhangpa to death by a strong sharp reed and threw his dead body into the Nungjeng pond. Another version is that Pakhangpa was killed by his own son Khuiyom Tompok in connivance with the Khabas (2003:90).

The Chothe folktales still highly speak of Khaba-nganba (Khoibu-Maring) to be the tribe that killed Pakhangpa. Chothe claimed that since early days the Maring are very skillful in religious-magic and witchcraft or sorcery practices (who practices even today). Kabui said after Pakhangpa died, Laisana fled and took refuge among the Angom (Tangkhul) and subsequently Khuiyom Tompok the eldest son of Pakhangpa succeeded the throne. All these suggest that Pakhangpa was probably killed by the Khaba-nganba conspirators helped by an internal person, where magical spell is also considered to be involved in the plot.

(i) Pakhangpa's Genealogy

From the above observation it is seen that many Meitei scholars have speculated and presumed different names to construct the true identity of *Chothe Thangwai Pakhangpa* or *Nongda Leiren Pakhangba* but proved to be unsuccessful because they could not ascertain his origin, identity and parentage authentically. Kabui said that 'the historicity of Nongda Lairen Pakhangba as king is clearly proved by the historical chronicles and his dynasty's genealogy. But with regards to origin, Pakhangba was a prince of mysterious origin; opinions regarding his origin and parentage vary from his being an Aryan prince from upper Burma to an adventurer from the Brahmaputra valley or the Himalayas to divine incarnate born to put an end to anarchy in the land, an illegitimate child of a clan chief, made a ruler by his foster father' (2003:75, 77). Thus, Kabui endorse that "The identification of his parentage has been quite a controversial problem" (*Ibid:* 77). The confusion and controversy over the identity of Pakhangba is obvious, since no complete historical record were made available to them on his origin and parentage. Moreover they have not consulted the *Chothe Thangwai Pakhangpa* (*CTP*) manuscript nor seriously analyses the oral history from the cognate tribes.

(ii) Pakhangpa's Mother

To many Meitei, Pakhangpa's mother is known as "Leinung Yaibirok" the literal meaning is 'from the interior enchanting stream' in Meitei referring to Leimatak river basin. Kabui said that according to *Khagemba Yangbi* text, Pakhangpa's mother was Leinung Yaibirok one born three times as queen and married to three chiefs/ kings. Similarly, *Chada Laihui* a book on genealogy of the queens of Manipur of Ningthouja dynasty mentioned Leinung Yaibirok as the mother of Pakhangpa. Then *Pakhangba Nongkarol* a text dealing with the death of the rulers also mentioned Nongda Lairen Pakhangba's mother as Leinung Yaibirok (2003: 76-77). Y.M. Singh and N.B. Singh from *Meihourol Lathup Latam* a sacred text said that the mother of Pakhangpa was "Liklabicha Nungtangnu" who was illegitimately touched by Luwang Langmaiba and was forcibly married to Puleiromba the Angom chief (see also Kabui, 2003: 77).

W. Ibohal Singh (1986) on the basis of the *Cheitharol Kumpaba, Moirang Ningthourol Lambuba* and *Leithak Leikharol* described that Pakhangpa's mother was called "Leinung Yabirok Yakha Chanu" it means in Meitei 'a lady from the interior group of enchanting stream area'. Singh said this Yakha/ Chakha group is believed to be of the neo-Tibetan or Tai or Shan group (amalgamated old tribes) who settled around the slanting downstream of the Yakha or originally migrated from Khamnung (*Khampa*) areas (1986:76-82, 266). This enchanting backward stream in Chothe is called "Tuipi" (lit. Main River). But the amalgamated Meitei called it as 'Leimatak', after the queen (Leima) frequently visited her ancestral place. This river flow westward to join Barak river unlike other tributaries.

Therefore, in accordance to the oral history, W. Ibohal Singh also believed that the people of Lei-Nung or Chakha/ Yakha (Chothe) are group of people who migrated to the south-western region of the state after a sequence of expulsion from the Tai by Tsi-Wang-Tsi in the 3rd B.C. who earlier occupied the *Khampat* region of the north-western Myanmar, originally belonging to *Kham-pa* tribe of eastern Tibetan (*ibid:* 77-78, 146-149). Y. Damshu (Stephen) based on his forefather's narration points out that *Leinung Yabirok Yakha Chanu,* is a Meitei dialect referring to Pakhangpa's mother by identifying with her birth place around the Leimatak river basin (Lungsuk). As seen above, all the scholars point their sources to one common thing, i.e. she was 'from the interior region of enchanting stream' (Leimatak).

The sacred manuscript *Chothe Thangwai Pakhangpa* (*CTP*) also states that Pakhangpa was an illegitimate son of Khamlang-Taobi (also known as Thamoilembi) the eldest daughter of Chothe King Tarang and Queen Lenghoinu, without specifying Pakhangpa father's name. They believed that Khamlang-Taobi was impregnated mysteriously by the intercession of their Principal Guardian God (*Lungchungpa*) the Dragon-Python (Para: 1, p.1). The various names of Pakhangpa's mother referred above are not a specific personal or birth name, except Lenghoinu, since it bears no any indigene Chothe name. Rather it is seen to be a common terminologies identifying with her birth place, group of people and the region she associates. This teknonymical is a tradition in the region where a person is often indirectly referred by nickname to show one's respect or politeness, despite knowing his/ her actual birth name. Such addressing style often confuses and misleads outsiders in identifying the actual person/ group of people, if one does not know the whole truth.[24]

There are also similar myths found among different communities about the mother of Pakhangpa. Mangpu Kilong in his paper, '*The Kom*' describes three similar stories of a tribal girl falling in love with a Serpent god. The stories seem to be a deviation of the legend of Chothe Thangwai Pakhangpa, since the elements and genealogy are related. Kilong states that a lady called "Chongnu fell in love with the Python God", and in another story of '*The Genealogy of Rengam the Hero',* he said "Shilnu, a girl cohabited with a Snake God, a daughter of Zetei" (probably Chote). He also points to a similar legend in '*Sherdukpen'* folktale written by N.B. Batra that, "a girl fell in love with a snake who was handsome in disguise" (2001:42-43, see also Batra, 1964).

Khiyang Manjou, besides other Chothe village elders like Mk. Neilut, H. Thambaljao, Y. Maipak claimed that Pakhangpa mother's name was "Daishin", the elder daughter of the great Chothe chief Surou (others knows him as Tarang or Nungkarakpa or Sanarakpa) and his wife Lenghoinu. Analysing the above views, the oral history, the *CTP* sacred manuscript and William Shaw writings: Pakhangpa's mother name as "Lenghoi" or "Nungmaidenga" seems to have been confused by some informants with Pakhangpa's grandmother (1929:47-48; Singh, 1993:153-154). While the second name "Nung-meidingu" carries two meanings; 'Nung-suk' (old Chothe village) and 'Meidingu' (Pakhangpa's nickname). The name suggests inferential name to identify Pakhangpa's mother by the valley people as a teknonymy tradition. The CTP sacred manuscript indicates that Pakhangpa was the illegitimate child of Khamlang-Taopi (Daishin), (Para: 91-93). She even visited her village and asked the villagers to perform the repentance ritual with the liquor (*Wangle zu*) to exonerate themselves from their past sins i.e., expulsion of Pakhangpa and his mother from the village (*Ipam Chothe ide khungang pumna hupna langei khumsheng khudingee ningol eina panthou khallei pamngapgi loidam manung-o*), (CTP-Para: 91-93, p. 47-48).

G. Kabui states that Pakhangpa's mother Daishin (Khamlang-Taopi/ Thamoilempi/ Leinung Yaibirok Yakha Chanu) was born three times queen and married to three chiefs (kings) or was associated with three great men in her lifetime (2003:77, 79). First, Daishin the eldest daughter of Tarang/ Surou fell in love with the mythical king the Dragon-Python God (the anonymous strange young youth) and subsequently bore a son Pakhangpa.[25] Since Pakhangpa was considered an illegitimate child, she and her son were cast away from their own village. Later, both Daishin and her son Pakhangpa took refuge at Moirang, away from the Khaba people of the north. There, she probably became one of the wives or concubines of King Kongding of Moirang, as indicated by her new name "Leima Thamoilempi" whose earlier name was known as Khamlang-Taopi. After Kongding's death, Daishin developed a close relationship with Puleiromba the Angom chief from northeast, for which the people considered her the consort of Puleiromba. Thereafter, she was known as 'Leinung Yabirok Yakha Chunu' (a girl from the interior region of enchanting stream) identifying with her birth place and the group she belongs. Except for the first person (mythical Dragon-Python king), the identity of the other two men/ chiefs viz.; Kongding and Puleiromba have established as historical kings, and as the foster fathers of Pakhangpa.

Some scholars even claimed that Pakhangpa had a younger biological/ step sister called 'Sira Khongthingnu' (Kongdingnu), probably a daughter of Kongding and Thamoilempi, but cannot be acertain (Singh, 1986: 269).

From the above analysis, it indicates that Daishin the Pakhangpa's mother belonged to Chothe tribe and was the eldest daughter of Surou (Tarang- chief of a Chothe village) and Lenghoinu. She is known by different names as: Daishin by the Chothe; Khamlang-taopi by the Khaba-Nganba (Maring) tribe in the north; Thamoilempi by the Moirang in the south; and Leinung Yaibirok Yakha Chanu by the later valley Meitei migrants of Imphal, Manipur.

(iii) Pakhangpa's Father

Scholars continued to speculate and presumed different names to identify the father of *Chothe Thangwai Pakhangpa* or *Nongda Leiren Pakhangba*. For example, Kabui writes that according to the genealogy of the Ningthouja clan the father of N.L. Pakhangba was projected to be Sentreng. But Y.M. Singh and N.B. Singh assumed that Sentreng was one of the aliases of the father of Pakhangba, and that the real father was Luwang Langmaiba, and the social father was Puleiromba the Angom chief (2003:78). Yet according to W. Ibohal Singh, Pakhangba's father was "Likleng" alias "Luwang Langmaiba" from a royal family of the Lei-nung tribe and held the post of Tupu a designation derived from "Lambu Tupu" (1986:274-275).[26] In Chothe layman *Lampu Tarpu* means 'the old village owner' or 'the old village chief'. In this respect, K.C. Tensuba contested W. Ibohal Singh's proposition saying that Tupu Likleng alias Luwaang Langmaiba as the father of Pakhangba might be a title given to one who was able to solve social problems at times, in short, a man of high thinking; *Lu* means the head or the intellect, *Waang* means high, and Laang-maiba means one who can set someone free from the dangerous trap... (1993:137). Tensuba's deduction only from the literal Meitei meaning shows incomplete.

However, Kabui pre-concludes that Tarpu Likleng or Luwang Langmaiba was an old man, a priest and the chief advisor who executed Pakhangpa's coronation (2003:85). But W. Ibohal Singh opinion on the reason for the invitation or selection for the chieftainship of the Leinung and Leihou is that 'Pakhangpa was the grand-son of Leihou chief' and son of Lambu-Tupu', is incorrect (1986: 274-275).

From the above examination, it points that Surou is the maternal grandfather of Pakhangpa's who was a respectable old village chief from Leinung-Yakha (Chothe *Lungsuk ching*) of Leimatak region. He was also known differently by different groups of people as; Tarang, Nungkarakpa, Sanarakpa, Lampu Tarpu and Luwang Langmaipa (lineage head priest).[27] W.I. Singh's has traced out Pakhangpa's maternal lineage that Likleng or Luwang Langmaipa or Tarang or Surou as his maternal grandfather, but not his father (instead of tracing his paternal lineage). So far nobody has traced out the name and identity of Pakhangpa's biological father, not even the Chothe people could tell, except that he was a mysterious young stranger. Thus, Pakhangpa father's identity remains anonymous and mysterious till date. The only human speculation is – Whether it was because of the rigid socio-cultural norms of the society during those days that the true identity of Pakhangpa's father was concealed in order to avoid serious consequences like death, war and feuds amongst them, or is it that the anonymous youth was a foreigner living in a village who immediately disappeared from the area out of fear

Table 20: Variation of Names Referred by Various Ethnic Groups to a Person

Sl. No.	Personal Identity	Chothe and other Cognate groups	In the South by Moirang/Ngangoi	In the North by the Meitei and other	In the Northeast by Tangkhul and other tribes migrants of Imphal
1	Chothe Thangwai Pakhangpa	a. Thangwai (Birth name) b. Mei-ngai (Nickname)	a. Chothe Thangwai Atengba b. Thingkri Nachouba (Defeater of Natoi Nachoupa) c. Thangwai Khongding (after succeeding the king)	a. Sentreng (Mythical name) b. Nongda Leiren Pakhangba c. Meidingu	a. Tubi Yoinongda Nongda Leiren Pakhangba b. Nongda Leiren Pakhangba (After coronation at Kangla/Imphal)
2	His (Pakhangpa) father	(Young handsome stranger)	Unknown	Unknown	Unknown
3	His mother	a. Daishin b. Chongnu c. Shilnu	Leima Thamoilempi	a. Nungmaidenga b. Khamlangtaopi c. Leinung Yaibirok Yakha Chanu d. Liklabicha Nungtangnu	a. Khamlangtaobi b. Leinung Yaibirok Yakha Chanu
4	His wife	Sunurempi	Leima Sunurempi	Laisana	Laisna
5	His maternal grandfather	a. Surou b. Lampu Tarpu	a. Tarang, b. Nungkarakpa c. Lambu Tupu	a. Tarang, b. Nungkarakpa c. Sanarakpa, d. Lambu Tupu e. Tupu Likleng f. Luwang Langmaipa	a. Tupu Likleng b. Luwang Langmaipa
6	His maternal grandmother	Lenghoinu	Lenghoinu	a. Lenghoi b. Nungmaidenga	Unknown
7	His step-sister	Sira Khongthingnu	Sira Khongthingnu (Kongdingmu)	Unknown	Unknown

soon after impregnating her, or was he afraid of the heavy penalty from the villagers and from Surou the brave king, is unknown?

(iv) Leima Sunurembi and *Thoukham-lei*

Significant evidences have already suggested that *Chothe Thangwai Pakhangpa* or *Thangwai Khongding* (*Thingkri Nachaoba*) or *Nongda Leiren Pakhangpa* to be one and the same person. Another evidence that firmly support is that all these three names mentioned above is found associated with only one girl 'Leima Sunurembi' the beloved wife of Pakhangpa who was also known differently by others as 'Laisana/ Laisna'.[28] Several other historical texts of Manipur also points that she is a distant relative of Poireiton. Accordingly, the *Moirang Ningthourol Lambuba* states that in the south before she was married, she was known by the Moirang as 'Sunurembi' the daughter of Hekhamba Nongyai Kokcha a royal family of the early-immigrant of the Poireiton group (Bhagashore 1982:98). Similarly, the CTP manuscript on many occasion stated that Thongnang Loinempa was the father of Leima Sunurembi of *Mayang chanu* (Bengali girl) the descendant of the new-immigrant group from the west who once temporary occupied the south-western region of Manipur at the foothills of Loiching (Loiyang/ Laimaton peak) or Lamangdong (Lamlanglon). It was also known by some as *Poireiton Chingkhong* in early days, but now called as Bishnupur (Para:42, 45-47, p. 22, 24-25). W. Ibohal Singh according to the *Cheitharol Kumpaba* said that in the north Pakhangba married a girl named "Laisana" of Tai origin who got mixed with the new-Tibetans who originally belonged to Poireiton group that came from Basa of Sena (1986:273, 305-308). So, the outcome of this marriage is stated by Kabui (2003) that Poireiton (leader of the new immigrant group) ultimately acknowledged the supremacy of Pakhangpa, and on his behalf, his younger brother Thongaren (Thongnang Loinempa) offered his younger sister Laisana (Lei-sena), who accompanied Pakhangpa to be his queen at Kangla.

The passionate love relationship between Pakhangpa and Leima Sunurembi is splendidly described in *Chothe Thangwai Pakhangpa* (*CTP*) and in *Moirang Ningthourol Lambuba* (*MNL*) manuscripts. Their passionate relationship is identified with '*Kharam Leishok A-ngangba*' (a kind of rare beautiful red flower grown in Kharam area), after a decree was issued in honour of her commitment. This indigenous red flower symbolises one's true love, like the red rose of modern times. Accordingly, it states that when Pakhangpa returned with his army from the fierce battle in the south-west hills, he gave that beautiful red flower brought from the conquest to his beloved girlfriend Sunurembi as a token of his true love. She, out of her deep admiration of his act, she thereby requested Pakhangpa to pass a decree to honour this significant gift by prohibiting any one from destroying the flower; and also forbidding any women, especially the Ngangoi groups of Moirang from wearing it on their ears; and whosoever disobey the decree should be penalised with severe punishment by shaving off their heads. Henceforth, the CTP described that later the Kharam red flower came to be known as "Kharam leisok a-ngangba leima Sunurembi Toukham-lei", though now commonly called only as '*Sunurembi Toukham-lei',* literally it means 'the forbidden flower' (Singh, 1982:94). Below is transliteration of the decree:

(*Hi eshabe, Moirang Ningthou (Chothe Thangmei Pakhangpa) ibungo shingel leirang ashibu karamnabu asuk phajabano, leirang ashigi maong machuga karamnabu asuk chunakhrabano ko. Aduga leirang ashibu Kege pakhang kanana hek chaillambada, masam kokpagi dandhi peduna chindanaba khambe-u, aduga Ngangoi chanurasingna karigumba na-da thetlabasu momnu nuja oibesingi masam samlang adu kaklaga arumba warak cheithang phangani haina yathang louthokpiduna chindanaba warol louthokpe-u haina khamjakhibagi warol hairakhi. Korou adu numitage houna Kharam leisok angangba leima Sunurembi Toukham-lei haina mingthonkhi),* (*CTP*-Para: 87, p. 45)

To continue, according to the Chothe oral history, Chothe Thangwai Pakhangpa being a divine person obliged not to marry Sunurembi despite the romantic affairs he had because his father the Dragon-Python God instructed him not to marry any girl in his lifetime, because if he does so, he would become mortal like any human beings. For this reason, it is said Pakhangpa avoided and deserted her for his heavenly abode. The CTP also described that Thongnang Loinempa (her father) was in low-spirits and unhappy with Pakhangpa when he deserted her or ignored for being an outsider. The native womenfolk also sympathised and encouraged Pakhangpa to accept her as his wife as they were a perfect match for each other (CTP-Para:29-41; pp. 15-21). This avoidance and dissertation period logically could be interpreted as the period of his long expedition in the north against the Khaba-nganba, in which his life was unpredictable. Further, the CTP manuscript described that Pakhangpa prayed the gods to create some obstacles for Sunurembi to discourage her from following him, but no physical harm should be done in any situation. On the basis, the gods created three obstacles to Sunurembi: firstly, the gods sent a big flood; secondly, wild forest fire; and thirdly, a ferocious tiger to obstruct her path. The CTP describes that she overcame all these hurdles, because of her wisdom, knowledge, patience and endurance. Even the ferocious tiger ultimately gave up obstructing the path and gave way to her. Since, she overcame all these obstacles even the Dragon-Python God sympathised and revoked and sent back Pakhangpa with consent to marry Sunurembi or Leisena.

It is believed that Chothe Thangwai Pakhangba married Sunurembi at Moirang hence the people of south addressed her as 'Leima Sunurembi'. So, in consonance with the available literatures, Pakhangpa after subjugating the northern tribes made his wife Leima Sunurembi as the Queen of Kangla (Imphal) on his coronation day before the three great kings/ chiefs on the first Saturday of Kalen (June/July), (Kabui 2003:84-85). Henceforth, the northern people, especially the Meitei called her "Leisena/ Laisana" (lit. gold flower from Sena) signifying respect for a woman of high status, instead of calling her Sunurembi.

Thus, the above explanations suggest that Sunurempi (descent lady) originally belonged to the Poireton group who came from Basa of Sena town of Bengal (Cachar or Selyet) whose immediate predecessors are an admixture of the new-Tibetan (Tai) of the southern Moirang group (Singh, 1986:305-308). She is also known differently by others as; Leima Sunurembi the beloved wife of Chothe Thangwai Pakhangpa by the Moirang in the south; and Leisena/ Laisana as the Queen of Kangla (Imphal) kingdom in the north. The term 'Leima' literally means 'mother of earth' often referred to a queen or woman of royal status/ birth. Both Leima and Leisena are synonymous terms but the variation is because of dialect variation since the Moirang and Imphal Meitei are ethnically different in origin.

(v) The Secrecies of Pakhangpa History

The genuine identity of Pakhangpa and his genealogical relation with the Chothe and Meitei; several proverbs, idioms, phrases and socio-religious decrees exist even among various indigenous tribes of Manipur like Kharam, Koireng, Liangmei, Maring, Kom, Tarao, Anal, Lamkang, Moyon, Monshang, etc. But the story is not shared for fear of condemnation or sacrilege. According to Thambaljao and Maipak, the most revered secrecies about the socio-religious history of Manipur as recounted by the early Meitei Purohits/ scribes is that, "The sacred history of Meitei is kept inside the Chothe basket" (*Meitei-gi, athuppa wa-shingdi Chothe lubak manungda lei*). Likewise, Roushi and Neilut also affirmed in their oral-history that "The history of Chothe ancestors is kept sacred inside the King's basket" (*Chothe-gi puwaridi ningthougi lubak manungda lottuna thamkare*), these are in Manipuri.

Both the averments indicates that the ancient history of Chothe and Meitei are hidden in the king's basket, definitely referring to the *Chothe Thangwai Pakhangpa (CTP)* sacred manuscript retained by the Chothe Village Council. But the above coded statements are in Manipuri language being the lingua-franca of the state, where the term *Lubak* means 'a bamboo storage basket' [(with dimension of (1 x 1 ½) ft (l x b)]. Such storage baskets (now unused) are usually made by Chothe and other hill tribes from a particular bamboo species called *U-tang* (lit. matured bamboo) where termites cannot destroy.

Certain superstitious taboos still observed by the Chothe and Meitei are: (i) No Meitei individual should ever kick any Chothe man nor touch them with his feet; (ii) No Chothe men should ever bear the palanquin for any Meitei, since the Chothe are their great forefathers.[29] Some Chothe elders believed that such taboo still entails. According to the Chothe, in early days they were treated with royalty by Meitei kings and nobles, and therefore there use to be always a reserved seat for any Chothe chief/ king or person of noble birth in the Manipur King's Court. This tradition was developed as part of the custom in honour and respect of Pakhangpa's mother's father, after his death the cognates, of Chothe tribe were given the same treatment (Mother's father or mother's brother is highly respected in Chothe society).

The confusion and contradictions frequently occurring with regards to hill tribes of Manipur is because the state is inhabited by multi-ethnic and cultural groups speaking their own dialects, thus resulting in wrong interpretation and references. This common error is evidently pointed out by McCulloch, as to how the tribals or Hills people of Manipur in early days were often referred wrongly by outsiders. He said, "all the Hao are the names used amongst the Meitei to distinguish the principal tribes, and though each of these tribes has a distinctive name of their own, often quite different from the Manipuri one, still as with the latter all are familiar, and as it is the name a stranger would be most likely to hear and use it" (1857:41). Other factors are like deliberate interpolation, distortion and manipulation by the latter Manipur kings and Purohits (scribes) or Meitei high priests during the Vaishnavism (Hindunisation) movement in order to claim their supremacy over the hills people by distinguishing themselves as the new superior ethnic group.

The concept of supremacy over the hills people by the Meitei politically, economically, religiously and culturally developed at much later period due to their scholastic advancement, unity and matrimonial supports from other hill tribes. According to some tribal oral history, in the past the indigenous (older) tribes are said to be much richer in their socio-culture and political system, though not materialistically. The earlier 'Mai-tai/ Meitei/ Meetei' the new immigrants are considered inferior racial group and were prohibited to occupy any hill territories, so they were driven to plain areas, who then established their settlements as hamlets at the foothills and banks of the Loktak Lake, subsequently that grew large in years. This indicates that upto seventeenth century the various southern indigenous hill tribes fully dominates and controlled the Manipur valley and its surrounding, till their complete dynasties' downfall by eighteenth century. This is one reason, why most of the early kings of Manipur bear indigenes tribal names.[30] In later social discourse many inter-marriages and feuds occurred between the hills and valley people, and a new group called 'Meitei' a conglomeration with various hill tribes came into existence by later nineteenth century.

With regards to the historical interpolation, S.N.A. Parratt asserted that the *Cheitharol Kumpaba* (*ChK*) the Court's Chronicle of Manipur was re-written twice; first during Garib Niwaz (1709-1748) and second at the time of Chingthangkhompa, alias Bhagyachandra (1759). She is also sceptical about the existence of this *ChK* manuscript to be in written form before Kyampa (1467-1508) as the standard of recording the events and deeds chronologically began in 1485 AD, after Kyampa met the Pong king of the Shan dynasty (2005:3, 5, 14). W.I. Singh also refused to accept the year of N.L. Pakhangpa's coronation i.e. 33 AD (76 Saka) as the first historical year considering it to be too early for reasons like geographical setting, population, genealogical calculations and archaeological findings, and presumed the date should be around 980 AD or later (1986: 41; see Parratt, 2005:5, 18).

Apparently from the historical perspective the distortion, inter-polation and manipulation of the socio-religious history of the Manipur (Meitei) began when Garib Niwaz's under the influence of Shanti Das Goswami imposed Hinduism on his subjects against Sanamahi the ancient Meitei religion. Garib Niwaz even went to the extent of forcibly burning down all the ancient historical records written in the Meitei script, where the history of Manipur was forced to rewrite in Bengali script (Parratt, 2005:14). It is also said that most hill tribes who had good relationship with the predecessor of Garib Niwaz were enraged for his action, and many stopped paying tributes to the later kings and left him. So, their age-old relationship got estranged due to frequent imposition of taxes and edicts on them.

Parratt also asserted that the serious twist and misinterpretation of Manipur history began from the early twentieth century, broadly classifying into two trends, both with clear ideological agendas. She said 'firstly, the early scholars like Phurailatpam Atombapu Sharma and his disciples writing on the history of Manipur were all highly influenced by Brahmanical Hinduism, which they seem to rectify their action later. Secondly, real damaged to the history of Manipur came from the Congress supporters after 1950, when the state merged with India and subsequent to integration of their culture with the Indian mainstream for political reasons' (2005:1-2). These evidences supports our contention that the genuine history of Pakhangpa and Manipur were distorted, interpolated, misinterpreted and re-written, especially by scribes as desired by the later kings of Manipur to claim the dominance and superiority of the valley (Hindu-Meitei) over the supremacy of Pakhangpa and hills peoples.

(vi) Pakhangpa's Mysticism

The sacred manuscript *Chothe Thangwai Pakhangpa* (*CTP*), the Chothe oral history and other literary works indicates the mysticism of Pakhangpa right from the time he was conceived till his mysterious death. First, mysticism is that he was mysteriously conceived and became an illegitimate child/ son of a Chothe girl (Daishin), whose father's identity remains anonymous. Secondly, the three miraculous escaped of Pakhangpa's life attempts made by his maternal grandfather (Surou) when ignorant about his divinity during childhood [i.e. (a) The enigmatic personality as to how he survived when left to die in the thick forest; (b) His deflection of a big boulder rolling down the cliff; and (c) His mysterious survival when crushed to death by the huge falling tree]. Thirdly, as an obligation to his father's command, Pakhangpa steadfast not to marry any girls and remained bachelor in order to immortalise himself (this obligation was revoked later). The CTP described that Pakhangpa deserted his beloved Sunurembi for several years. Thongnang the father of Sunurembi expressed his displeasure to Pakhangpa for that action; while the womenfolk pleaded Pakhangpa to rethink and marry Sunurembi (CTP-Para: 20).

It is most probable that Pakhangpa's commitment to bachelorhood might have led to calling or identifying him by the valley Meitei as "Pa-khang-pa/ ba" (*Pa-khang*, lit. means Virile youth/ Young bachelor). But on the other hand, the term 'Pakhang' is also seen associated with the clan "Pakan" of Anal tribe, Chandel district (located on southeast of Moirang). Some Moirang people must have assumed Pakhangpa to be from the clan of Anal tribe, or his mother must have assumed it, since both fled from Langthabal area towards south after they were expel by Khaba-nganba of the northern group. Such presumption of a title must have given an opportunity in concealing his true identity being an illegitimate child without a father/ clan's name, thus acquired the name 'Chothe Thangwai Pakhang-pa'.

There are also many other folktales describing Pakhangpa's mysticism. T.C. Tensuba said that Pakhangpa was a divine being, believed to be Dragon-Python; God by day and Human by night (1993:46). He described that Laisana was the most beloved wife of N.L. Pakhangpa, but she was unhappy with him because he did not invite her during the daytime transaction of the Royal Council meetings as he acted like *Lai* (God) in the affairs of administration. But Pakhangpa did not forbid her from joining them at the night-time gathering of the Royal Assembly as he acted like *Mee* (man or ordinary layman). Because of such reasons and his in-different attitudes, Laisana who was unhappy and offended him twice, asking why he treated her in such manners. She also accused Pakhangpa with hidden wives; or as she was of low origin of Poireiton (the immigrant group) that he avoided her (1993:136; Kabui, 2003:89).

This mystical belief is supplemented by Naorem Sanajoaba that the Dragon-Python god has supernatural power to transform himself into anything like a stone, a tiger, a dog, a human being, and could even take human birth at any time and place (1991:104). So, even after his death, he is believed to appear in such forms at certain places as a sign of his divinity, and those places are treated as sacred places by the believers.

Lastly, Pakahngpa's death is still shrouded in mystery with different versions like; he was killed by the Khaba (Koibu/Maring) tribe; by his son; by his wife; by the conspirators; some claim he disappeared in the western hills side, etc.

The mythical anonymity of Pakhangpa's father too plays an important role in the Chothe religious belief and practices. The Chothe still uphold their indigenous religious belief and continues to practice their ancestor-worship like any other indigenous or Tribal religion of the world, although some Hindu elements have been acculturated and assimilated. In other words, the divinity of Pakhangpa and his mystical father formed the intricate bases of the Chothe indigenous religion linking to their genealogical myth.

Thus, Pakhangpa's birth and life is much alike with the mysticism of the Christian Biblical story of Lord Jesus Christ, who was born of a Virgin Mary through the intercession of the Holy-Spirit; so also, in the case of Krishna the Hindu gods is believed to be mysteriously conceived by Divine power of Vishnu, or in the case of Buddha of Buddhist. We see all these great religious leaders are endowed with Supernatural Powers and Grace mediating as the avatar or the incarnate of God, thus showing the similarity of world myths. Since, the Chothe revered their ancestors from their mythological perspective it re-instil their beliefs and practices in the person of "Chothe Thangwai Pakhangpa" as the avatar of their guardian God of earth *Pu Lungchungpa.*

Notes

1. *Myth and Modernity*: Hans Blumenberg's Reconstruction of Modern Theory. Author(s): Bernard Yack Reviewed work(s): Work on Myth by Hans Blumenberg; Robert M. Wallace, The Legitimacy of the Modern Age by Hans Blumenberg; Robert M. Wallace, Source: *Political Theory*, Vol. 15, No. 2 (May, 1987), pp. 244-261: Sage Publications, Inc. Stable. URL: http://www.jstor.org/stable/191677 Accessed: 22/09/2008 02:50.

2. *Chothe*: Among the Mizo, a clan called "Chawhte" found in the south-western part of Mizoram is considered a relative of the Chothe/ Chawte of Manipur. But since they have been completely assimilated to the Mizo like the Hmar living in Mizoram the genealogy is difficult to establish now. The Mizo (Lushei) speaking groups considered Chote or Chawte as one of their missing clans of the twelve. The irony is that, Chawhte and Hmar are considered as tribes in Manipur, whereas in Mizoram as clans.

3. *Kanshu*: There is a province name called "Kansu" in south-western China, which the Chin-Kuki-Mizo speakers trace their pre-historic origin. The Chothe also uses such similar names in their oral narrations like Kanshu-Kanrung for a place and personal names, associated with the past.

4. *Huipi-thoranga/ Hurpi-thoranga*: In Chothe 'Huipithoranga' lit. means 'the five men that sprang out' (*'Hui / Hur'* means 'a hole or a cave'; *'Tho'* means 'sprang out', and *'Ranga'* means 'five'. Some argued it is seven men or clans not five. Such mythical cave is referred by the Chin-Kuki-Mizo speakers as "Chhinlung" or "Shinglung", claiming the place to be somewhere in southern China.

5. *Lungleh*: According to Hmar tribe of Manipur the Lungleh-waishu is around the Barak River in Jiribam near Silchar, Assam. The Hmar tribe also shares similar history, migration and language with Chothe. But according to Chothe elders based on their folktales claimed that the place indicates could be somewhere around Lungleh or Champai district of Mizoram bordering Myanmar, since they have migated northward from the south passing Aimol (Aizawl). Both Chothe and Hmar share similar language, though not exactly same. For example, water is called as *'Tui'*; Rice as *'Bu/ buh'*; plain people as *'Vai/ Wai'*; and hot river water flowing as *Tui-sarung*, etc.

6. *Sacred-grove*: The present sacred-grove of *Chothe Thangwai/ Thangmei Pakhangpa* of Lamlanghupi (Chothe) at Bishnupur has been, Ordered by the Governor of Manipur, Imphal on 16th June 2007, as the 'Protected Historical Monuments and Archaeological site', of No. 5/24/99-S(AC), Under Sub-section (3) of Section 4 of the "Manipur Ancient and Historical Monument and Archaeological sites and Remains Act, 1976", published by the *Manipur Gazette*: Extraordinary No. 145 Imphal, Thursday July, 2007 (Asadha, 1929: 14). On the basis, brick fencing had been constructed around the sacred-grove as the village received financial assistant from the Govt. as per the order and to stop the encroachment of the area from the neighbouring Meitei Khuman villagers.

7. *Natoi Thingkri Nachaoba*: *'Natoi'* in ancient Chothe means Thigh; *'Thingkri'* means Clean or Wipe out or Pierced by a stick; and 'Nachoupa' in Meitei means Big ear man. It may have different Chothe latent meaning which is unknown now but the last term signifies a tribal warrior, since hill men in olden days usually wore big heavy ear rings and so has big ears.

8. *Khaba-nganba/ Poi/ Fhalam/ Maring*: They are considered the original Meitei of Kangleipak/ Manipur as known by different names, whose origin may be traced to Kachin country who move down south and move up north-west. *Khaba* is pronounced as "Kaba" by Kachin. The tragic hero 'Khamba' in the romantic epic of *'Khamba-Thoibi'* of Moirang/ Manipur is claimed to be from Khoibu-Maring tribe. The name *Khaba-nganba* is believed to be a name given by the Tangkhul to people who occupy the North-west hills of Manipur.

And the name 'Maring' is believed to be a generic term given by the Chothe, derived from 'Mei-ring lu-ngei' meaning 'one who steal live fire' to indirectly refer to some Poi/ Fhalam groups who took asylum in the Chothe territory during migration and left secretly by taking even the charcoal fire from their bonfire place. Now the original Khoibu-Maring tribe inhabits in the southeast of Chandel district Manipur, after Pakhangpa ousted from Kangla (also see *Poi-reiton*).

9. *Maram*: It is my inquisitiveness that even the Maram Naga tribe of Senapati district could probably be part of the Khaba-nganba or a section of Maring and Liangmei cognatic group looking from the linguistic and cultural aspects. Since some Maram people do share their sure-name or title as "Khaba/ Kaba" to their names? I am sure they don't originally belong to Tiinizdii or Mao-Poumei speaking groups.

10. *Thangwai/ Thangmei Pakhangpa*: In Chothe the term *Thang* or *Chang*, means 'Virile/ healthy/ mature person', and *Wai* means 'bright'; while *Mei* means 'fire or tail'. In two accounts of CTP, King Khongding of Moirang is referred as Pakhangpa's foster father. This is probably because Kongding married Pakhangpa's mother (Daishin/ Thamoilempi) after he was born, or she became Kongding's concubine when they took refuge in Moirang after they fled from Langthabal. Khongding being without an heir to the throne Pakhangpa succeeded him after his death being the step-son. Pakhangpa acquired the new title as "Chothe Thangwai Atengba' (the aide to king Khongding) and also earned a name "Thingkri Nachaoba" as the subjugator of the great Chothe King Natoi Nachaoba (also see *CTP*-Para: 25, p.15; and MNL chapter -19). Later, because of his successful conquest and defeat of the Khaba-nganba in the north, the poets and singers of the valley people gave him a new regal title on his coronation day at Kangla (Imphal) as "Tubi Yoinongda Nongda Leiren Pakhangba" (Kabui, 2003:85). The word "Tubi Yoinongda" seems Bodo-Cachari phonetic to mean "Leinungda Yabi-rok" (Tubi=Yabi; Yoinongda = Leinungda) referring to his birth place by honouring his mother's origin "Leinung Yabirok Yakha Chanu" and maternal grandfather (Singh, 1986:76-82, 266; Kabui, 2003:76-77).

11. *CTP:* These quotes are from the abridged manuscript of *Chothe Thangwai Pakhangpa* (*CTP*) after having been read and compared with the original *Chothe Thangwai Pakhangpa* manuscript by two experts namely, Dr Laishram Imoba (Assistant editor of 'Ereibak', a daily local newspaper) and M. Gourachandra (founder of 'People's Museum, Kakching'). The reason being the language used in the original manuscript is of very ancient, cryptic, phrase, idiom or in poetic forms as compare to the translated abridged manuscript which is somewhat simple and comprehension.

12. *Khuman*: In early days, the Moirang principality was formerly known as "Kege-Moirang" (Chinese silk producers) but later was predominately dominated by the royal clan of *Khuman*. And since Pakhangpa lived and also succeeded King Kongding (his foster father) of Moirang, some latter Meitei presumed Pakhangpa to be from the Khuman clan being a dominant group. This Khuman is equated with the Chothe Mareem/ Marim clan by some to bring into relationship. These supporters claimed that the small-pox marks on their face is their trademark for their clansman, religiously pointing to the mythical tale that was caused by the mixture dropped on the (unknown) Pakhangpa's father face while courting his mother in the jhum field (see the legend of Pakhangpa story). All these assumption are seen as an inference version of Moirang's people who tried to incorrectly establish the genealogy of Pakhangpa with them, since he lived amongst them. Denying all such allegation, Pakhangpa after assuming his Kingship/ Emperor at Kangla established himself as the Head of a new clanship "Mangang" the Seventh Royal Clanships of Manipur, at Lammangtong/ Bishnupur (see CTP, Kabui).

13. *Chakha-khong Mareempa*: The early Meitei generally identified the indigenous tribes like Chothe, Kharam, Koireng, Poi, inhabiting around Thangching peak and Leimatak river basin as 'Chakpa' or 'Chakha-khong' (*Chakha* or *Yakha-khong* means stream, probably referring to backward stream of Leimatak river). The name *Mareempa*, probably suggest another great Chothe chief from Mareem clan. Thus, it points that Pakhangpa's mother (Daishin/ *Khamlang-Taopi / Thamoilempi*) came from the country of *Chakha-khong Mareempa*.

14. *Langthabal*: Tensuba opined that Nongda Leiren Pakhangba (Chothe Thangwai Pakhangpa) is son of Leinung Yabirok, who married Laisaana the daughter of one in the line of Poireiton, and who established the first capital at Langthabal hill in the Hangjing hills range (900 Mtr. M.S.L.), (Tensuba 1993:134-135). Langthabal is around Mayang Imphal about 6-7 km south of Imphal. The place has much religious significance as the first historical/ ancient capital of the valley. The place is also connected with the Chothe folktale called, '*Asha Changnu: A lady who transformed into an animal*', where one of the king's huge boat made by the Chothe was mysteriously lost in the northern Loktak Lake near Langthabal hill, but it appeared later at some place. Much later, some Chothe from southwest migrated north, and before moving further down southeast occupied around this place and named it as "Yangpalkung". This place is evident as Moirangthem Rajendra pointed out that the settlement at Langthabal was known as "Chothe Yangbi" to others. Rajendra said much later, after the Chothe abandon the area it was given to Meetei-Pangal (Muslim immigrants) from Bengal who came as soldiers during Khakempa in 1606 (2008: 30). But this period could be much later probably by 18th century.

15. *Meitei (Mai-tai)*: To speak bluntly, today's' Meitei/ Meetei/ Manipuri of Manipur valley are conglomeration of various old and new tribes/ communities belonging to proto-Tibeto-Burman and Aryan speaking groups. They do not belong to one specific tribe or racial group, but a composite of many formed the Meitei ethnic group. But the original Meitei is believed to be the Poi/ Loi (Poireition group) or the group known by Khaba-nganba/ Fhalam/ Khoibu-Maring tribe who first occupied the Imphal valley by crossing the western hills. Some claim the Loi's of Andro, Phayeng and others are the earliest setlers of the valley. In due course, batch by batch various new immigrant groups like the Thai-ahom, Aryans also began to flock into Manipur valley from different directions including the Bodo-Cacharis, Bengalese and Muslims from the east and west, who later acculturated and assimilated linguistically, culturally and religiously by political subjugation and inter-marriages with the dominant tribes of the time. Subsequently, by latter 18th century with the new religious upheaval of Hindunisation in Manipur the Bodo-Cacharis (Vaishanavists) and other assimilated groups in the valley under political subjugation were identified as the "Meitei" (Outsiders).

    The term 'Meitei' is believed to have derived from the words 'Mai-tai' or 'Mee-atei', where 'Maitai' means 'Paste/ Chandol appliers' who applied paste on forehead (Hindus), and "Mee-atei" means 'Outsiders or Different people' which owes its origin to Chothe, Koireng and other cognatic speakers of Manipur, being dominant indigenous communities who settled on the surrounding valley hills. In earlier days, they generally develop a coded form of terming and identifying others by their peculiar traits. Later, when the new culture and religious movement (Hinduism) reached its peak by 19th – 20th century by forced acculturation and assimilation, the term 'Meitei' gained its ground as a new cultural entity. The genealogical picture of Meitei of Manipur is also pointed out by S.N.A Parratt that 'the Chakpa and the Poi/ Loi were assimilated, later some hill groups formed alliances with them. The early part of the *ChK* is essentially the story of the expansion of the Meitei across the valley and hills of Manipur, and the gradual acculturation and assimilation of the *yeks* (clans) and tribes into their kingdom' (2005:3).

Linguistically, the spoken Meitei language owes its origin to the Maring (Khabanganba), but now is admixture of surrounding tribal languages like Chothe, Koireng, Liangmei, Anal, Tangkhul, etc. The ancient Meitei Mayek (script) is considered to have brought by some Pong (Thai) people that shows similarity to the Chinese script. Culturally, the Meitei traditional religious costume wore in *Lai Harouba* festival owes its origin to the Kege-Moirang (Chinese) people. It is believed that Pakhangpa brought the Moirang attire along with him when he became the king of Kangla/ Imphal kingdom. Politically, the counting of chiefs (*Thing-tepa*) by scrolls and counting of years (*Cheitharol Kumpapa*) is still practice by the Chothe. Religiously, the Meitei (Poi/Loi) indigenous religion *Sanamahi* is practiced till 18th century before the forced conversion to Hinduism. Therefore, some Meitei may be able to trace their genealogical roots to specific hill tribes. Thus, Kabui concludes that 'the history and origin of Meitei is shrouded in mystery (2003: 15, see also Shaw 1929: 47-48, Parratt 2005:1-2).

16. *Taibelou Pukphat Sapeilou*: According to *CTP* manuscript this truce or treaty of "Taibelou Pukphat Sapeilou" made near Khoijuman (Thongjourok river), Bishnupur town between Chothe Thangwai Pakhangpa and Thokchao the eldest son of Koubrurel Angom-ngagi (Angam of Tangkhul) is seen to be the most fortunate and a turning point for Pakhangpa to defeat the Khaba-nganba the northern group (Singh 1982: 97, CTP: 90, p. 46).

17. *MNL*: The manuscript *Moirang Ningthourol Lambuba* (*MNL*) of Chapter -19, well elaborates the nature of its people, landscaped and its devastation, its tactics, costumes and methods of warfare of that period. It described how Pakhangpa ousted the great Chothe King Natoi Nachoupa and subdued his country in the Nungsuk battle.

18. *Lungsukbung/ Nungsuk ching*: According to *MNL*, Chothe Thangwai Pakhangpa by breaking all the traditional political and kinship ties first plundered and burnt the whole village of Koireng and defeated their brave warrior Nungnangchong. The war was so devastated that the entire atmosphere of the area was covered with black smoke. It further said that Pakhangpa's name and famed did not end just there as he continued to attack *Hoirei kha pangda* too, a nearby village of Koireng (Singh 1982:90-91). Then, Pakhangpa later gathered all his brave warriors of Kege-Moirang and assembled like a fence on the border sides and attacked the great country of Chothe located on the five ridges of the high mountains separated by the five rivers and the five valleys, and defeated the great Chothe King Natoi Nachaopa in one of the most fierce and devastating battle of "Nungsuk/ Lungsuk ching" (*Lanpham ashida Chothe gi Ningthou Natoi Nachouba koubabu maithiba perakkhi*). It is said that because of the fierce battle even the nearby Kharam village fled away (*Kharam khungangshu pumchai*

chaikhaikhi), (ibid: 92-93; *CTP*-Para: 84, p. 43). Thus, it states that Pakhangpa after defeating the great Chothe King Natoi Nachaopa one of the great kings of south-western region in the battle of *Chothe Nungsuk-ching (Lungsuk lan),* acquired the title "Thingkri Nachaopa" symbolising the victor king and subsequently succeeded King Kongding of Moirang. The word 'Thingkri' or 'Thinkgri' is unclear probably an ancient Chothe term for 'speared man', while 'Nachaopa' refers to any tribal leader with big ear lopes (see notes 7).

According to the Chothe oral history, Pakhangpa's attacked on the south-western groups of people and against his own people in the battle of *Nungsuk ching/ Lungsuk bung* is said to be his retribution primarily for personal reasons of ill-treatments and humiliation he and his mother suffered during his childhood. The humiliation accordingly are like rebukes, assaults, accusation of being illegitimate child or fatherless, banishment from the village, the mockery and scoffing at his protruding tail as *Meitingte* or *Meingai.* Kharam and Koireng neighbouring communities also became victims because they refused to give food and shelter when her mother Daishin escaped among those villages in search of her lover to elope, besides his political motives. The last three paragraphs of *CTP* manuscript described that Pakhangpa's mother Daishin (Khamlang-Taopi or Thamoilempi) after the devastated war went to her parent's village and explained about the past events and asked them to perform a rite with their best wine (*wangle zu*) for the recourses (Para: 90-91, pp. 46-47).

19. *Poirei/Poireiton/Loi:* The name Poirei is also associated with a prince, son of Queen Peyai of Ashong village near Moirang, who is a brave warrior with a huge structure of Poireiton origin. Their roots like Chothe may be traced to Kachin of Poi. Some archive materials point that they are immigrant group or traders from the north-west of Moirang trying to pass the Manipur valley to go to Kabaw valley via Manipur (Iril) River. Pakhangpa subjugated and brought them under his direct control in south. Some said Poireiton group entered Manipur by Old-Cachar road from the west and occupied the Leimaton foothill (Loi-ching) and known as *Poireiton chingkhong* by some, while locally people called it as 'Lamlangtong', but now it is known as Bishnupur town. But some claimed another group of Poi (Poirei) or Fhalum/ Maring entered Manipur at much later period from the south-west. Probably, the group must have scattered during their long stay and some must have migrated north and established settlements around Kangla-Tongbi (north of Imphal), where the Liangmei and Tangkhul tribes must have identified them as *Kaba/ Khaba-nganba.* After Pakhangpa defeated the *Khaba-nganba* many fled far away to the eastern hills and they are now known as 'Khoibu-Maring' tribe. But those who are scattered in and around the valley are still known as "Loi" identifying with their early settlement's name of 'Loi-ching'.

20. *Angom-ngagi:* The term "Angom" of Meitei clan is believed to be a mispronunciation for "Angam" by the Bodo-Cachari immigrants, probably referring to the descendants of "Angam Puleiromba" the great Tangkhul chief of the Northeast. The meaning 'Angom' in Meitei is blurry. Mayonmi Shimray of Khangkhui, Ukhrul said in Tangkhul, "A-ngam" means 'steep' or 'be a winner', commonly use as a prefix or suffix in a person's name.

21. *Kansurol*: There are folktales that say Makan Kansurol was a great Chothe chief. One of their settlements called "Kansui or Kanshu" (Brave fighter/ warrior) was posthumously named in memory of his greatness by his descendants (kin groups) during their sojourn to south-east, Chandel district. The name clearly suggests a Chothe indigene name, since it relates to one of the early progenitors in their genealogical myth. Similarly, some Chothe leaders felt that certain words such as 'Tao' should be read as 'Thao'; and 'Maringpa' as 'Mareempa/ Mareempa', probably pronunciation and spelling errors made by non-locals (CLAM, Souvenir 2000: 3).

22. *Tubi Yoinongda Nongda Lairen Pakhangba*: See *Chothe Thangwai Pakhangpa* the endnotes no. 9.

23. *Mangang*: Pakhangpa by virtue of his Divine power and military skills defeated the Khaba-nganba of the north and established himself as Emperor of Manipur valley by combining the two dominant principalities of Moirang and Kangla (Imphal) by consolidating all the confederate kingdoms of east, south, south-western and northern kingdoms. Thereafter, he declared himself as head of "Mangang" the new clan-ship as equal among the confederate Ningthouja (Royal) clans. The Mangang of Ningthouja clan is equated with 'Yuhlung' clan of Chothe. W. Ibohal Singh (1986) in a section 'Mangang' of his book said they are groups of people who mainly inhabited around the Lammangdong (Bishnupur) area in early days. It points nearer to Pakhangpa's genealogical root/origin/place of birth. But Tensuba said that N.L. Pakhangba was the founder of Mangaang Salai (Clan), although he descended from Taang-Shaang Leela Paakhangba since the ancient Meitei composed an eternal formula for the Meitei that the three prayers: (1) Prayer for Mangang Kuru, (2) Prayer for Luwang Kuru and (3) Prayer for Khuman Kuru were strictly prescribed for the Meitei since time immemorial (1993:136-137).

24. *Misnomer*: The frequent misnomer, confusion and paradoxical terms, names of persons and places and its variation found in many of the Manipur historical texts is because of the interpolation, misinterpretation and also in the nomenclature or style of the syllable, syntax, semantic and morphology of the term used by various multi-ethnic groups in the state, that is understood only by few or by their own groups resulting in confusion. For example, the metamorphosis names of Pakhangpa; many are confused with his posthumous names given by different ethnic groups on the credibility of an event, incident, his extra-ordinary feats or trademarks or talent or achievement, birth or kinship (see Singh, 1986:271-2). Likewise, many ancient names or places or stories are confusing because their meanings are not clear and certain mythical elements are later added to it usually by the folk narrators or writers. To be precise, in *CTP* manuscript Pakhangpa's grandmother's name had been written as "Leng-heinu", but in Chothe and other similar linguistic groups of Chin-Kuki-Mizo, a girl is usually called as "Hoi-nu or Boi-nu" (sweet girl) or "Thei-nu" (smart girl), but not as "Hei-nu" which has no meaning (see CTP- Para:1, p.1). Similarly, Pakhangpa mother's name was called 'Daishin' (Cool/ Accumulative girl) by Chothe. But the Imphal Meitei knew her as 'Khamlang-Taopi/ Thaopi' and by the Moirang people as 'Thamoilembi', a teknonymy referring to her birth place or personality. From the linguistic point of view, the two latter names does not bear a Chothe indigene, it is probably Poi or Tangkhul terms. Another error is

"Tupu" that probably means 'Tarpu' (old man) to refer to Pakhangpa's grandfather (see Singh, 1986: 274-5, also see Notes 21).

25. *Anonymity*: It is the anonymity of Pakhangpa's father and his mysticism that Chothe indigenous religion survived till today as ancestor-worshippers. Perhaps, if the identity of Pakhangpa's father was known even by few people it must have been deliberately concealed because of the extreme rigidity of the tribal custom and tradition or cultural norms practiced in the past. For example, according to Chothe custom if the concern person did not come and claim his illegitimate pregnant lover (girl) or the illegitimate child within the stipulated time, no amount of fine can compromise in the future for the shameful and humiliation act. The person would be treated as death, though alive. In case a relationship is re-established both would be expelled from the village.

26. *Lambu Tupu*: In Chothe and other similar Chin-Kuki-Mizo linguistic speakers the term *Lampu* means 'land owner' (*Tupu* has no meaning, but if written as 'Tarpu' it means 'old man/ elderly person', *Tar-* old and *Pu-* masculine gender term for aged person). The suffix of 'bu' is used by Meitei while Chothe used 'pu' as 'Ka-pu' = my grandfather, 'Na-pu' = your grandfather. The term *Tar-pu* is often used as prefix in referring or addressing any old/ elderly man using the eldest child's name as 'Tarpu Wailum-pa' (old man of Wailum's father/ grandfather). Such aged persons because of their life-long experiences are generally considered knowledgeable and wise in society, and often occupies high political position and status in the Village Council as advisors. So, the outsiders in ancient days must have referred and designated them as 'Lampu Tarpu' (lit. The old village land owner) because of their geographical knowledge. This suggest that Yuhlung Surou (Tarang) being the chief/ leader of a village was referred as Tarpu Tarang, the maternal grandfather of Pakhangpa.

27. *Luwang Langmeiba*: According to the Chothe oral history, Pakhangpa's maternal grandfather Surou (also known by others as Tarang or Nungkarakpa or Likleng or Luwang Langmeiba) and his relatives often helped Pakhangpa and his mother materially and militarily. Here, Surou is identified by some valley people as *Luwang Langmeiba*, associating him with the Luwang royal clan of Meitei and as a famous priest/ magician. This Meitei Luwang clan is equated with Thao clan of Chothe. It is not certain whether the scribes inferred him to be from the Liangmei tribe (another dominant cognatic tribe of Chothe inhabiting in Tamenglong district). In earlier days, the Liangmei are believed to be a cognatic group of Chin-Kuki-Mizo who migrated from south towards north. Their admixture with the Tinyimee Naga (Mao-Poumei) group in the historical process have made them much closer to Nagas. Some Chothe elders believe that the Liangmei and Puimei (Inpui) tribes of Manipur, and Riang tribe of Tripura and Mizoram suggest cognates, supported by their genealogy, language and cultural similarities. Another significant Chothe custom observed is that in case a girl bore a man's child through an illicit relationship and they did not marry in future, such illegitimate child is often brought up by the girl's parents or maternal grandparents, rather than the boy's parent who normally refused to accept and bring up.

28. *Sunurempi/bi*: Pakhangpa's wife Sunurempi/ bi or Laisana is sometime confused with Chingurembi the wife of Naothingkhong. W. Ibohal Singh said Chingurembi

was a Bengal princess, daughter of a Sena prince of the Senas of Bengal who settled at Lamangtong (Bishnupur) at the time of marriage, which the Poirei took as Mayang principality (1986: 305-308). In earlier days the inhabitants of Bengal at Lamangtong principality were known as 'Basa' and not as Mayang, a generic term derived from 'Mai-haang' meaning Dark face. It is most probable that Pakhangpa and Naothingkhong both marry a Bengal girl from the same region but not the same girl, since Naothingkong's period comes later compared to Pakhangpa. This shows political and matrimonial relationship was already established amongst various ethnic groups, before Pakhangpa marry Sunurempi.

29. *Taboo*: See the details in *Taboo* section in the following Chapter 5 of the thesis 'Chothe Indigenous Religion and Culture: A Sociological Study' by the author.

30. *Historic king's names*: Most of the early historic kings' of Manipur such as, Taothingmang, Naophangpa, Sameireng, Naothingkhong, Aayangpa, Yirengpa, Senahongpa, Loiyumpa, Tapungpa, Punsipa, Marampa, etc. of the Kangla (Imphal) principality significantly bears pure indigene names or cognatic names as claimed by Chothe elders. While the names of the early kings of Moirang principality like Fang Fang Ponglenghanba, Iwang Telheiba, Laiphangcheng, Ura Ngangoiba, Laiya Punshiba, Tushemba, Kongding, Nungnang Tomba, Thanga Ifan, Kaba Purang, etc. considering contemporary rulers of Kangla principality is seen different in the nature of their names. This indicates that they were of different ethnic origin from the linguistic and cultural point of views (see list of Kings, Parratt 2005: Tensuba 1993:172-73). There are many muzzy histories that speaks that the early historical kings of Imphal (Kangla) are close kins of Chothe and other cognate groups like Kharam, Koireng till the 18th century as they lived together and fought in their territorial expansion, battles and conquest in the east and west. The disassociation of matrimonial and political ties between hills and plain peoples began with their dominance over the hills peoples, the primogeniture issues in the palace and the advent of Hinduism in 18th century. Since, the latter kings are occupied with their political hegemony they failed to pay their gratitude to the hills people for the support and help received in the past. Thereafter, the allied hills tribes began to live independently as an entity without jeopardising the valley people in and around the valley at the foothills. Despite many learned persons in Manipur who knew the real history of Manipur or the origin of Meitei and the distortion story by earlier scribes, many remained silent spectators unable to speak the truth for fear of repercussion and consequences, which is why the Manipur history remains unclear and controversial till today.

CHAPTER - 5

Chothe Religious Belief System

Introduction

The Chothe believe in monotheism, the Supreme Almighty God (*Thangvan Rengpa*). However, their belief shows polytheistic in nature. Their religion, like some ancient religions of the world is cosmologic, naturalistic, animistic, totemic and ancestor-worshipper in nature. They also believe in a host of gods and goddesses or spirits like any indigenous tribes of the world. The Chothe cosmologic, naturalistic, animistic and totemic beliefs are also similar to many groups like; among the Ao, Angami, Lotha, Khasi, Jaintia, Garo, Apatani, Mishmi, Mao, Maram, Maring, Meitei of the North-east Indian tribes; or among the Santhal, Baiga, Todas, Gonds, and Coorgs of the mainland India tribes, and also among many Western and European societies. The polytheistic nature of belief among most indigenous tribes is related for their physical and emotional needs, security and protection.

Therefore, Verrier Elwin asserted that the Baiga pantheon is exceedingly varied and elastic with no exclusiveness about it and so they naturally worship everything they can, in order to be on the safe side (2002:54-55). Choudhuri also said that the Santhal have a number of pantheons known as *Bongas* or deities apart from a host of ghosts and spirits, some are worshipped by the community in public places while others like the Marang Buru and Gossain Era are worshipped by families as family gods (1987:25). Playfair too discussed various types of offerings, sacrifices and worship; how the Garo give attributes to the creation of the world, while others are for those who control the natural phenomenon like the destiny of man from birth to death as governed by a number of divinities whose anger must be appeased by sacrifice and whose good offices must be entreated in like manner (1975:80).

V. Elwin's statement on the Baiga polytheon or nature of worship seems to be the most important belief facet for many indigenous polytheistic and animistic believers. J.H. Hutton likewise points out a strong polytheistic view that the belief held by the indigenous tribes are not "mere vague imaginings of superstitious and untaught minds, but the debris of a real religious system, a definite philosophy, to the one time prevalence of which the manifold survivals in Hinduism testify, linking together geographically the Austro-Asiatic and Austroloid cultures of the forest-clad hills where the isolated remains of the original religion still hold out in an unassimilated form" (quoted from Elwin, 2002:54).

Thus, the indigenous polytheistic religion appears to be the earliest religion, as it exists in its crudest form, defined and structured to its best by maintaining a close relationship with nature, thereby balancing the eco-system unlike the modern religious belief system that focus only on individual spiritual aspect. According to Chothe mythology, it is said in the past when man and beast roamed around the world man and gods had direct relationship. The gods treated man like their alien friends from a different domain, so also man; where man live by day while the gods by nights. The communication and interaction with gods and spirits is usually done by the priest through the magical words/ incantation who responded by signs, dreams, senses and even revealing sometimes. Many such indigenous religious aspects may be testified by the Chothe indigenous religious belief and practices as paradigm.

Chothe Pantheon: Cosmic and Nature Worship

The Chothe in principle believe in monotheism, yet practices polytheism in daily lives. They believe that *Thangvan Rengpa* (the Heavenly God) is the Ultimate Supreme God, but at the same time they did not ignore their ancestor's spirits. They also honour, revere and worship the Seven Primary Cosmologic and Natural Elements of the World as their Principal Gods. Such belief is seen practiced by the ancient Chinese, Hindu, Greek and Roman, Egyptian, Mayan, Inca, Aztec, etc. (Ash, 2006:160-163). The Chothe Seven Cosmologic and Natural Elements are: (1) the Heaven or Sky God, (2) the Earth God, (3) the Sun God, (4) the Moon God, (5) the Wind (Air) God, (6) the Fire God, and (7) the Water (Rain) God. So, they may be identified as Cosmic or Natural worshippers too.

Of all these Gods, the Chothe considered the 'Heavenly/Sky God' i.e. *Thangvan Rengpa* as their Supreme Almighty God, or the most Powerful Ultimate God. He is also addressed as *Chungthing* (lit. The God above of pure element), and at other times used as *Apu Leihu* (lit. The Ancestor God or the God of forefathers), meaning 'Lord of lords'. The Chothe believe that *Thangvan Rengpa* or *Chungthing* or *Apu Leihu* is the Creator of the Universe. He is Omnipotent, Omnipresent and the Benefactor God; the Controller of the Human Destiny, the Giver and Taker of all life forms on earth. Acknowledging His greatness as the Supreme Almighty God, He is not directly interfered for His greatness. Prof. Vanlalnghak said even the Hmar people called the Supreme God as 'Khuonu-Khoupa' or 'Chunga-Pathein' the creator and sustainer of the Universe and does not directly interfere in the day today affairs of mankind and in such manner no special sacrifice is made for Him (2005:41). This is one reason why most scholars claimed that tribal religion is polytheistic instead of identifying as monotheistic because the reverence is not practice regularly despite acknowledging His greatness. They failed to see the intricate understanding between the Supreme God and ordinary human beings, since men do not want to simply interfere in the activities of the Supreme God for minor concerns. This behaviour is reflected in the daily working functions of any human social institutions of society, where the common man does not simply approach directly the Head or Boss of an institution unless seriously required rather he first deals with the subordinates in solving his problems. Likewise, men first pay more attention to lower gods by appeasing them since they usually come in contact and suffers the burn of certain ailments caused from their social intercourses. Therefore, rites and rituals performed becomes an act of reconciliation to cure human ailments. Thus, the tribal religion is regarded as ambiguous and vague by many scholars.

Wailum Parpa (my respondent) said in early days the priest or the head of the family usually makes a devotional prayer outside the house before any major rituals are performed to their Heavenly God early in the morning just when the sun rises:

1. Inn- Thouna Ashe (Morning Devotional Prayer of the Priest)

"Thangvan tengpe la-i, abur hongpa sand siki le-o,
Kaming rel-o, kaming hem-o, kaming chum-o...,
Adam keita, husung relleh huiwand bommae,
Ta-kup leh, u...rr...rr...".

[*In free translation:* "O, Almighty God, the Heavenly King the one who opens the door of death and life. Tell my name, turn my name and straighten/correct my name. People say that I am a curer in the village, and if the outsiders learn about my successful work, they flock to me because when I spell the magical words in your name, all evils flew away like u..rr..rr.." (Source: Wailum, mp3 record No. 4-2)].

The Chothe believes that *Pu Lungchungpa* or Pakhangpa is considered their Principal Guardian God on Earth. The term *Lungchungpa* literally in ancient Chothe means 'one who sits above the rock', symbolising the 'Dragon-Python king' i.e. the 'Rain God'. The laymen being a serpent refer him as *Ruipi-Santai Rengpa* (lit. The horned python king with fireballs).[1] Chothe believes that the Almighty Supreme God entrusted *Pu Lungchungpa* to be their Guardian God, being the only ethereal God among the Seven Celestial Elementary Gods with equal power that is tangible, visible, adaptable and approachable to the human beings. The concept and nature of interrelationship between the Dragon-Python God and with other Heavenly Celestial Gods is described in earlier Chapter Four (see *Chothe Genealogical myth*). Since, the Dragon-Python God/ *Lungchungpa* represent the ethereal Gods, he is considered as the Emperor on Earth. So, the Chothe believe as their Supreme Guardian God the protector and benefactor on this earth.

In Chinese, the Dragon King is known as *"*Lungwang*"* lit. the 'Rain God', also known under four names of direction as: *Ao-shin* (north), *Ao-chin* (south), *Ao-kuang* (east) and *Ao-jun* (west), (Channa, 1998:144; Ash, 2007:160). Linguistically, in ancient Chothe (being Tibeto-Burman speakers) it suggests that "Lung-wang" or "Lung-chung-pa" (lit. Lung = rock, Wang/ Chung = high/above) implies the Dragon-Python God as one of their ethereal Gods. The Mayan of Mexico called it "Kukulcan" (feathered Serpent God), and the Inca of South-America called it "Kon" (God of Rain and the Southern Wind), (Ash 2007:161). All these myths signify the similarities. The Chothe in view of their *Genealogical Myth* and being ancestor-worshiper believes that "Chothe Thangwai Pakhangpa" the historical king of Manipur is the son or avatar or the Divine incarnate of *Pu Lungchungpa* the Dragon-Python God. Thus, they revere, adore and worship him as their Guardian God. They believed that any false promise made by any person to their God *Pu Lungchungpa* at their sacred-grove is immediately responded either by sudden death or illnesses.[2]

In some ancient religious-historical texts of Manipur it is written that the Chothe and the Meitei worships *Pu Soraren* (the Sky/Sun/Lion God). There is also a reference in the *Chothe Thangwai Pakhangpa* (*CTP*) sacred manuscript that they invoked '*Chingnu nong ningthou*' literally in Meitei 'the rain king of hill peoples' (*CTP*-para-1, 24, 26-29). However, the Chothe elders said that *Soraren* literally means 'the Lion King' (since 'Sora' means 'Lion' and 'Ren/g' means the 'king'). This implicates that the Chothe and other cognate hill tribes god has magnificent strength and power like the Lion. It symbolises bravery and absolute power that decide the fate and destiny of all mankind. Tensuba said that *Soraren* refers to the god or spirit of the sky, the unlimited extent that represents the Heaven. The early Meitei sacrifice oxen to the Heaven or *Soraalen* in the open space (1993:122-123). Similarly, Sushanta Talukdar said that the ancient folksong of Bishnupriya refers a lot to *Sorarel* in the *Rain-Invoking songs* (1450-1700), and also in *Madoi-Soralel songs* (1500-1600), as the king of all the gods who has seven daughters.[3] The term *Sora-reng* is believe used by the Bishnupriyas to implicate the tribal god 'ferocious like the lion king'.

From the perspectives of the *Chothe Genealogical Myth,* rites-of-passages, parturition rites, child-naming and death ceremonies all indicates that the Chothe revere, honour and worship the Cosmologic or Celestial Elements like; the Heaven, the Earth, the Sun and the Moon including the Stars as Powerful Gods. While the Rain/ Water, Wind/ Air, and Fire are considered the Earthly Ethereal Gods for its indispensable Natural sources of life, without which they believe that any life form on this earth would not be possible to exist. So, the Chothe believed that these Cosmo and Natural Elements combine to form what is life on earth. They considered the thunder and lightning, storm or cyclone and water whirlpool are caused by these Powerful Gods. They conceived that it is beyond the human mind to comprehend and explain these supernatural phenomena, since no man has the power to control these elements at his own will. Therefore, the Chothe gives due reverence as an awesome Powerful Celestial or Ethereal Elementary Gods of life. The Chothe Cosmo believers through their *Pu Lungchungpa* (*Pakhangpa*) offer thanksgiving prayer and seeks blessing for good weather and prosperity, protection and peaceful co-existence with nature. Durkheim rightly said that "There is no religion that is not a cosmology at the same time that it is a speculation upon divine things. If philosophy and the science were born of religion, it is because religion began by taking the place of the sciences and philosophy" (1915:9).

There are three types of places/lands for the deaths. My Chothe respondents said that their ancestors believed the bright stars are the souls of their great ancestors who died long before and dwells amongst the Heavenly Gods. They said all the death men does not go straight to Heaven (*Thangvan lam*) but only righteous men does, while the wicked one goes to the Land of Death (*Athi lam*) or Hell, and some whose fate cannot be decided are stuck in the Middle-path of God's land called *Leihu lamjai.*

Ancestor Worship: It is obvious, from their genealogical myth and their legend that the Chothe since time immemorial, honour, adore, venerate and revere their ancestors like many ancient tribes. Although today, it is not widely practice but the nature of ancestor-worship is deducible from their ritualistic observances. In the strict sense, they did not revere their ancestors like they revered their Higher Gods *Thangvan Rengpa, Lungchungpa* (*Pakhangpa*), *Sanamahi* and *Leimaren.* But they show gratitude and respect to their ancestors by honouring and paying homage for their great contribution in building their society by offering food, drinks and sweets at their burial or tomb. Often a prayer is sought, especially by the family members on the death anniversary to help ward off against evil spirit and misfortunes. The kins also shows respect during their benedictory and valedictory ceremonies i.e., before and after any major festivals like *Innampei rhin* and *Achui rhin* festivals.

Special commemoration of death anniversaries celebrated by the Chothe are known as *Yairitha rhin, Theilhong* and *Hungdoi rhin* (in Meitei *Kriton*). These death anniversaries are ritualistic ceremonial feast organised by the decease family to honour the deceased with love, gratitude and prayer by offering food and drinks to God by inviting friends and relatives. And assuring his/ her death soul a peaceful rest in the abode with their ancestors in the land where the death belong. Tomalsing Yuhlung (my respondent) said "the *Inn-thinkpa* the 'House-Purification' ceremony is observed on the fifth day after the death ceremony. But the main death anniversary/ commemoration (*Theilhong*) is usually held on any auspicious day within three months, now conducted within three years for socio-economic reasons". According to him, "since the main death ceremonial feast (*Theilhong*) involve heavy expenditures for the grand feast and elaborate ritualistic offering of food and drinks many cannot afford to perform it on time, besides other socio-economic reasons. The food and drinks offered is divided into three shares; the first for their Almighty Supreme God (*Thangvan Rengpa*) represented by their Guardian Dragon-Python God of earth (*Lungchungpa/ Pakhangpa*); the second for their great ancestors (*Pu-Pi*); and the third for the evil deities/ spirits (*Tharou-leihu*) of the earth".

The Chothe treat their Guardian God *Pu Lungchungpa* (*Pakhangpa*), his wife *Pi Leima* (Queen- the mother of earthly beings) and his personal bodyguard *Pu Potlungpa* (the angel who guard the rock) as their ancestor gods representing their Heavenly Gods and performed a special offering and divination known as '*Leihu pot tampa*' (lit. gifts for the gods) at their sacred-grove by the village priest on behalf of the community. Tomalsing Yuhlung said the third offering was to appease the evil spirits, so that, they do not disturb the deceased soul on the death journey. So, when Chothe performed any merit feast or sacrificial offerings the food and drinks are offer in three categories: first to their Heavenly Gods, second to their ancestors and third to the evil spirits. This is seen in the rites of *pheiroi-khapa* of *Lamleh lethoipa* the village ritual, child-naming and funeral ceremonies.

In case of traditional death/ funeral ceremony, either the priest or assistant-priest always proclaims loudly to the death's spirit in each ritualistic offerings (like while wrapping up the corpse before taking it to the cemetery for burial) that some of the gifts in the coffin are meant for the deceased himself, others for the deceased friends, relatives and great grandparents whom he is supposed to give it when he met them on his/her death journey, if they would ask for it. As seen in certain movies, Sino-Tibetan speakers or Mongoloid racial people similarly practice speaking to the death spirits like Chothes in death ceremonies.

The Chothe have death commemoration songs called *Meebo laa,* dedicated in honour of their great ancestors or clan's head for their outstanding contribution to their society. These *meebo laa* songs are forbidden to sing anytime. They can be sung only during the three death commemoration feasts mentioned above and during *Innampei rhin* festival.

Family Gods: The Chothe venerates the family gods like *Sanamahi* and *Leimaren* inside the house. *Sanamahi* (lit. molten gold) meaning 'the god of wealth and protector' is venerated by families. His resting site is located on the extreme south-western corner of the house. Similarly, *Leimaren* (lit. merciful queen/mother of earth) meaning 'the god of fertility' is also venerated. The spot is located on the north-west house pillar, near the back door. This belief and practice is believed to have borrowed from the latter Meitei before.

Forest Gods: The Chothe refers any forest gods as *Ching leihu* (lit. Mountain/ Hill gods), while the Meitei term it as *Umang-lai* (lit. forest gods), both implies the same meaning. Sometimes, even the water gods/ spirits (*Tui leihu*), the goddess of wealth and prosperity (*Lairenma*) are club together among the forest gods. Since the Chothe believes that the forest gods comprising many benevolent and malevolent gods/ demigods/ spirits resides around huge rock, mountain peak, giant tree, dense forest, brook/ spring side or pond, etc. and have certain supernatural powers to harm or cause misfortunes to mankind. As a result, the Chothe perform appeasement rites and rituals by addressing to these forest gods when contacted 'to be on the safe side', so that no serious harm is done to them for their misconducts or trespasses. The Chothe thus, revere these lower gods because of their phenomenal powers. Practically they did not worship them unlike their principal Cosmic Gods but build a close mutual inter-relationship, believing that man and gods dwells together in this world.

The water rituals of "Tui-thoipa" and "Tui-humpa lethoi" are performed to the water (river or spring or pond) spirits. The Chothe believes that drinking spring/ pond water from unknown source is always considered unsafe. So, one is asked to splash the water three times with his hand before he drinks it, to signify permission from that particular water spirit. They believe that if a person disrespect, he would suffer from certain water or air borne diseases like measles or viral fever inflicted by the angry water spirits for contempt. In case a person seriously falls sick, a priest makes a divination and offers an appeasement offering to the spirit. We know the Chothe, from their genealogical myth and folktales (like *Lungkang*) revere any unusual type of huge rock (*Lung-pi*). The Chothe performed a rite called *Ru kokna lethoi* (Rain invoking rite) like the Hopi tribes of Melanesia when there is no rain or drought during the plantation season. They offer a fowl's egg, some uncooked rice and red flowers including a rupee coin, all placed on a banana leaf in the north-western corner of the paddy field and invokes the Rain (cloud) god for rain. But no dance is performed like the Hopi.

Shunglung: In Chothe the village pantheon that guards the four village gates or gods of four directions is known as "Shunglung" lit. Wrapped stones. These deity's sites are marked by a symbolic stone in each direction especially around a tree. These sacred area is identified by bushy environment and on the border of the village. Some people called these deities as 'Bambu' borrowed from Rongmei tribe, instead of calling as 'Shunglung'. They are specifically known as: *Shunglung-Nashu* (deity of East direction), *Shunglung-Nata* (deity of West), *Shunglung-Mai or ma* (deity of North) and *Shunglung-Thangting* (deity of South).

A similar kind is observed even among the Mayan of Mexico, Belize and Guatemala that called it "Bacabs", as 'gods of the four directions'; *Mulac* (North), *Cauac* (South), *Kan* (East) and *Ix* (West), (Ash, 2007:161). The Chothe perform an appeasement rite called "*Lou-houpa*" (lit. throwing away the waste/ medicine) to these *Shunglungs* on the eve of any main festivals i.e. before and after the benedictory and valedictory invocation ritual, seeking protection against outside evil forces that tries to enter and disturb the village. However, a special sacrificial ceremony called *Lamleh lethoipa* (lit. main village road ritual) is carried out annually exclusively for these four directions deities (*Shunglungs*), soon after their *Innampei rhin* festival of the following Saturday, by offering a dog and a fowl to show their gratitude for protecting the village from external evil forces.[4]

Other pantheons of malevolent forest gods/ spirits are like *Thei-nompa* (ghost that shake fruit trees), *Tingtricknu* (elf), *Heloi* (seven sisters' elf), *Lam meithanpi*, (fireball gods) etc. They believe if a person happened to encounter and suffers from certain hallucination or is in trance, a divination is consulted by a priest to their Guardian God to find out the specific god or spirit that inflicted the person. On the basis of the divination's findings, all these gods or spirits are appeased by sacrificial offerings, but not worshipped at all.

Concept of Three Worlds

The Chothe believes in three types of worlds. They are: (1) *Thangvan Reng lam* – The Land of Heavenly God, (2) *Athi-lam* – The Land of Death, and (3) *Leihu-lamjai* – The Middle World, on the way of land of Gods. The first two worlds may be equated with the Christian concept of Heaven and Hell. H. Hiyangsing a respondent said that "Yes, Chothe religion have the concept of heaven and hell. We believed that after our death, God from heaven will come down and also take us up through the golden ladder' (respond based on question no. 3, set-B, Does the Chothe have the concept of heaven and hell? If so, describe).

However, the concept of Third World or "Middle-World" is vague, though found mentioned among some ancient (tribal) societies of the world. According to Chothe, this 'middle-world' refers to a special 'firmament' place between the two worlds of: Real (Earth) and Unreal (Heaven-Hell) where some called it as the 'Under-World'. They believed that the souls of certain death persons are trapped within this under/ middle-world temporarily like spirits/ ghosts, considered as neither 'living nor death' waiting for their final judgement.

The Chothe eschatology is that all the dead men's souls do not go straight to the Land of God (Heaven) as soon as they die. Only the just, the good and the righteous people who had lived a good moral principle life and had done remarkable service to mankind during his lifetime on earth goes straight to the Land of God and dwells with the Heavenly Gods. While those who are brutally cruel with serious criminal records like murder, homicide, suicide and disdained by the society for their cruel intension goes to the Land of Death (Hell). Certain types of people whose lives are not as good as the first nor as bad as the second category, but had died accidentally in sleep, fire or water, or killed by wild animals are considered as the intermediate group whose souls are trapped in the Middle-World of God's land (*Leihu-lamjai*). These trapped souls are assumed to have certain powers to interfere with human beings in different ways as they can become demigods. The distinctive character about these spirits is that they can see and influence mankind while on the contrary the human naked eye cannot see them. But some priest claimed they can see and sense their presence.

Another example that indicates the existence of the Supreme God and the concept of the Heavenly kingdom i.e., Land of God and Land of Death is found in *Louchou* festive song, as rendered by Chongdin and Wailum:

> "*Kareng-ngo hange, kareng-ngo jung-nge,*
> *Lamal la kareng hakthing nge,*
> *Rengchung-nga ayang mo-ae,*
> *Thangvan jaiya sholhapilam mae, ...*".

[*In free translation*, 'Our king has started his journey, and he is on his way, to the festive centre where we all waited for him. Though we waited long for him, there is still 'Someone else' (God) above all the kings, (who is far greater and more powerful than him waiting for the time, when he comes he will judge all men equally on the basis of the actions), and He will give eternal rest at the Centre of Heaven'].

Soul

According to E.B. Tylor (1873), all living beings have a soul "anima" and "animism" meaning 'the existence of soul'. Thus, he propagated that belief in animist is the foundation of all primitive religions. Though many scholars argued against his concept, yet many accept the fact that all living beings possess *anima* or soul. The Chothe call this *anima* or soul "Tha-wai", an intangible bright thing that reside within the body or in the heart (*Lung*). The Chothe believe that the day a child began to breathe forth inside his mother's womb he is endowed with a soul by the creator. This soul becomes active only after birth and continues to grow as he grows up, and perishes with his death in the form of spirit. Durkheim firmly stated that "The soul is not in the breath; it is the breath. It is the part of the body where it resides is only one" (1915:243).

In Chothe belief system, these remarks of existence of soul in the body and its significance are seen in the child-naming and death ceremonies. The soul in the body is given an identity, a name when it come (born) into this world, and is given a ritualistic farewell as when it left/died/expired. Interestingly in certain cases, if a person suffers from certain illness/ weaknesses or often falls sick during his lifetime 'Personal-Rituals' like *Thawai kokpa*, *U-sil lethoi* and *Ai-ring thapa lethoi* are performed to re-strengthen his soul since the Chothe believed such symptoms are infliction caused by evil spirits for certain reasons.

The concept of soul and spirit, according to Chothe is that as long as a person is alive his soul exists within his living body. But once the person dies his departed soul is conceived to transform into a spirit. They believe that all the death men's souls did not go straight to Heaven or Hell. It depends on his/her goodwill life on earth. Perhaps, if a person's spirit is believed to be trapped in the Middle-World between the two worlds; real and unreal, his spirit is considered as a ghost (*Bhoot*) 'the walking shadow/soul'. They believed until and unless the family or deceased relatives prayed and performed 'appropriate farewell ritual' for such departed soul the spirit will continue to remain in the firmament and hunt humans.

Many Chothe claimed sighting or being hunted by a spirit or ghost (walking shadow) in many occasions. They said certain spirit used to appeared or hunt before the family members or friends in their homes, especially at night time or in their dreams. Some claimed sighting such spirits in the kitchen looking for food and drinks. Some said it appeared to them in their dreams to warn of certain danger coming in their way but cannot easily comprehend until it had occurred as they cannot communicate verbally. The Chothe believe that if the deceased family is being hunted or disturbed even after 1-2 years of the death ceremony the spirit must have come out of his grave through a hole. In such cases, the family members may inspect the graveyard, and if found, should fill the hole immediately. Then an appropriate ritual should be performed by the village priest at his dying spot or at his graveyard depending upon the circumstances, assuring his death and to rest in peace. The Chothe believe that if any unnatural death like suicide occurred in a family they consider it is a generation curse upon the family for a serious crime or blunder committed by their ancestors. So, until and unless a proper ritual is performed it would continue in the family line generation after generations. And this final death ritual called *Athi thong keina lethoi* (lit. rite for closing the death's door) is again carried out, often secretly by the deceased's family at the earliest. This ritual is considered a must since they believe in the immortality and reincarnation of the soul. The concept of the soul is further discussed in Chapter Six under '*Death Ceremony*'.

Some Chothe elders said that certain professional priests and priestesses (*Thiempu/ thiempi* or in Meitei *Maiba/ Maibi*) who acts like sorcerer or local medicine man captured the spirits of the death and extracts secret information (some by trance) requesting the spirit to reveal the thought, intension and past life of intended person. These spirits are believed to have certain power to inflict harm upon an enemy or heal or cure, if appeasement offerings are made accordingly to them. These spirits act as a medium (power) in the art of witchcraft. Such spirits are captured using magical words by befriending and confiscating part of their body or asset, and with an assurance to release them after their errands are carried out.

Totem: Definition

According to Emile Durkheim, the term "Totem" originates from the Ojibway an Algonquin tribe of Northern America, and refers to an object of an animal or a plant whose name the clan bears (1915:103). Similarly various scholars like, Sigmund Freud (1952) and Arnold Van Gennep (1960) have given different concepts and definitions on totem. But since, the term is loosely used by many, G. Van Der Leeuw has defined totem as:

1. The group bears the name of the totem;
2. The totem is accounted its ancestor;
3. The totem involves sundry taboos, such as
   (a) The prohibition against killing or eating the totem, except in specific cases or under special conditions;
   (b) The prohibition against intermarriage within one totem group (exogamy), (1963:79).

Besides, in its entirety, *Webster's Dictionary* define totem as, "a natural object, usually an animal that serves as a distinctive, often venerated emblem or symbol - usually a means of personal or spiritual identity".

It is obvious from the above definitions that a totem is an emblem of an object, such as an animal or plant or insect that serve as a symbol for a family or clan attached with a certain kind of personification. For example, the Native Northern Americans still practice the tradition of carving their totems like eagles, crows, owls, etc., out of a wood and painting them according to their colour, and thereby paying their homage and attribution on the death commemoration day by ceremonially erecting the 'totem poles' at a particular place.

(i) The Chothe Totems

The Chothe, like any indigenous communities of the world have different types of totems. Even today each clan maintain their obligation and allegiance to the contract made with their totems as before. Some totems have similar beliefs and practical aspects in the relationship with other societies though it differs in its story since the culture and myth varies from one society to another. Such variation in meanings is remarked by Levi-Strauss (1972) who talks on 'Natural Law of Similarity' that myths of different cultural groups belonging to different parts of the world are similar in many ways.

Each totem shows its distinctive characters from the other with regards to their habitat and physiology. Some Chothe totems are similar with some of the Native Americans (Red Indians), Indigenous Aborigines of Australia, New Papua-Guinea of Pacific Islanders and were also believed to be prevalent throughout Europe, Africa, and Asia.[5] Based on the above criteria, totems are classified into different types as: (1) Land-animal totem, (2) Water-animal totem, (3) Air-animal totem, (4) Reptile totem, (5) Insect totem, and (6) Vegetable or plant totem.[6] Accordingly, the land totems are like the beaver, otter, bobcat, bear, deer, fox, horse, cow, ram, lion, tiger, panther, wolf, bear etc.; and the water animal totems comprises like the dragon, fish, frog, seahorse, etc. The air animal totems are like eagle, crow, bat, hawk and dove. The reptile totems include salamander, chameleon and turtle. The insect totems comprise of praying-mantis, dragonfly, spider, firefly and butterfly. However, certain kinds of animals are symbolised as emblems and identified with a particular country like the Peacock of India, Kangaroo of Australia, the Olive leaf of Canada, etc. But such animals or plants are unique symbols or trademark representation of a country's beauty and pride for its abundance or rareness. These symbolic animals and plants are, however not considered as totems since they have no religious significance. But, the Lion of the British, Scottish and Punjab (India), the Eagle of the American (Army) and the Dragon of the Sino-Chinese are in broad sense mythically connected as totem of the people. In view of the above, the Chothe clan's totem and its taboos are described below as provided by the Chothe informants:-

1. The Tiger (*Kamkeirang* or *a-Kei*) - is considered the totem of *Makan's* clan. The Makan are forbidden from killing and eating any stripped animals belonging to the tiger or cat family and its

sub-families. The origin of this totem may be traced to their Chothe genealogical myth. Accordingly, it is believed that the first Chothe man that came out of the mythical cave wearing the stripped shawl *awa-ampi* was from Makan clan who confronted the Tiger and forced him to swear that whosoever eat or kill any of his kins would lost all their 32 teeth, by assuming both are cognate due to similar body stripes. As per the deal, the Makan members observes the obligation as an allegiance to the Tiger, and claimed to share the tiger's character of bravery, courage and fearlessness.

2. The Hornbill (*Phuirang*) - is the totem of *Khiyang/Khiang/Hiyang's* clan. This totem is about a girl who turned into a hornbill, connected to a folktale *'Ata Sari'* (The Seven Brothers). Despite her best effort, sincerity and dedicated service rendered to her seven brothers she felt she was always scolded, humiliated and accused by her brothers for being insincere and negligence in her duties. So, out of her helplessness and desperateness she wished and prayed to God to be like a hornbill, thus, became a hornbill. Since, the seven brothers belong to Khiyang (Hiyang) clan they owe not to kill or eat any hornbill and its species like the bulbul, whosoever disobeyed would not survive long. Most Naga and Kuki tribes also do have different stories connected with hornbill.

3. The Black Praying-Mantis (*Ahang-Yuishom*) - is the totem of *Mareem* or *Marim's* clan. This totem is associated with the folktale *'Shoma-reng'* the locust king. It is said that *Shoma's* husband was lazy, stubborn and stupid who even spent all her hard earned wealth and resources. Despite her hard work they remained very poor, who could not even effort to replace her old black sarong (*nek*). Because of her extreme poverty and lazy, stupid husband she felt terribly humiliated and embarrassed to face society. So, she decided to do away with her life. While grieving helplessly and praying for help she suddenly transformed into a black praying-mantis (*Ahang-Yuishom*). Since, Shoma married to a Marim man, they are forbidden to kill and eat any praying mantis and its kind. Till today the Marim are said to be lazy and idealist who depends on their wife.

4. The Otter (*Sachou*) - is considered the totem of *Thao* clan. The otter signifies clever and hardworking person. This totem is connected to a folktale *'Ahu maichoupi'*. Accordingly, one of the lineage head of *Thao* clan hosted a grand feast during a drought season and engaged some *Khiyang/ Hiyang* youths (as *Maksa*) to take in charge of water. These youth when they went to fetch water could not locate any water source. Suddenly, they saw an otter (*Sachou*) and asked him. The otter after much persuasion, reluctantly agrees to

tell them, only if they accept to his condition that they would not harm or kill him or his kind in future. The youths agreed to his condition and swear to the otter, after which he took them to the water source. Just then, when the otter bids farewell and about to enter his borrow; one of the youth caught hold of his tail and attempted to kill him. Luckily the otter's tail slipped off from the youth's hand and escaped death. This angered the otter, and so he blocked the flowing water and diverted it to another direction. The youths, as such, could not fetch enough water for the grand feast and return exhausted. When the host *Thao-pu* and the villagers questioned the youths about their water, the leader (from *Khiyang* clan) explained about the broken breach made to the otter. Learning the story, the *Thao-pu* accepted the otter's curse to befall upon him and his clan on behalf of the *Khiyang's* clan, assuming the reason of his feast. As such, the Thao members obliged not to kill or eat otters (*Shachou*) for fear of aftermaths.

5. *U-chikte* - a kind of small brown bird, is considered the clan's totem of *Yuhlung/Zulung*. The bird is usually found among thorny bushes. The bird signifies calm nature and independence. Accordingly, once during a famine the bird helped the Chothe find food and saves them from starvation, and also by providing their eggs. The little red feather below its neck is believe to be the bird's blood caused from an injury as caught by thorns while helping to find food for the Yuhlung man. Therefore, the members of the clan are prohibited from eating this specific bird and its kind as an allegiance of brotherhood.

6. *Shirsim* - is considered the *Parpa* clan's totem. It is a kind of wild vegetable grown in the forest. Accordingly, they said that during a drought season the people survived by eating this vegetable for many days as it was found grown at a particular area only. As a result, the *Parpa* man being the leader of the group took the responsibility to protect it from being plucked and eaten in future by their clan members.

7. The Swallow (*Pingprou*) - is considered the totem of *Rangshai/Riang's* clan. On the basis of the legend, the Rangshai consider that the bird is one of their ancestors or cognate who turned himself into a swallow in a magical fight to protect his clan's reputation. Henceforth, the clan's members are forbidden to eat or kill the house swallow. It is a taboo even to chase away from their houses.

The Chothe totems are seen as brotherhood. It is an emblem, a symbolic representation of an animal or plant or insect related to their clans by various mythical tales. They believe that specific clan members share certain similar characters and behaviours of these totemic animals, birds, plants and insects. Some still believe that if a member has strong faith in the totem of his clan, he can obtain inspiration, power and strength for those who share with Tiger or otter alike. They also believe that if they dreamt of their totem or comes in contact, it signifies that their totem is trying to communicate a sort of warning or danger to the concern person. Such similar totemic beliefs are seen among the Native Americans like Iroquois, Cherokee, Apache and Algonquin, and even among the North-east tribes of Naga and Kuki (like Mao, Ao, Angami and Hmar, Thadou speakers).[7] For Chothe, totem is one that remains with a person for life, both in physical and spiritual world. Besides the above mentioned totems, most Non-Christians Chothe believe that they have their own totemic influence of certain animal's spirit like mouse, cow, elephant, tiger, cat, eagle, etc, affecting their life and nature, sometimes acting as their guardian angel through one's intuition.

Table 21: Distribution of Chothe Respondents who Believes in Totems

Category	Youths (20- 40) years		Matured adults (40-60) years		Vill. elders above 60 years		Total	Percentage
	M	F	M	F	M	F		
Yes	18	8	34	8	28	6	102	51
No	38	14	29	6	11	-	98	49
	56	22	63	14	39	6	200	100
Total	78		77		45		200	100

The Chothe does not worship, revere or adore the totems like their Heavenly Gods. But the sacredness of their relationship lies in their allegiance and adherence to the promise made once upon a time with this animal, plant or insect that originates from certain circumstantial incident, with a belief that such totems are related to their ancestor spirits when man and gods dwell together in this world. So, the Chothe believes that after being helped by such totems from the bondage of cursed or rescued them from certain misfortunes both agreed to share the same clan by becoming like blood-brothers or cognates. Such events led them treat the totems with respect as their ancestors or relatives or alien loyal friends by obligating to their allegiance of the oath made earlier. This is because they believe in life after death or re-birth or re-incarnation of the soul in different forms.

Therefore, the Chothe consider these totems as sacred and taboo - forbidden from killing and eating one another, or from being deconsecrated. Even marriages within the relative clans are forbidden for the above reasons. Such belief is seen more attached with the village elders or senior citizens than the younger generations. Graebner rightly points out that the ancestor of a clan was born from the animal group, but sometimes it is the other way round that at one time animals belonged to the human clan. There is probably an animistic signature when people believed to turn into their totemic animal upon death. Often the totemic relationships seen are quite indistinct: the totemic animal is regarded as a friend or companion of the clan, so the rule is a prohibition against killing or eating such totemic animal, and also to maintain the exogamy (1924: 55).

Out of 200 respondents, 102 (i.e. 51 per cent) of them said "Yes" and believe in totems, while 98 (i.e. 49 per cent) said "No" and did not believe it (see Table 17). The data variation shows that there are higher numbers of respondents among the youth and matured adults who said "No" as compared to the village elders. The reason is that the present Chothe youth or younger generations are mostly educated and Christians who have modern outlook. So, they consider totemism, taboo and norms as superstitions despite their elders (parents and forefathers) still having a strong belief and attachment to it.

Superstition: Sign, Omen, Dream and Curse

Superstitious beliefs are universal. They are found in every society whether primitive or civilised. They co-exist with religion. But the intensity of belief defers from culture to culture, since some culture are more superstitious than the other. Superstition exists even among families or individuals irrespective of religion. The term superstition, according to the *Oxford English Dictionary* (1989) is derived from the Latin word *Superstitio,* meaning "standing over" from being awed, unreasonable or having excessive belief in fear or magic, especially foreign or fantastic ideas. The term superstition, to medieval scholars, means belief outside or in opposition to Christianity. But today the concept is applied without foundation or in contravention to scientific and logical knowledge.[8]

There are innumerable superstitions of varying types and degrees based on signs, symbols, omens, numbers, letters, colours, days, months, events, directions, names, totems, sighting of birds and animals depending on the perception of a person or society. It is this perception that defined the individual where he stands among the crowd or society. Anything and everything can be taken as superstitious belief by relating to his experiences, but not always since, it cannot ascertain about the happening at will. Certain hypothetical belief which is unexplainable or that opposes common belief is considered as superstition. Faith, in such hypothetical belief plays a major role in the perception and deception of variant superstitions. Mysteriously, many similarities of superstitions are found among different cultural groups of the world, like the myths discussed by Claude Levi-Strauss (1972).

Since, superstition exists in almost every cultural group with varying degree of beliefs and frequency of practices it is very difficult to classify them accordingly. Superstition, simple or complex shows many similarities from one society to another. The Chothe, as explained by them have innumerable superstitious beliefs that may be classified as Lucky or Unlucky; Auspicious or Inauspicious; Favourable or Unfavourable on the basis of Signs, Symbols, Omen, Numbers, Colours, Days, Directions and Birth name of a person that greatly affects their personality. But there are some individuals who intentionally ignore and try to avoid or reject such beliefs without completely disproving it. For example, atheists and the agnostics consider any kind of superstition as 'co-incidental event'. Such sceptical opinions are also common among Chothe elders and matured-adult individuals from certain incidents since they experienced, seen or heard, but not willing to admit openly their belief. However, the attitude of scepticism among the younger generation with any superstition is less in such semiotic belief. They are less apprehensive or un-bothered by directly rejecting or ignoring any types of signs and symbols. For example, a young boy does not bother seeing a black cat crossing the road, which may be unlucky sign or a bad omen for some elders. A contrasting belief also exists among the Chothe members. For example, a particular sign or number or colour may be considered lucky for a person, but proves unlucky for another. Therefore, the belief in such signs, symbols, colours, numbers and dreams are not universally uniform. They vary from individual to individual, or society to society, on the criteria how one views, understands and interprets his/ their perceptions and experiences.

Opinions on the nature of superstitious beliefs differ from individual to individual amongst the Chothe population too. The Table 18(i) shows that the majority of the followers of Chothe indigenous faith i.e. 40 respondents of the total 200; 28 (i.e. 70 per cent) said "Yes" and expressed their belief in various superstitions, while only 12 (i.e. 30 per cent) said "No" and did not endorse superstition. Similarly, Table 18(ii) shows that out of 160 Chothe Christian respondents, as many as 98 (i.e. 61.25 per cent) respondents said "Yes" and believed in different types of superstitions, while 62 (i.e. 38.75 per cent) persons said "No" and did not believe. This statistic indicates that many Chothe Christian population still believe in superstitions.

However, Table 18(iii) shows that out of a total of 200 respondents both followers of indigenous and Christian faiths; 126 (i.e. 63 per cent) persons believed in various types of superstitions, while 74 (i.e. 37 per cent) of them considered they did not believe in any types of superstitions. The figures indicates that despite many Chothe being converted to Christianity the majority are not yet completely free from superstitious beliefs. Interestingly, looking by the Tables 18(i and ii), it shows that the number of youths/younger generation are less superstitious than the elders in both the categories of Christian and Indigenous believers.

Table 22 (i): Followers of Indigenous Faith who Believe in Superstitions

Category	Youths (20- 40) years		Matured adults (40-60) years		Vill. elders above 60 years		Total	Percentage
	male	female	male	female	male	female		
Yes	6	4	5	4	7	2	28	70
No	4	4	1	2	1	-	12	30
	10	8	6	6	8	2	40	100
Total	18		12		10		40	100

Table 22 (ii): Followers of Christian Persons who Believe in Superstitions

Category	Youths (20- 40) years		Matured adults (40-60) years		Vill. elders above 60 years		Total	Percentage
	male	female	male	female	male	female		
Yes	25	8	34	5	22	4	98	61.25
No	21	6	23	3	9	-	62	38.75
	46	14	57	8	31	4	100	100
Total	60		65		35		160	100

Table 22 (iii): Distribution of Chothe Respondents who Believe in Superstitions (Both Followers of Indigenous Faith and Christians)

Category	Youths (20- 40) years		Matured adults (40-60) years		Vill. elders above 60 years		Total	Percentage
	male	female	male	female	male	female		
Yes	6+25= 31	4+8 = 12	5+34 = 39	4+5 = 9	7+22= 29	2+4 = 6	126	63
No	4+21= 25	4+6 = 10	1+23= 24	2+3 = 5	1+9 = 10	-	74	37
	56	22	63	14	39	6	200	100
Total	78		77		45		200	100

1. Lucky and Unlucky Signs

The Chothe believe that if a person on his important journey or business trip or mission happens to step out his house, with his left foot first or he re-enters the house to get something he had forgotten, it is considered unlucky sign. Similarly, incidents like if a person notices a cat (esp. black) crossing his path, a woman combing her hair, walking under a pole-bar or a ladder, or touching a sweeping broom accidentally by leg/ while being swept, sweeping a room before leaving the house, etc., all these actions are looked upon as bad omen or unlucky signs with objection, defeat and loser. They relate the broom with a witch.

On the contrary, if a person notices a girl fetching water, a calf sucking its mother's milk from behind (between two legs), being greeted by an elderly man, etc., are all considered good and lucky signs. Similarly, the western Europeans also believed that if a bride meets a lamb, a dove, a spider, a policeman, a clergyman, a doctor, a blind man or a black cat on her way to her wedding ceremony is unlucky. But if the groom gives a coin to the first person he sees on his way to the church or if the bride or a child cries during the wedding service it is considered lucky. Dating back to Victorian times seeing a chimney sweep on the way from the church is believed will bring good luck.[9]

The Chothe elders like M. Khundo and H. Ibochou said sexual intercourse before any game is unlucky. They said if a sportsman, especially a footballer or a volleyball player had sexual intercourse either with his wife or with any girls the night or just before the game, he is considered polluted. Therefore, he or his team will probably lose the game, even if he or they are positively on the winning side. Their explanation is that a 'woman is an evil', since she can be easily influenced or possessed by evil spirits, and capable of seducing man to bring downfall. Many claimed that since they have experienced such downfalls, they repeatedly warned the young village players to avoid such immoral activities during any major tournaments, so that, such disgraceful defeat does not happen on them for silly reason.

Numbers and Colours: The Chothe believes in astronomy. So, numbers play a very important role in their lives. Generally, they follow the 'binary-pairs' counting method as 'Chaang - Si/Thi' (Matured-Decay or Ripe-Death), or 'Chaang – Waie' (Right side – Left side), where '*Chaang*' means 'matured/ripe/right side or odd number', and '*Si/thi* or *Waie*' means 'decay/death/left side or even number'. The Chothe, when counting equates any *Odd numbers* with right side - considering good and favourable, and any *Even number* is equated with the left side - considering unfavourable, even or unlucky.

This Chothe belief may be contrary with other societies. For many European and American countries, the number Eight (8) and Friday the Thirteenth (13) are considered unlucky. The Romans believed the number 13 as a symbol of death and destruction. But for the Mayan and Aztecs of Central America and the Chinese it is a sacred and a lucky number (Ash, 2007:172). For the Christians, triple six (666) is believed to be the "Number of the Beast" or Satan's number. Tetraphobia or the fear of four is widespread in China, Japan, Korea and Hawaii and so the use of number 4 (four) is minimised or avoided as far as possible because the Chinese word for '4' (*si*), sounds nearly the same word for death (*s*).[10] But for the Chothe and some indigenous tribes the number "Seven" (7) is the most important and powerful number as it relates to their 'Seven Cosmo-Natural Elements' or the mythical 'Seven Heavenly Gods', etc. The significant of Number-Seven among the Chothe is seen with their 'Seven clans' also reflected in the 'Seven items' in the sacrificial offerings for the 'Seven' Cosmo-natural elementary Gods.

The Chothe also believes that their luck depends upon colours. Some colours are believed to ward off evil spirits and protect them from certain injury, accident, illnesses, evil eye or witchcraft. So, many do wear colours of their own choice like a talisman in clothes, metals and gems on the basis of their personality (*rashi*) since they believe to be good and comfortable. The Chothe village priest wear white dress along with their traditional shawl and head-gear while performing benedictory or valedictory ritualistic ceremonies. The colour of their ritual flag is normally white. But for certain rituals related with evil resolve, a kind of horizontally striped flag mixed with; red, black and white colours is used, signifying the three domains of – Mankind, Evil and God, or the ignorant man, bad and good scale.

The Chothe believe that wearing any shining metallic objects ward off or protects a person from any kind of harm or misfortune or evil (witchcraft) acts like colours do. So, both men and women wear ear-rings and necklaces made of gold and silver, bracelets made of brass and copper. Some wear amulets prepared by a priest around their arm or waist with a belief it deflects or averts evil spirits (borrowed from Meitei). They believe that if one's necklace, ear-ring, finger-ring or bracelets made of gold, silver or brass becomes dull in colour it indicates ill-health due to internal or soul's weaknesses. Precious gem-stones like diamond, emerald, ruby and sapphire are also considered as a good talisman. But they believe that one should wear such gem-stones according to one's character or personality (*rashi*), if not the person may suffer from certain illnesses due to its incompatibility.

2. Auspicious and Inauspicious (Days and Directions)

The Chothe believes in astrology. Certain days of a week, months of a year, numbers and geographical positions are very important, since they believe their lives are influenced by cosmic elements, relating it as auspicious and inauspicious. Champu Mareem (68/M) said "The birth day and date of a child/ person is a very important criterion to determine the right day for any ritual or ceremony like merit feast, marriage, starting day of any business enterprises or for any important journey, etc." The western people also believe that marriage in January is roar and rime, September is golden glow, smooth and serene life will go. December is cheer, love shines brighter from year to year. The general auspicious days for the weddings are: Monday for health, Tuesday for wealth, Wednesday's the best of all, Thursday brings crosses, and Friday losses, but Saturday - no luck at all.[11]

This way, the Chothe considered 'odd numbers' (*chaang*) meaning 'matured/right' as auspicious and favourable, while the 'even numbers' (*si*) meaning 'death/decay' as inauspicious by binary counting method. Accordingly, Monday, Wednesday, Friday and Sunday are considered auspicious, while Tuesday, Thursday and Saturday are considered inauspicious days, so also the months and directions. Depending on the nature, certain rituals that involve black magic or witchcraft are performed on 'Even' days only with a belief that the days are favourable for the evils. Monday, Wednesday, Friday and Sunday are auspicious to make journey to the north and east directions, while Tuesday, Thursday and Saturday are auspicious to go west and south. It is said that in olden days the Chothe like the ancient Greek always consult divination and performed sacrificial offerings in order to find out the ominous signs including month and direction before they wage and fought any wars and battles.

3. Favourable and Unfavourable Signs

Like any auspicious and inauspicious days, months and directions there are also certain ominous signs that are considered favourable and unfavourable by the Chothe.

Village or House Site: The Chothe believe that January-April is the most suitable session for constructing a house or establishing a village. They always performed an egg-divination (*artui jan*) on any auspicious day (Sunday, Monday, Wednesday and Friday) to find out for any ominous signs on the selected spot, soon after they surveyed a suitable site for the construction of a house or establishing a new village. This superstitious belief is described by T.C. Das too in 'Divination' that the Chothe perform an egg divination at the new settlement (1945:41). Perhaps, if the divination shows favourable result, another ritual called *Lamthing lethoi,* (land purification rite) is performed on any auspicious day, to cast away the evil spirits from the chosen area. A similar procedure is practice in locating and establishing a new village site. The logic behind favouring these months (January-April) by them is that the season is considered plentiful since it comes after the harvest and moreover, the season is dry and warm. The Meitei is also believed to follow suit with this belief.

Ancestral Names: The Chothe firmly believes that some of their ancestor's names are endowed with certain charisma which may or may not be suitable in re-naming or giving it to their grandchildren. For example, Tarik Yuhlung said that Marcus Marim (18 yrs) son of Manhoi Marim (56 yrs) of Khongkhang village was named as "Langshu" a name belonging to his deceased great grandfather. Tarik said, Langshu (Marcus) suffered from frequent illnesses for about four/five years during his childhood, where his sickness cannot be diagnosed despite giving full medical attention. So, some village elders began to doubt about the child's name, since it belonged to his great grandfather a famous Marim priest (magician or medicine man). Though the villagers are all Christians, they were later convinced of their traditional belief that the boy might have suffered because he could not carry the charisma of his famous grandfather. So, his family re-perform the traditional child-naming ceremony and re-named him "Marcus" a Christian name by wearing him the *amtoi think* (a kind of wild turmeric stalk) on his neck, thereby requesting the spirit to leave the boy without harm. Thereafter, Tarik said the boy Marcus gradually recover from his illness and grew up to be a healthy 18 years old person now. The Chothe, likewise performed personal rituals like; *Iring thapa, U-sil lethoi* and *thawai kokpa* to cast away an evil spirit if they believed that a child is possessed by a spirit or his soul is being disturbed by some spirits.

Twins: The Chothe are sceptical about twins. When a woman gave birth to twins of boys or girls they considered good and favourable. But if they are cross-twins, a boy and a girl, they considered unfavourable for the family. They believed that in case of cross-twins, usually one of the child dies earlier at the time of birth or when young, and the surviving child often suffers from miserable sickly life as though he/ she misses something. They believe twins souls are attached together like the faces of a coin, whatever happen to one has a direct effect on the other in taste, choice, experience and sicknesses. They called it dualism of soul.

Some Common Superstitions of Chothe

1. The Chothe believe that turmeric, garlic, *Kuchu-leiham* (a kind of wild herb) human's urine and faeces repels evil spirits or ghosts, since it is disgusting and pollutant. Whenever their dreams are bad and apprehensive of evil spirits they used to keep those first three things below the mattress or hangs in front of the door. When a journey is taken to a strange area or thick forest they would either carry or apply them on their forehead. Some burned the dry leaf of *Kutchu-leiham* as incense and also apply the ash on the forehead while travelling at night with a belief that the smell dispels the evil spirits.

2. The Chothe still believes in the saying that if any Meitei man kicks any Chothe person, and did not apologies he would suffer from certain misfortune very soon. Besides, they forbid any Chothe person to be a palanquin bearer for any Meitei king or Royal persons. They also believe that only the rightful person like a king can sit in a litter (Pic.107).[12]

3. The Chothe believe that if a person dreamt of a big silvery fish or his right palm itches, he gets money. But if one's foot is scratchy they expect an un-scheduled journey.

4. If a person sneezed during lunch or dinner, they believed people are gossiping or back-biting him/ her. If the number of sneeze is odd they believed to be a positive remark, and if even number a negative sign. But if they shared the belief with others after the moment, the intensity of bad remark is believed to lessen. Similarly, if the muscle on the left arm involuntarily tremble or move, it means a quarrel or a fight would occur. But if it is on the right arm it means a serious discussion on serious issues. They also believe that if one accidentally spilt salt, a fight or argument would take place. To undo the harm, they should toss some salt over the left shoulder with the intension for no harm.

5. The Chothe believe that if a rooster crows at an unusual time, especially in the evening or at mid-night and another rooster responded from a different direction, then they anticipate the news of elopement, a sign that a youth is planning to steal a girl.

6. It is auspicious if a bee stings a person, a belief he will not suffer from any illness for the whole year, so they avoid killing honey bees. This belief seems connected to science.

7. If a winter bird (*Ngabek*) hovers or flies to and fro above a house, Chongdin of Ajouhu believes that it is a sign that an animal or a bird has been trapped in his net. He is optimistic of a good dinner when he sees such sign.

8. If a person suffers from epilepsy or stammering or some kind of delirium or hallucination he is considered under the possession of an evil spirit or spell of a witch. So, accordingly they seek a divination and performed ritual. The Chothe believes that baffling or dumb-fooling the person during hiccups helps cure. They baffled such persons with unusual act or shocking stories, so that he gets shock or astonished (annoying the spirit) and released the person. This is commonly practice by elders on children/ youth.

9. Some Chothe believes that if a person found some money on his way and happens to pick up, it brings him bad luck and often incurred more losses. So, some did not take such dropped money. Yet, some took the dropped money and replaces it with a stone at the exact spot for no repercussion to occur on him.

10. According to Mrs. Urumleima (Margaret) as told by her grandparents said if one notices a snake carrying certain type of grass/ herb in its mouth one should managed to identify such grass/ herb with a belief that it is capable of curing and healing its poison and can even resurrect a dying man from any snake bites.

11. The Chothe believe that if a dog comes charging to bite at you, one should immediately sit down and (pretend to) throw a stone or a stick instead of running. This belief is related to their folktale, *'The Dog and the Eclipse'*. Besides these, there are many others superstitions belief practice by the Chothe.

i. Ominous Sign and Symbol

Ominous signs and symbols are important elements in Chothe belief system. If a person notices certain ominous sign and symbol before any important events, they have to read whether it is auspicious or inauspicious sign. Arthur Stanley Pease in, *The Omen of Sneezing* says that sneezing, unlike others that are more persistent and widely diffused ominous significance, throws some light upon the attitude of the Greeks and Romans rather than their interesting customs. According to him the belief that sneezing possesses an ominous significance appeared very early in many texts like in the *Odyssey* of the Greeks and Romans. He said that the belief and disbelief in the omen of sneezing is remarked by great philosophers like Plutarch, Aristotle, Socrates and Cicero, etc. in various writings (1911:429-432). The Chothe considers that if the number of sneezed is odd it is a good sign, but if it is even it is bad. Similarly, Campbell Bonner (1906), in *The Omen of Herodotus* described that "a dream of losing a tooth forebodes death. If the tooth falls out without pain, it signifies the death of a friend or a distant relative, if it gives pain, a near kinsman will die" (1906: 236). There are innumerable sign and symbol of omen, some may be distinctively similar in many ways, but the nature of interpretation differs from person to person and from society to society. The Chothe often consults an expert like the priest or priestess (sorcerer) when any ominous sign is observed. They also perform divination with a fowl or a pig or a dog before any major festivals or war campaigns or family or personal rituals to see for any ominous sign. The detail is given in Chapter Six - *Religious Practices* (rites and rituals section). However, it is hoped that the readers will be able to better comprehend and understand the nature, degree and types of Chothe ominous signs from the description below.

The Ominous Sign of *Maharani Sana Leirum*: Khongkhang Chothe village is entirely a Christian village but still many believe in superstitions. One common superstitious belief is the ominous sign of "Maharani Sana Leirum" meaning 'The queen's gold ear-ring'.[13]

According to Khiyang Khedon (F/o Khetrichou) of Khongkhang, the then king of Manipur had gone to Kabaw valley in Myanmar (Burma) for some official purpose. But since he did not return at the expected time the worried queen came down looking for her husband (the king) and visited the Khongkhang Chothe located on the Indo-Myamar (Burma) road near

Tengnoupal peak after learning that they were her distant relatives. Since, she was given a warm reception and hospitality she felt so indebted that she took out her own gold ear-rings and gave it to their chief (*Hulak*) as a token of her love, appreciation and gratitude with an assurance that the ear-ring is the souvenir of their bond of friendship (see Pic.17). On the basis, they claim that whenever some unfortunate events happened in the village they found something unusual in the ear-rings on checking. For example, Khedon said one of their newly appointed chief did not live long after an unfortunate accident occurred on his coronation day; one of the ear-rings slipped off from his ear while ceremonially wearing it to symbolise his chieftainship. He also said that the ear-ring sometimes changed its colour from bright to dull yellow, and whenever it changes the village experienced chaos and disturbances.

The Khongkhang elders said the village council used to check the queen's gold ear-ring once/twice annually for any ominous signs like change in colour or mark. This checking is done especially when they felt that their peaceful village was disturbed or is in chaotic situation. The inspection of the gold ear-ring is carried out only on Sundays, considering as the most auspicious or holy day of the week. Another story is that a hundred years ago the left gold ear-ring developed a crack, and that was considered as a warning of a serious quarrel that broke out amongst the villagers leading to disintegration of the village into two groups (now re-united). When the second crack was noticed adjacent to the first cracked a major crisis occurred in the village. Later when a section of the cracked portion of the left gold ear-ring split the village suffered from the Naga-Kuki Crisis (1989-1997) that forced them to relocate their village. It is because of such ominous signs of the gold ear-rings and co-incidents that the villagers still believed in the queen's assurance.

They said that the village was earlier known as "Mouhulon". But it was re-named as "Khongkhang" derived from "Khongkap" meaning 'footsteps', in Meitei. The new term owes to the queen as her expression after her visit to the village because the steps prepared for her were ladder like steps. The queen's gold ear-ring is successively taken cared by each new village chief. That time it was under the custody of Kh. Manichandra (56) the village chief.

The Omen of a Barking Deer: The Chothe believe that if a deer barks toward the village, it indicates an ominous sign that some well-known person like a village chief/elder or a leader probably would die. If not, a serious village dispute or misfortune may befall upon the villagers. On the other hand, if a deer barks toward another village it indicates that they will receive death news from the villages of that direction. Heshu Aji (37/M from Sajubo Mao village) said the Mao and Lamkang tribes of Manipur also believes that if a deer barks in and around a village, the enemy attacks the village or they faced serious internal crisis. But some agnostics viewed such events occur because some hunters have killed either the mother or partner, or the deer had lost its way in the dense forest and was signalling help out of fear.

The Omen of a Falling Banner: Maipak recounts about an event occured on 21st January 2007 when an ominous sign (falling of the banner) was ignored by their youths met with a bus accident. He said that *The Emmanuel Catholic Church of Lamlanghupi, Bishnupur* celebrated its Silver Jubilee (25 years) on 19th Jan. 2007, and some youths (volunteers) from Tampakhu Chothe village (Chandel district) stayed back after the celebration. So, on 21st January they decided to send them home by hiring a local bus jointly by the *Catholic Youth Organisation* and the *Catholic Church Committee of Lamlanghupi*. So that very afternoon the youths boarded the bus happily, and as the bus was moving out of the village road the "Jubilee's banner" that was still hanging across the gate of main village road suddenly snatched the string and fell on the ground, and the bus just happen to over ran it. Some villagers who came out to bid farewell saw this ominous sign and including some women-folks requested the youths to cancel their journey while some warned them to be careful. But since the youths were all in high spirits they pay no heeds, who replied nothing would happen to them. Unfortunately, within an hour the village elders were informed by some friends from Bishnupur town that their bus had met an accident and the injured ones had been taken to the *Regional Institute of Medical Science* (RIMS) hospital, Imphal. Later, Maipak learnt that the youths were joking and dancing inside the bus, some were intoxicated, but luckily none of them died in the mysterious accident although most of them suffered from minor injuries.

Death News: The Chothe have their own perception to know different types of omen for death news. In early days, sighting a crow and vulture was considered a bad omen of death. According to Chongdin Thao of Ajouhu, if he heard the *Baibek* bird (Koel family) howl or cry at any time of the day, it brings him death news of his kins or friends of afar. Similarly, if a honey bee comes hovering and mumbles especially around a person's ear, he believes the bee is conveying him some desperate message from a distant relative. Many Chothe like him believes that when such things occur they often get bad or sad news like death, serious illness or an accident concerning friends or distant relatives within few days. They believe that such birds and bees act as messengers sent by benevolent gods/ spirits on behalf of the concerned person or family members because of the helplessness situation in difficult times.

The Tragic Landslide at *Ahu Tuitrit*: The Ajouhu of Central-cluster group claimed that the tragic landslide at *Ahu Tuitrit* occurred few hundred years ago that led them to de-populate was the punishment of their Guardian

God *Pu Lungchungpa* (Pakhangpa).[14] They said that the punishment was because of their arrogant and selfish village chief.[15] Accordingly, the chief was cruel, selfish and arrogant who divided the village *Ahu Tuitrit* into two groups viz., the rich and the poor, and celebrated their annual festivals at different places. On one of their annual festival of *Achui rhin (Jarr rhin)* there was heavy incessant rainfall. Mysteriously, the area in which the rich group were celebrating their festival was suddenly swept away killing most of them in the landslide, while those few poor groups who celebrated on the narrow ridge survived. They said their God had shown many signs and warnings to that village chief but he seems to ignore it. So, the present Central-cluster group claimed they are the descendants of those poor people who survived the mysterious tragedy.

The Sign of Makan Roof: Roushi Parpa said when Ajouhu settled at *Ahu Lunghor* there was another mysterious event among the group which took place in the early days. Accordingly, he said that the roofs of all the Makan houses were blown away in one stormy night, whereas the houses belonging to other clans' members were not affected at all. They believed that it was a kind of ominous sign from their God *Lungchungpa* to the members of the Makan clan, who had wrongly swear. After the incident they shifted the village to a nearby place.

Ominous Sign of Wild Bird and Animal: The Chothe believe that if any wild animal like a deer runs through the village or any strange wild bird enters a house it is considered a bad omen. They believe that such animal/ bird are sent by the evil spirits as spy/ messenger to inspect whether the village or the house is still occupied by humans. Whenever such animal or bird entered the village or a house they did not spare its life on account of the superstitious belief, that if they released freely or let it escaped the evil spirits will intrude and bring misfortunes and disturbances to the village/ family, or even death considering the village or the house is unoccupied. Such ominous sign is seriously taken by Chothe and is still practice.

H. Thambaljao and Y. Tomalsing of Lamlanghupi describes an event that "Some three centuries ago when their forefathers settled near *Laimaton* peak on the south-western hill range a bewildered deer ran through the middle of the village in the afternoon and escaped after a chase to the other side of the village. The deer look frightened but saw no hunter behind. Soon the village was attacked by the neighbouring Rongmei tribe after the incident."

Another event occurred again at Lamlanglon (an old settlement) several years after the previous incident, when most of their men were away in the field. They said in the evening a young deer run through the village, but when some untrained young village youths simply attempted to kill, the deer had escaped. Then when the elders learnt about the deer's escaped they sense that some misfortune would soon befall upon them, but pretend to ignore for mere coincidence. But within few months the village had a general meeting for some reasons, and unexpectedly a silly quarrel broke between two young leaders belonging to different lineages as an ideological conflict. This silly quarrel later flared up and created rival parties, since both were unwilling to compromise. Subsequently, the village was divided into two rival parties irrespective of clans and lineages, and began to celebrate their festivals separately, although they are now reunited.

According to H. Dimho (36/M) of Lamlanghupi, in October 2006 one rainy night a strange wild bird flew inside his house and he was surprised to see the unusual thing. When he was about to chase it away, his eldest son (Hiyangdi) five years old went and informed his grandfather. Then, he was ordered to capture the bird and call the village elders to discuss the reason of the bird's visit and also confirm the bird's identity. Dimho, who initially did not believe the various sorts of superstitions and taboos, thought that the bird had accidentally fly inside his house attracted by his house light since the evening was stormy. He said after hearing various ominous stories he became sceptical because that week he was in bad terms with his wife. As decided by the village elders, the bird captured was killed and cooked. And just before lunch was served a priest performed a simple rite *Chathak-paypa* (feeding the gods) by offering little piece of the bird's meat, rice and wine (*zu*) to the gods, by seeking protect from whatever misfortunes that would befall upon them and Dimho's family. Dimho and his family members were forbidden from eating the bird's meat.

Later, when I enquired the reason why Dimho was forbidden to eat the bird's meat? H. Gulapsing one of the Chothe elder said any misfortune that would befall on Dimho and his family members will be received by them, even death, with a belief that they are old and have lived long enough. But Dimho is still young, healthy, and has young wife and children and he should continue to live life longer. It is understood that the elders have taken the place of Dimho's fate for the matter, from the past ominous belief and experience that any entry of wild animal or bird inside the village/ house brought them misfortune and disaster if let loose or escape it. Hence, Chothe kill such wild animals/ birds, contrary to Mao tribe of Manipur.[16]

The Ghost and the Dog: The Chothe believes that dogs have the capacity to sense and see a ghost or spirits of the death. So, they considered an ominous sign if a dog howls frequently at night or delves the soil. According to Mrs. Y. Atonsicha (89), if a dog howls at night it means that the dog had sense or seen ghost/ spirit moving around the area. And if a dog delved the soil at a particular spot it signifies of hunting the spirit where it had disappeared. When such things happen to a family's dog they considered that the ghost or evil spirit is trying to intimidate the dog, for the misfortune to come. While delving the ground symbolises digging of a graveyard. She said some people mixed little of the delved soil in the dog's food with a belief that the spirit will not intimidate the dog again by assuming to have killed that spirit. But if the dog still persists howling despite scaring off the spirit even with loud drum noises or fire or fire-crackers, then they may consult a priest/ sorcerer, and if necessary may perform divination and ritual. In certain cases, that dog may be sacrifice in place of human being by letting its blood ooze, like in *Anam kokna lethoi* (a ritual to free the suppressed soul).

Dreams

Dreams are conceived as a sequence of images, sounds and feelings experienced while sleeping, strongly associated with *Rapid Eye Movement* (REM) sleep.[17] The contents and physiological purpose of dreams are not fully understood, though they have been a topic of speculation and interest throughout the world. Many people have sought meaning in dreams or divination through their dreams as a point of reference. This has been described physiologically as a response to neural processes during sleep, psychologically as reflections of the subconscious, and spiritually or religiously as messages from God predicting the future. Generally, dreams are also considered as prophetic or omens of particular significance. Many cultures practice dream incubation, with the intention of cultivating dreams that were prophetic or contained messages from the divine. For instance, the ancient Greeks constructed temples they called *Asclepieions*, where the sick were sent to be cured. It is believed that cure would be affected through divine grace by incubating dreams within the confinement of the temple. In ancient Egypt, priests also acted as dream interpreters. In the Holy Bible there are also incidents recorded where Joseph and Daniel acted as interpreters of dreams to the Egyptian kings as revealed to them by their God.[18]

The scientific study of dream is known as "Oneirology". Science claimed that a human spend a total of about six years dreaming during an average lifespan, which is about two hours each a night. It is unknown where in the brain dreams originate. It has been hypothesised that dreams are the result of *dimethyltryptamine* (DMT) in the brain.[19]

It is said dream interpretation began as part of psychoanalysis at the end of the nineteenth century: the perceived, manifest content of a dream is analysed to reveal its latent meaning to the psyche of the dreamer. Sigmund Freud (1900) in *The Interpretation of Dreams* made the first attempt of explaining the causes of dreams. But later Freud and Carl Jung identified dreams as an interaction between the unconscious and the conscious.[20] J. Allan Hobson and Robert McCarley in 1976 suggested a new theory that changed dream research, challenging the previously held Freudian view of dreams as unconscious wishes to be interpreted. The activation synthesis theory maintains that the sensory experiences are fabricated by the cortex as a means of interpreting chaotic signals from the Pons. They proposed that in REM (Rapid Eye Movement) sleep, the ascending cholinergic PGO (*ponto-geniculo-occipital*) waves stimulate higher midbrain and forebrain cortical structures, producing rapid eye movement.[21]

The activated forebrain, synthesises the dream out of this internally generated information. They assumed the same structure that induced REM sleep also generates sensory information.

Whatsoever science may lead us, but like many primitive societies of the world the Chothe also accept that dreams are messages from their divine God, spirits of their ancestors or deceased relatives or friends. Some considered it as a medium of conveying the problematic situation, a sign forewarning about any misfortunes that would soon befall either on him or someone related, while others view it as mere sub-consciousness from past experiences and deep thoughts. Based on the dream's nature, his belief and experiences one may interpret it according to the essence of the dream and the rationality. This way, same dreams are sometimes interpreted differently depending on one's perception. Since, there are innumerable types of dreams and its meaning the root cause of a dream is still speculated and it remains as unsolved mystery till today, although it differs from person to person. Among Chothe, complicated dreams are often interpreted by the priest or village elders. For example, seeing house construction, flowing of clean water, bathing, climbing over a hill, etc. are considered good signs, while dreams of falling in a pit, chased by an animal indicates unlucky sign. If one dreamt of catching a big silvery fish, he is expected to get money. Some of the Chothe respondent's dreams are given below:-

M. Chongdin of Ajouhu village said that he still believes in divination and dreams, even though he is a Christian now. He said "Just before my sick brother died, I dreamt of my brother being handcuffed by some soldiers and taken away to unknown place. In the morning when I got up suspicious, just then, a relative came and informed me that my brother had expired. So, I was asked to kindly visit my brother's house at the earliest for the necessary traditional death ceremonies". Similarly, he said that if a wild cat captured a fowl and ate it in his dream, one of his relative used to die (the above is freely translated).

Kh. Khedon (85/M) of Khongkhang said that, "If I think about my jhum field and slept that night and dreamt of a banana tree with three co-joined fruits, I use to fetch a good harvest that particular year. But if I dreamt of making a rope, it indicates I have to go and clear the creepers in my jhum field. But if I dreamt of a war, it means that wild animals like monkeys and wild-boars are destroying my paddy or vegetables. Perhaps, if I dreamt that my jhum is being harvested by other people, it indicates a sign of bad harvest".

Kh. Hamunchou (68/M) of Chumbang said that, "Each time I dreamt of one of my molar tooth falling, an elderly person used to die". According to him, if he dreamt of such dreams, then the next day he expects the death news of his aged relatives, either from nearby or afar. He retorts that if he dreamt of a big river with large amount of clean water, it indicates a lucky sign, and if he undertakes any enterprise on such days it prove successful, since clean water indicates positivism. On the contrary, dirty/ murky water indicates inauspicious. Such dreams are common among many Chothe. But it is very obvious that most of them though Christians still believes in ominous signs, while the younger generation with less experiences are less bothered about such signs, omens and dreams (see Table 18).

Curse

Some Chothe still believed in curse or generation curse. Accordingly, if a person out of joke/ anger/ quarrel insults and humiliates to shame, especially grandparents, maternal uncle, aunty or any aged person, it is believed that the concern person/ people will definitely receive the curse if those elders happened to curse the person for their disrespect. They believe such curse continued to last seventh times or in seven generations of the family line. When such curse returns to the family, it is known as "*Sirap Mapok Lehpa*" meaning 'The return of the generation curse'. The Chothe said generation curse are often in the form of suicide, incest, marriage-breach, premature death, blindness, physical deformation, handicap and other shameful or detrimental problems that disgraces the family status. For example, Thambaljao said that kicking or insulting, especially to a maternal uncle, or a Meitei fellow kicking a Chothe person are considered a very serious offence and is taboo in terms of socio-religion. A curse by them is said to have direct manifestation upon the assailant's children like death or physical deformation that disgraced his family for obvious unpleasant reason. It is said until and unless the assailer compromised or performed a repentance ritual to the doer the generation curse will continue to remain. Since, the majority of Chothe are now Christians they tried to ignore it when such misfortunes befall with a belief that it was a co-incidental event, thereby discarding it.

According to one of their folktale '*Moirang Sirap*', many Chothe elders believe the first major plague that occurred in Manipur when settled at *Chinapung* in sixteenth-seventeenth century A.D. is assumed to be the curse of an old Chothe widow who married to a Kege-Moirang (Meitei) man. According to Hongpa, 'This old widow came to visit her parent's village (a Chothe village) on the northwest of Moirang. On her returned journey, she was dropped by some Chothe youth who left her by the eastern bank of the Loktak Lake alone. Despite her earnest request to accompany till her house, they refused by telling her that they too had to row back home and would be late. The old widow got furious at the very attitude of the youths for their insolence. So, she shouted back cursing the youths to lead a short life and die in the wilderness for their selfish act. Later a plague came and took thousands of Chothe lives. The Chothe believed that it was the old widow's curse, since it occurred soon after her death. The subsequent plaques that occurred in 17th and 18th centuries in Manipur killing thousands of Chothe and others are also considered as generation curse and the punishment of their Guardian God *Lungchungpa/Pakhangpa* for their notoriety and recklessness in the used of magical charms and spells in battles and wars on others. The Chothe elders still believe that the cause of their present de-population status is credited to generation curse; curses given to their forefathers by neighbouring ethnic tribes in the past for their barbarism, brutality and extreme atrocities during their rage, plunders and wars of defence and conquest.

Taboo

Etymologically the word "Taboo" traces back to the *Tongan 'Tapu'* or the Fijian word *"Tabu"* meaning "Under prohibition or Not allowed or Forbidden". The word *taboo* drawn from *tapu* is said to have dated back to 1777 A.D. as mentioned first by Captain James Cook, an English explorer on his visit to a friendly African Island (Tonga).[22] A.R. Radcliffe-Brown gives us a better picture of the term that was first scientifically explained in an article, '*Taboo*' by James Frazer in the ninth edition of the *Encyclopaedia Britannica*. Accordingly Radcliffe-Brown said the English word "Taboo" is derived from the Polynesian word "Tabu" which simply means "to forbid or forbidden", and can be applied to any sort of prohibitions. A rule of etiquette, an order issued by a chief, an injunction to children not to meddle with the possession of their elders may all be expressed by the use of the word *Tabu* (1972:73). Such a logical story is similarly seen among many of the primitive societies of the world.

In Chothe the term "taboo" may be understood as "Asei-Asi" meaning 'Forbidden from doing unpleasant things' or 'Prohibit from doing Even or left sided things'. The logic of the term *Asei-asi* implies a warning to a person that 'one should avoid doing unpleasant/ unfavourable things considered unfortunate/bad/deadly/evil/even or left side'. For example, touching a corpse, incest, patricide, kicking elders, or desecration like shitting at sacred places, stealing/destruction of sacred objects, etc. It derives from the perspective of their past bad experiences (after which they tag as superstition) forbidding certain unfavourable behaviour of a person so that one conforms to their socio-religious norms.

Sigmund Freud (1950) described in his essay, *Totem and Taboo* a link between forbidden behaviours and the sanctification of objects to certain kinship groups. He also stated the only two universal taboos are viz.; incest and patricide, which form the eventual basis of modern society.[23] This is no doubt, incest, patricide and homicide, etc. are universal taboos. Alfred L. Kroeber said that Freud's thesis proposes certain psychic processes tending to be always operatives and finds expression in wide-spread human institutions. Among these processes would be the incest drive and incest repression, filial ambivalence and the like (1972: 25).

In view of the above, taboo for Chothe may be classified into two: Religious taboo and Social taboo, as defined by their socio-religious norms. Example of religious taboo are: unsanctioned priest cannot perform a village ritual, a person deconsecrating the deity's sacred objects, etc. The Chothe have rich folkways and courtesy behaviours because of which the social norms are check and followed till today in certain ways.

Certain social action that negates or demoralised a person or family's reputation are seen as social taboo, with a belief that such action brings misfortune, disgrace, bad luck, illness or even death to the doer. In short, the Chothe social taboo specifically means the Do's and Don'ts acts that are acceptable or unacceptable by the society in their social-relationship like, incest, breach of marriages, disrespect to elders or actions with certain repercussion.

The Chothe forbids a woman from eating bee larvae or crab or half-hatched eggs during her pregnancy, with a belief that if she does she would definitely suffer from miscarriage. This belief applies even to certain animals like bitches and pigs too. By their experiences they did not simply ignore such taboo, which science needs to prove.

For the Chothe to bury any person of unnatural death in their common cemetery is a social taboo. They prohibit taking unnatural death body inside the village or house. For example, if a man/ woman dies committing suicide by hanging (*Ruijand thi*) or dies in wilderness outside the village killed by wild animal (*Lamthi*) such persons are buried separately outside the village cemetery and outside the village boundary. They believe, if buried together the dead spirit haunts or disturbs family members and others. If proper death ritual is not performed the effect seems to have chain-reaction on the next generation of the family. For such fear, the Chothe no matter whether the person is good or bad is buried outside the village cemetery. Therefore, extra rituals like house purification, village area purification and a special final death rite are performed accordingly by the village priest, so that such misfortune does not repeat again in his family or amongst the villagers.

Y. Chongkan of Khongkhang said it is a (social) taboo for his village to keep any newly constructed house unoccupied for months or years for fear of misfortunes. This way, one is asked to inaugurate and occupied the newly completed house at the earliest or at least make fire everyday inside the house on the pretext of occupying it, where conflicts between man and gods does not arises. Otherwise, they believe the evil spirit comes and claim the house, which later may cause misfortune or even death upon any family member.

Thus, religious taboos are rules that strictly prohibit/ forbid anyone from performing any kind of ritual activities to their God at the sacred-grove other than the ascribed village priest/ assistant-priest, without prior permission of the village council. Deconsecrating on sacred objects, urinating and defecation at sacred places. Touching corpse, pronouncing a deceased name, eating, drinking or bringing something polluted inside the house without washing/ bathing/ smoking oneself with fire after touching a corpse are all religious taboos. To cut and burn banyan tree is considered a religious taboo by Chothe for fear of misfortunes.

Certain social taboos observed on village gates ritual day (*Lamleh lethoipa*) are:

1. *Lajek* - forbidden to weave or start a new cloth in a loom machine.
2. *Shangjek* - forbidden from rice plantation.
3. *Neemjek* - forbidden from *Neem* (a kind of yeast plant) plantation.
4. *Abaijek* - prohibited from yam plantation.
5. *Aithingjek* - prohibited of ginger plantation.
6. *Aishanjek* - prohibited of turmeric plantation and,
7. *Annajek* - prohibited from gathering or planting any kind of vegetables.

It signifies that the villagers should not engage in any social activity on such specific day for fear of varied misfortunes. But these taboos have become lenient due to the passage of time. There are also innumerable socio-religious taboos and superstitious belief practiced by Chothe which is partly described in *'Rite-of-Passage'* in the following chapter.

Ghost and Spirit

The Chothe believes in the existence of benevolent and malevolent spirit or ghost. According to them, the 'soul' (*Thawai* - 'His Life/Soul/ Light') of a man transforms into 'spirit' (*Thawai mee* - 'His life/soul's shadow') only after death. So, a spirit is considered the soul of a death man i.e. the shadow of one's life, who is unable to reach either the Land of God (*Thangvan/* Heaven) or the Land of Death (*Athi Lam/* Hell) since his spirit is believed to be stuck temporarily in the Middle-World (*Leihu lamjai*) between real and unreal worlds.

In Chothe, the dual concept of soul (*Thawai*) and spirit/ ghost (*Thawai mee* or in Meitei *bhoot*) is that the 'soul' inhabits within the living body which is 'His life', while the 'spirit' (His life's shadow) exists outside the individual's body after death. The notion is that the soul has a home (body) but not the spirit, which is homeless like an orphan that wanders from place to place trying to find a body to occupy. At times when such encounter happens, people consider as being haunted or possessed or intimidated. Perhaps, if the soul of a person possessed by an evil spirit ventures out during his/ her sleep that soul is assumed as 'spirit'. The perimeter between the two concepts is very narrow. As such, when a man dies his/ her soul goes straight to Heaven or Hell according to one's life performances on earth. But the soul that cannot enter either of the two worlds and is stuck in the middle-world becomes a spirit (*Thawai mee*). Often a spirit/ ghost that exists in the middle-world is equated to unnatural death or those that died untimely in wilderness (*Lamthi*) unsatisfied or with unfilled dreams and desires. T.C. Das also said that "The most prolific sources from which evil spirits have been and are still being derived is unnatural death" (1945:201).

They said some professional Meitei priests and priestess captured these spirits by possessing a piece of their valuable body parts and used them as sorcerer during divination to prophesy the secret life activities of others. Elizabeth Colson also described that the Tonga people term their ancestor spirits as *Mizimu* who act as the agents of sorcerer between ghost and mankind, dependable on living, not independent like malevolent ghost who cause evil. They are mostly kinship members and helped only the kin groups, and even choose their own descendant to give their names too (1972:484-85).

The Chothe characterised spirits into benevolent and malevolent depending on its nature. Spirits that are good, approachable and helpful with the socio-economic life are regarded as benevolent spirits, while those that are mischievous, harmful, cruel, destructive and evil in nature as malevolent/ evil spirits. Some of the benevolent spirits are considered their ancestors who still live in the middle-world and have not yet immortalised like gods. They believe unless the specific final death ritual '*Athi thong keipa*' (lit. Closing the death's gate) is performed accordingly the malevolent spirit prolonged their stay unsatisfied, disturbing the concern family members. These spirits are communicated only by specialised priest who negotiate and bargain their death, regrets and grievances. This indigenous concept of soul or spirit is similar to a Christian belief, where the *Roman Catholic Church* observes a special prayer day for all departed souls on 2nd November as "All Souls Day" every year.

The Chothe believe that the ghost or spirit one often sighted, met or heard noises at certain places are usually connected to some kind of mysterious unnatural or premature death from a tragic accident, fire, drowning, and parturition or killed by wild animals. H. Thambaljao, Y. Maipak, Miss. H. Hoirei and many others claim to have sighted or met different types of spirits or ghosts. They consider the wandering spirits who are harmless are benevolent, while the mischievous are treated as malevolent spirits like *Theinompa, Lamhel, Suttrai, Cheijunpa* and many unknown ghosts.

Table 23: Chothe Respondents who Believes in the Existence of Ghost and Spirits

Category	Youths (20-40) years		Mature adults (40-60) years		Vill. elders above 60 years		Total	Percentage
	M	F	M	F	M	F		
Yes	21	12	36	9	30	6	114	57
No	35	10	27	5	9	-	86	43
Total	56	22	63	14	39	6	200	100
Grand Total	78		77		45		200	100

Generally, these malevolent ghosts are believed to have existed long before, died under similar fate and the cause of their death cannot be ascertained. The Chothe have a way of identifying these mischievous spirits as male or female by the nature and types of their behaviour and targets. According to them, female spirit/ ghost often target children, young boys and handsome men, while the male ghost targets young girls and women. Their habitat are often identified as haunted areas marked by marshy or dense area or spring site, accident prone areas, places where vehicles frequently broke down, or old empty house. Since they claimed to have sighted these spirits often at such places especially on cloudy nights, at dusk, midnights, or quite hours. These malevolent ghosts may cause illness and even death if one rebuked or threatens them. John Middleton said that "The Lugbara, an African tribe constructed shrines for their ancestors and any disrespect shown to them could collectively send sickness to the living, and are said to do so if offended by lack of respect and consideration by their descendants" (1972:489). Melford E. Spiro, however speaking from the sociological perspective said that "The *Ifaluk* of the Central Carolines (Micronesia) who fear and have anxiety of their malevolent ghosts (*alus*) for bringing ill-luck or sickness, which makes them dysfunctional in their society has a latent function, manifested in the form of social order from being aggressive and misbehaving within their society" (1972:479-82).

Out of 200 respondents, both followers of the indigenous faith and Christian as many as 114 (i.e. 57 per cent) of them claimed to believe in the existence of ghosts or spirits, while 86 (i.e. 43 per cent) indicated that they did not believe in ghosts (see Table 17). Here too, the number of respondents in proportion to the age-groups who said "No" are more with the Youths than with the other two age-groups of Matured-Adults and Village Elders who said "Yes".

Thambaljao describes one of his experiences that "In early days, our village area was filled with bushes and shrubs. One evening in 1938 when I was a young boy, I saw shrubs fighting like bulls in the pasture behind our village while I was looking for my cows and buffaloes. I was so petrified and amazed to see those shrubs fighting. I can even hear the sound of the bull's horns clashing. So, as I went closer to have a look out of curiosity, they move further away from me and later faded and disappeared. But when I reached the spot I saw the shrub plants in their own places". He also claim to have experienced of sand thrown by the spirit (*Theinompa*) from road side, sighting of evil fire-balls (*Lam meithanpi*) near the river-side and mountain cleavage, and heard of baby's cries around marshy and bushy areas of his village. Below are some common stories associated with malevolent spirits:

***Theinompa* (The Spirit that Hurl Granules):** According to Chothe, this mischievous spirit teases people by throwing granules/ pebbles/ sand to passersby from bushy fruit trees grown along the road side. The victims are assumed to be young ignorant or fickle minded people. They believe that a person can cast away such malevolent ghost/ spirit occupying the area if too annoying. But he should followed certain conditional rules, that is, perhaps if the ghost threw the sand granules at him he should collect it in a piece of cloth or shirt and then go home straight (and he should avoid communication with anyone on the way until the task is over), and then he should fry the sand granules collected in a pot. Meanwhile, the spirit is expected to come begging for the sand granules knocking by the door or making noises until the granules are return. It is believed that he will not be able to see the ghost with his naked eyes but will be able to sense his presence with the unusualness around the house. Therefore, when such things happen, (on the pretext that the spirit is around the house) he has to tell the spirit not to mess up with him or with any of his family members in future, and suggest the spirit to relocate his present hideout or face dire consequences, and then only, he may throw away the sand granules outside the house. It is warned that one should not over annoyed the spirit by retaining the granules overnight for he may invites more troubles. They believe that such ghost does not enter the house or inside the mosquito net for fear of being trapped. The story reflects the weaknesses of spirit/ ghost, their life style, nature of existence and how one can overcome fear and cast them away.

Lamhel: It means 'mischievous/ naughty' spirit. Actually, it refers to any forest ghost/ spirit that guard a particular forest area. Perhaps, if a person wish to use a plot of forest area for jhum cultivation he should first performed a simple appeasement rite before clearing it otherwise they believed the field would not bear much fruits. So, in order to find out whether the area will be favourable or not, a divination may be consulted for signs. But if a person dares such forest spirit or ignored while travelling in his territory such spirits often mislead the way by hallucinating the person/s. This spirit's wife name is called as *Sutrai*, commonly known as *Sutrai-lamhel* because of his mischievous nature (see Das, 1945:192).

Sutrai: Literally it means "Hovering vagina", to mean 'Lecherous woman'. Thus, it implies to a spirit of a loose character or lecherous woman (*Sutrai*), often who died during parturition/ child birth for obvious reason of immoral act. They believe that her spirit normally appears in white dresses enticing man by the road sides, especially at dusk or on cloudy nights before full moon. The term also applies to a bastard child (*Sutrai-te*) or the spirit of a death bastard child directly relating to a lecherous woman, who is characterised by high promiscuity with different partners or who abort and threw away her bastard child in the wilderness to die. Since in early days the social norm were very rigid the Chothe believe that if a woman dies during her child birth it is a curse either due to her fault or her predecessors' promiscuity behaviour. Such dead woman and child are buried outside the village cemetery considering as unnatural death or possessed by evil spirits. The existence of bastard child's spirit is identified by a baby's cry, especially in the evening at dusk around a brook side or marshy areas of the village. The interesting phenomenon about this spirit is that one can hear only the baby's cry from a distance and can never be seen. If one gets closer to the spot to find the baby, it suddenly echoes back from another direction mysteriously confusing people.

Lamtaipa: Another powerful forest spirit/god that guards a specific territory of an area and residing around the deep forest gorge or river side is known as *Lamtaipa* (lit. the guardian spirit of a land or the wild spirit that wonders around the village boundary). T.C. Das in connection to a legendary story of "*Angte and Ansu*" (about two missing persons who went to the forest and never returned home) mentioned that the Chothe in early days performed an annual ritual *Lamtaipa* for such spirit/ god in the month of *Inga* (June-July), (1945:193). This ritual is also called as *Tuithoipa* (*Tuikuk-thingkuk*), where only the village council members went down to the main village river/ stream and sacrifices a pig. This offertory ritual is to appease the spirit for protection against harm and misguidance of the people.

Chei-junpa: It literally means a 'stick-thrower'. It refers to a kind of malevolent spirit that throws virtual bamboo stick from a bushy place playfully up in the air. It produces a peculiar sound like '*Blu-urr*' when heard, but mysteriously the stick cannot be seen with the naked eyes. They said it occurs at any time of the day or night, especially when still and quiet. The sound when strike is consider deadly. The spot may appear bruise and terribly painful.

Tingtricknu: Literally it means 'the woman who breaks sticks'. It refers to 'an old elf or witch' that lived around bushy area or stream identifiable only by the sound of collecting fire woods (breaking sticks). She is known for alluring young boys and taking them to her hideouts by hallucination, thereby making the boys looked weird, stupid and ridiculous. They seem to resemble in character a witch or elf (*Helloi* the seven elfs).

Helloi: This spirits refers to the 'seven elf's sister or witches' that has the power to disguise as human beings. The youngest is said to be the most prettiest of the seven elf's sister. They mainly inhabit places around stream side, bushes, dense forests, huge trees and marshy areas who roam during day and night times. If they noticed any man loitering alone around their territory they often duped him with their illusionary magical power, trapped and feeds him with worms and insects, where the victim enjoyed as delicacies items like meat or fishes. In real, the victim appears to be suffering from some psychological disorders. Superstitiously, the Chothe dares not simply marry girls of seven sisters for fear of impoverishment.

They said that if a person happens to meet an elf (spirit) in disguised human form, and later he became apprehensive of its nature and wanted to find out the truth, he is asked to secretly bend down and look at between his two legs. And it is believe that he can see the true nature of the world and will be able to distinguish between the real and imaginative world. If it is the elf or disguised spirit, he will see the elf's leg hanging above the ground and her feet will be in opposite from the normal position.

Lam-meithanpi: It literally means 'land/ forest fire lighter'. But it means 'fireball spirits'. In olden days, when population was thin and the jungles were dense, many elders claimed sighting of big fireballs moving around playfully at strange places, especially at night near mountain cleavage of river-side or gorge. Though science claim such fireballs to be methane gases, but those who have experienced and witness the incident with their own naked eyes disagree the science hypothesis, because of the mysterious nature it displayed.

The Banyan Tree of Khongkhang: During my field trips to Khongkhang village, I inquired from Y. Neisim (29/M) why most of the villagers are prohibited going at night around their banyan tree grown near their playground? This question was raised since a friend of mine (P. Hiramani) warned me not to go to that place considering a haunted place. After much persuasion, Neisim reluctantly said that according to his elders, the spot seems to be where human sacrifices were carried out in early days, since they found many human heads around the tree when the playground was levelled by a bull-dozer (JCB engine). The elders believe that the heads could belong to some ancient travellers or early soldiers of Manipur or the Japanese soldiers who marched from Myanmar (Burma) side during the Second World-War. He said many strange things used to happen around the area. Rev. Namhatlung of the Liangmei tribe a visionary even told them that the banyan tree was owned by a male evil spirit. The spirit often comes out at night, dupes and mesmerised boys when seeing any girl (irrespective of biological relation) who came to fetch water alone or for dating or for other purposes. A boy or a man being possessed by the evil spirit easily seduces the girl often leading to force sex or rape. In such kind of incident, the boy and the girl are forced to marry. But for reason of consanguineal/ cognate, the boy is punished with a fine of a pig/ cow for the crime committed. Such cases resulted in serious family conflicts for the breach of marriage rules or illegitimate marriage, by ignoring that the spirit is the sole cause for such incidents.

Besides, these common stories of malevolent spirits or ghosts mentioned herein, there are several nameless spirits which the villagers identify according to their mischievous behaviour and peculiar character. If a new spirit is spotted around the village or at certain location, it is usually assumed that a person had died of unnatural death at the spot due to certain reasons. There, rituals may be performed by a village priest on the request of the deceased family, so that the deceased's soul may rest in peace and does not disturb anymore.

Notes

1. See, S.M. Channa (1998: 143-144, 156); also see, Chapter four in the section – 'Brief Analysis of the Chothe Genealogical Myth'. *Nongta Leiren Pakhangpa* is a new name of *Chothe Thangwai Pakhangpa* given by the valley Meitei poets mythically on his coronation day to mean 'the Dragon-Python who knows the father/ God'.

2. *Swearing at the deity's site*: Many Chothe irrespective of whether Christian or non-Christian still firmly believes that if any guilty person made a false promise at their deities' site or sacred-grove in the name of their Supreme Guardian God *Pu Lungchungpa/ Pakhangpa,* either the accused or the accuser, who is guilty will suffer according to his oath. My informants Pr. Roushi and Y. Lungle said few neighbouring Meiteis from Waikhong (near Sugunu) who are guilty and swore at their old Ajouhu (Purum Khullen) settlement's deities' site suffered from severe illnesses, some became cripple and paralysed, and some even succumb to death.

3. *Madoi-Soralel songs*: E-Pao.Net http://en.wikipedia.org/wiki/Kangla_ Palace. Accessed on: 17/6/2009

4. See, *Lamleh lethoi:* It is the main village gate ritual. The detail is provided in Chapter Six.

5. *Totem Animals:* (http://www.crystalinks.com/totemanimals.html), Accessed on: 19/8/08.

6. *Animal Totem Power:* Discover Your Animal Totem Symbol, Introduction written by StarStuffs. http://www.starstuffs.com/animal_totems, Dated: 19/9/08.

7. *Legends of America:* A Travel Site for the Nostalgic and Historic Minded (American legends: Native American Totems and Their Meanings), Copyright © 2003-2008, www.Legends of America.com, Dated:19/8/08

8. *Superstition:* (http://en.wikipedia.org/wiki/Superstition, Dated: 10-11-2008).

9. *Good luck - bad luck:* Superstitions and sayings of unknown origin (April 1861). Customs, Lore and Legend of Other Clare Days: Superstitious Beliefs and Charms (http://www.clarelibrary.ie/eolas/coclare/ history/beliefs_charms.htm), Dated: 10-11-2008.

10. *Superstition:* From Wikipedia, the free encyclopedia (http://en.wikipedia. org/ wiki/Superstition. This page was last modified on 5 November 2008, at 14:03, Dated: 10-11-2008).

11. *Good luck- bad luck,* (http://www.clarelibrary.ie/ /history/beliefs_charms. htm), Dated:10-11-2008.

12. Some Chothe believe that certain old sayings and superstitions still exists and cannot be ignored. Example, Chothes should not act as palanquin bearer for any Meitei, since the Chothe are their forefathers'. Despite such belief, recently a group of Meitei came to Chandolpokpi and Ziontlang villages of Chandel and shot some historical movie (*Pidonu*). The Chothe king was acted by a Meitei actor but some palanquin bearers were hired Chothe Christians. As a sign of disapproval *Pu Lungchungpa* or *Pakhangpa* the Chothe guardian god appeared Himself on 6th November 2011, and left his footprint image on the road. The footprint remains for a week (see pictures No. 105 and 107). The Chothe being now Christian and the Meitei claiming superiority seems to have ignored such old belief. It is said that after a ceremonial prayer was performed it disappeared mysteriously.

13. The identity of the queen or the owner of the gold ear-ring (*Leirum*) cannot be ascertained till date. But base on folklore and history of Manipur, Thambaljao said it could belong to King Pamheiba's wife, if not Chandrakriti's wife, since they frequently visited the Kabaw (Shan) valley, Myanmar during the 18-19th century.

14. *Ahu Tuitrit:* Village settlement No. 53 is found mentioned in the *Chothe Golden Jubilee Souvenir,* 2002.

15. The Chothes claimed that in olden days their ancestors were brave warriors, who fought bravely defending their land. Some are considered cruel, ruthless and barbaric in nature during their raids and plunders towards their enemies. They claimed to have defeated and escaped many times from their enemies baffled by their magical charms; like by letting their drums and gong beats itself in the village to signify a festive celebration while fleeing. According to ancient tradition a village cannot be attacked during a festive celebration, if done, they attacker is consider weak. They believed that such superior and arrogant attitudes in the

use of magical witchcraft and cruelty on their enemies have later caused depopulation as a result of curse and punishment.

16. However, this particular Chothe belief is contradictory to the Mao's belief. According to P. Lokho Savio of Kaibi village and Heshu Aji, the Mao forbids killing such bird or animal that entered the house, on the basis of their myth and on humanity ground. According to them, the Mao considers such bird or animal as their relatives seeking help and protection from human friends, since they escaped from their enemies or evil spirits. Accordingly, both claimed such wild bird or animal appeared sickly or frightened. The Mao tribe, unlike the Chothe release such bird or animal to a safe place after treating them well or healing the wound, if any.

17. *Dream*: From Wikipedia, the free encyclopaedia. (http://en.wikipedia.org/wiki/ Dream). Date: 10-11-2008.

18. *Dream interpretation*: From Wikipedia, the free encyclopaedia. (http:// en.wikipedia.org/wiki/ Dream interpretation), accessed on: 10-11-2008.

19. *Dream*: From Wikipedia, the free encyclopaedia. (http://en.wikipedia.org/wiki/ Dream). Date: 10-11-2008.

20. *Dream interpretation*: From Wikipedia, the free encyclopaedia. (http:// en.wikipedia.org/wiki/ Dream interpretation), accessed on: 10-11-2008.

21. *Dream*: From Wikipedia, the free encyclopaedia. (http://en.wikipedia.org/wiki/ Dream), Date: 10-11-2008.

22. *Taboo*: From Wikipedia, the free encyclopedia. (http://en.wikipedia.org/wiki/ Taboo), Dated: 24/4/2009.

23. *Ibid.*